THE NEW INTERNATIONAL WEBSTER'S POCKET GRAMMAR, POCKET GRAMMAR, SPEECH & STYLE DICTIONARY

OF THE ENGLISH LANGUAGE

TRIDENT PRESS
INTERNATIONAL

Published by

Trident Press International

1997 EDITION

TABLE OF CONTENTS

INTRODUCTION

For real communication to take place two or more people must, for a time at least, share some portion of themselves with another. It is irrelevant whether the sharing is intellectual or personal and whether the communication is unspoken, spoken, or written.

Communication is more than a two-way street: it is a meeting of minds. Whether listeners and readers agree or disagree vehemently with another person's statements, an interaction takes place, or there has been no communication. Effective speakers often ask their audiences to participate in some way; a speaker may request a show of hands or a verbal response. An audience may spontaneously communicate its amusement, restlessness, or appreciation by laughter, coughs and noisy movement, or applause.

Even written communication—by necessity a rather solitary activity—implies involvement of at least one other human being whose comprehension of what has been written is necessary for communication to take place. For the reader to simply see words is not sufficient: that person must understand what has been written.

The word communication is derived from the Latin word *communicare*, which means to impart or participate. It is the participation implied in the origin of this word that holds the key to success for anyone who would communicate by whatever means.

No one ever communicates perfectly—as anyone who has ever played the children's game known in some areas as "gossip" or "telephone" knows all too well. But, to the degree that the meaning received matches the meaning intended by the sender, communication does take place. In academic settings, the efficacy of communication between instructor and student is put to the test, literally and frequently. Communication skills are also tested daily in the workplace and in the home.

In the workplace, letters, memos, and reports must express clearly the thoughts and facts each writer is seeking to communicate regardless of whether the writer is employer or employee. Failure to do so can harm one's career and drastically affect the size of one's bank account.

Equally important are the unwritten forms of communication. The salesperson's success depends on his or her ability to hear what the prospect is communicating both with the spoken word and with unspoken signals.

These unspoken signs are even more critical in the home. Babies manage to communicate their needs quite well even before they have learned the language of their families. However, communication is much easier on everyone once they have mastered a rudimentary vocabulary. A large part of their early success with acquiring language must be attributed to the attentiveness of their parents and other caregivers.

Listening and reading skills, as well as the unspoken forms of communication, comprise an important part of a person's ability to communicate. That is why attention must be given to each form of communication before the more detailed exploration of the creative arts of speaking and writing.

UNSPOKEN COMMUNICATION

Forms of Unspoken Communication

What is it that adults and older children use to understand a baby's needs and wants? The same clues are the ones looked for if summoned to the principal's office—or even on a first date. These clues include context, body language, and touch.

Context

Context is so important that we rarely think about it consciously. An infant waking from a nap may cry out because of physical needs or simply to receive attention. We walk into a room and an awkward silence ensues; we wonder if we were the topic of conversation or if those already in the room were having a private conversation that cannot be continued in our presence.

Body Language

Body language is what the other person sees even before he or she hears a word, but it is also those messages that continue to be transmitted unconsciously throughout any encounter. Is the teacher smiling or scowling? Is Aunt Jane affirming or disapproving? Does a wave of the hand beckon or bid farewell?

Each person's body language speaks a message that at times may conflict with his or her words, but correctly interpreted the unspoken message is the more honest. Perception of another person's message includes assimilation of at least some information about his or her facial expression, stance, and gestures. In fact, studies have shown that first impressions based on body language and appearance are often determinative in job interviews.

Distance and Touch

Distance and touch may be considered part of body language or apart from it as separate forms of unspoken communication.

Distance is both physical and psychological. Two people talking across a table in a conference room are physically more distant than two colleagues would be if discussing something in the corridor, but the physical distance is not the only determinant.

A supervisor who is larger than his or her employee and who stands with hands on hips and feet apart blocking the doorway of the employee's small office is consciously or unconsciously practicing intimidation. In response, the employee will usually back away if there is room—a natural reaction to the other person's threatening behavior.

Strangers in proximity—on the subway or a park bench, for instance—will place possessions between them, turn their bodies away from each other, and avoid eye contact, thus erecting both physical and psychological barriers.

Touch, essential to the healthy development of infants, remains a particularly strong form of communication—even when stylized in such forms as the handshake or dance. Each society has its rules and taboos about touch. These govern not only who may touch whom but also under what circumstances and where on the body.

Observe Unspoken Communication

To sharpen your perceptions of unspoken communication, try watching a television drama with the sound turned off. See how much of the story line you can pick up from the context, body language, distance, and touch. Try the same procedure with a news broadcast. As you go about your daily activities, be aware of the silent messages people are sending.

Try to determine the messages your body is sending. Catch a glimpse of yourself in a window or mirror. Was your head down, your face grim? Were you standing erect with a pleasant, interested look on your face?

Abraham Lincoln is credited with the observation that most people are as happy as they decide to be. Of course, there are times when laughter is inappropriate, and a mindless grin is never attractive, but if the person you see in the mirror does not appear to be a person you would want to work with and know as a friend, perhaps it is time for serious self-evaluation and change. Attitude and appearance can be changed, and the importance of either in effective communication cannot be overestimated.

Use Unspoken Communication

Context

Appearance counts. Dress appropriately to the situation. Whether you want the attention of a den of cub scouts or the board of directors at the bank, dress the role you are filling. Make the most of your physical appearance through attractive hairstyling, clean and well-pressed clothing, etc.

Body Language

Your facial expression should reflect the emotion being expressed verbally. As a listener, use your face to show interest; as a speaker, use your face to reinforce your statements.

Make eye contact, but do not stare. Look away when you begin to speak, but look back at the other person as you finish—to hand the conversation back to him or her. This is not to say that you do not look at the other person while you are speaking. Think of your eyes as a part of your communication tools, just as your voice is.

Do not let your posture give a different message than your words. To convey interest in the speaker, lean forward with your back straight and your arms open. Disinterest is reflected when you turn your body away from the speaker. Folded arms in front of the chest indicates resistance to the ideas or personality of the other person. Slumped shoulders or a bowed head may mean submissiveness or depression.

Use appropriate gestures. Nod agreement. Avoid aggressive gestures. Note the gestures of your listeners. Fidgeting and hand-wringing usually reflect anxiety; foot-tapping denotes irritation.

Keep an appropriate distance so the other person is comfortable with the space between the two of you. When overdone, leaning forward, proximity, and eye contact are expressions of aggression and dominance. Use touch to convey warmth and emotional support as when comforting a bereaved person, but be wary of touching beyond the firm handshake in the business world. The optimum personal distance varies with relationship, gender, and culture.

When speaking, use a resonant tone and moderate volume. Vary the pitch and rate of speaking.

Before dealing with a person from another part of the world, try to learn as much as possible about the customs and practices of his or her culture. Especially avoid violating taboos, but do not overgeneralize. For example, a person from Egypt may be a Muslim (the dominant religion in the country), but he or she may be a Coptic Christian with quite different religious customs.

For further material on unspoken or non-verbal forms of communication, you may wish to read *Body Language* by Julius Fast (New York: Pocket Books, 1970). This was the book that popularized the concept of body language.

Eye to Eye: How People Interact edited by Dr. Peter Marsh (Topsfield, Mass.: Salem House Publishers, 1988) is a fascinating collection of very readable articles by contributors in the United States and Great Britain. Illustrated with many colorful photos and charts, this work translates scientific research about body language, personal space, cultural differences, etc. into language anyone can understand. It also includes information about office furniture arrangement, friends, and family patterns.

SPOKEN COMMUNICATION

Spoken language, although learned in the family, is modified in myriad ways. Visitors to the home, neighbors, radio, and television usually influence vocabulary, pronunciation, and grammar even before a child sets foot in the classroom. Consequently, almost everyone develops an informal language and a formal language. The first is for everyday conversation at home and with friends. The second is for more formal occasions such as a speech or a job interview.

Success on these formal occasions depends on preparation. Just as Liza Doolittle in *My Fair Lady* was transformed from an uneducated flower seller to a "lady" through instruction by Henry Higgins and her own hard work, so too can anyone learn how to give an effective speech or successfully use an interview to obtain employment.

Learn to Listen

The easiest way to learn to send effective messages is to start by receiving messages. Concentrate first on participatory or active listening. This is a skill that improves with practice but consists primarily of shifting our consciousness from ourselves to the other person—from what we plan to say next to what he or she is communicating now.

The principles are largely common sense—although studies show that we apply them less than 20 percent of the time. Try these listening techniques when talking with one or two people:

- Concentrate on other people while they are speaking.
- Look them in the eye. Do not turn your body away from the other person or keep scanning the area behind him or her.
- Lean forward slightly.
- Note the other person's body language.
- Respond to what the other person says.
- Do not counter a question with another question or shift the topic suddenly, but do ask about what has been said to learn more about the other point of view.
- Occasionally rephrase what the other person has said, and ask if your understanding is correct.

In situations where a formal presentation is being made, such as a class or workshop, observe the speaker. Listen to discern the organization of the presentation; watch the body language and gestures. Note mistakes, too, and determine how you would avoid them if you were giving the presentation.

Pronunciation

Just as important as the written word is the spoken or sounded word. The sounded word precedes the written word by thousands of years, and of course without the one there could not be the other. And just as there are correct ways to use words in writing, so are there correct ways to sound them in speaking.

English is supposedly a phonetic language. That is, the letters of our alphabet stand for sounds, and the way words are spoken or pronounced is supposed to correspond to the way they are spelled. In practice it does not always work that way. In the early years, English was more or less phonetic, but time has brought drastic changes in pronunciation, while changes in spelling have not kept pace. It is the gulf that has been created between pronunciation and spelling—widened during the last several centuries by the invention of the printing press—that has transformed English from a phonetic to a most unphonetic language.

To fill this gulf, our dictionaries respell countless thousands of words according to the way they are actually sounded in practice, and they construct elaborate phonetic alphabets that correspond to the true sounds. The dictionaries do not always succeed, however, since there is considerable difference in the way people speak. Still, the dictionaries are our only guide, and if you follow the phonetic respellings of a reputable dictionary, you will be sure of pronouncing words correctly in most instances.

In the United States, there are three more or less distinct types of pronunciation—the northeastern, the southern, and the northwestern. Even when pronunciation differs from the norm or standard as given in dictionaries, it is nevertheless considered correct and proper as long as the pronunciation is used by the educated people of any one of these regions.

Common Errors

Do not sound the *t* in most words ending in *-sten* and *stle*.

fasten
wrestle
chasten

Do not sound the *t* in the following word:

soften

Beware of dropping the *g* in words that end in *-ing* and in *-ength*.

believing *not* believin'
thinking *not* thinkin'

Beware of dropping the letters, *d, t,* and *l.* Even in the South, the practice of dropping these letters is regarded as incorrect by educated Southerners.

old *not* ol'
just *not* jus'
self *not* se'f

Beware of dropping the letter *r.* In New England and the South, correct pronunciation sanctions the substitution of the short *a* for the letter *r* in certain words. But to drop the *r* altogether in these words is regarded as uneducated (not *do'* for *door* or *fo'* for *for*). In these same regions, on the other hand, pronunciation allows for the perfectly proper *r* in words such as *car* and *farther* to be dropped.

Beware of the so-called intrusive *r.* Do not insert an *r* in a word where it does not belong, nor between two words when one word ends with a vowel and the following word begins with a vowel.

spoil *not* spurl
law and order *not* lawr and order
the idea (*not* idear) of it

The Speech

Having taken advantage of any opportunities to observe speeches and presentations, you already have a head start on giving one, but you may be wondering how you effectively communicate with more than one person at a time. The solution is simple: you must be in command of the situation at all times. You achieve this goal through extensive preparation and rehearsal. The following steps can help you prepare:

Complete Guide to Speech, Style and Grammar

Know Your Audience

Learning as much as possible about your audience is the equivalent of listening to the other person in a dialogue, but this may require research. At the very least you need to give considerable thought to who these people are and what they are interested in and how you are going to hold their attention while informing them about your topic. Learn all that you can about your audience before you write your speech.

If you will be speaking to a small group of strangers (as in a sales presentation perhaps), ask for the names and titles of the people who will be in the group and try to establish in your mind the relationships between these people. Are they all on an equal plane, or do you have one or two decision-makers and their subordinates? If the latter pertains, identifying the decision-makers and watching their responses during the presentation will enable you to be more effective.

If the audience is known to you (as a class or club), think about the individuals in the group. List all that you know about the group. This includes age, sex, special interests, but also extends to how well the members of the group know each other and how they relate.

Select Your Topic

Even if you have an assigned topic, you must decide what the purpose of your presentation or speech is to be. Write it down. Having this purpose clearly in mind will influence every aspect of your presentation.

Gather Information

Collect the information you are considering using, including your own knowledge. Make notes of the facts and statistics as you gather them. You may wish to use index cards as they are easy to rearrange, or a presentation program on your computer.

Sort out the information you have gathered. Eliminate all that does not advance your purpose. Ask yourself how much detail should be included in the presentation. Try to determine how much your audience already knows about your topic. Too much detail will bore your listeners; too little will decrease your credibility with them.

Make an Outline

Construct your outline, but leave the introduction or grabber, as it is sometimes called, for later. As you prepare the outline, be prepared to change it. This is a beginning effort, not your final draft.

As you list your points, do not hop around; try to have a logical relationship between the points you wish to make. If you have difficulty with the outline, simply list the points you want to make, then mark the items that are major points. Ask yourself if these points are of equal weight. You may need to make one subordinate to another or pull up one of the items you had not marked as a major point. Then decide on the order in which you wish to use the points, saving the most important or persuasive for last. (See the section on "The Outline" on page 205 and the section on "Types of Writing" on page 72.)

Review your outline to make sure that every item is true to your purpose and that the structure of the outline gives a logical flow to the presentation.

Write the Presentation

As you write the presentation, try to treat it as if you were talking to the decision-maker in the group. Pretend you are sitting across the table from this person. Keep your writing simple.

Use a speaking vocabulary. Keep your sentences short. Avoid tongue twisters.

With these ideas in mind, begin to write the presentation, but skip the opener or grabber unless you have thought of the perfect opening while you were gathering material or preparing the outline. Often the opening is the last to be written. Concentrate on writing the body of the presentation using your outline. Be positive in your statements, and use facts.

Signal that you are about to end as you begin the conclusion. Make it strong, persuasive and clear. If there is an action you want from your listeners, make sure they have no doubt as to what it is.

If you have not already written the opening or grabber, that is your next task. This part of the presentation is usually written last so that it perfectly reflects the total tone and content of your speech. Like the lead in a newspaper story, your introduction should grab the attention of your listeners and make them want to hear what you have to say.

The introduction should relate strongly to the audience's interest and knowledge; it could be a direct statement (audience oriented, of course), a vivid example, an important and authoritative quotation, impressive or frightening statistics, or an anecdote. Be careful with humor, however; it can cause you to lose a substantial part of the audience before you have really begun.

Review the speech that you have written, checking it against its purpose and keeping the previously mentioned guidelines in mind. Rewrite as necessary.

Prepare Visual Aids

Visual aids greatly enhance any presentation so if the setting permits, create visual aids that will allow you to use sight as well as sound to get your message to your audience. Visual aids used properly add to the credibility of your presentation. (Remember these are used to help the audience understand the material being presented, not to help the presenter.)

Keep any visual aids simple: dramatic photographs or videotape can verify and emphasize some of your points. A simple bar graph or pie chart can graphically illustrate statistical material.

Your audience gets to hear your spoken words only once and then those words are gone. If understanding does not take place as the words are being spoken, chances are it never will. Good visual aids can cut the time needed to convey an idea and increase the understandability of the words being spoken.

Keep each illustration or chart to one idea or concept. Check to make sure that each visual aid you plan directly supports the related text material. Having decided what equipment will be needed—overhead projector, slide projector, or video cassette recorder—check to see that such equipment will be available to you at the site of the presentation. Then prepare the material in the most attractive manner possible.

Rehearse

The importance of rehearsing the presentation, not just once but several times, cannot be overemphasized.

- Rehearse aloud with your visual aids. Record a rehearsal of your presentation.

- Rehearse in front of a mirror.
- Finally, rehearse in front of co-workers or knowledgeable friends.

Critique each rehearsal and make any necessary changes in your presentation. In addition to adjusting the content of the presentation and the wording, consider your rate of speaking (nervousness can make you speak too quickly, so practice controlling your speed), pitch (not too low, not too high), and your volume.

Give attention to your body language. Try to be natural, but do stand straight. Move only when there is a reason to move. A change of stance can make a transition, for example.

Gestures may be expansive and welcoming or restrictive and forbidding. In communication the former is generally preferred to the latter. As you make a presentation, hand movement can help you tell about an experience or teach a procedure, but do not cover any part of your face with a hand or arm. Even if there are no lipreaders in the audience, everyone will hear better without obstruction. Banish any nervous mannerisms or unneeded gestures from your performance.

Practice making eye contact.

Plan what you will wear just as you plan what to say. At the office the correct attire for both sexes is a business suit, but women need to beware of appearing unfeminine or too feminine, according to recent studies. To present in a class, wear your neatest attire. When an audience likes what it sees, it is more attentive initially.

Set the Stage

View the space in which you will give your presentation as early as possible if you are not already familiar with the room. You need to be able to see all the people in the room, and they will need to be able to see you. If you are using visual aids, everyone in the room needs to be able to see your screen.

Rules for the optimum viewing area suggest that the distance from a projection screen to the closest viewer be two times the width of the screen and that the distance to the farthest viewer be not more than six times the width of the screen. Video monitors may be used at greater distances if the monitor is elevated (or the audience is seated in tiers) so that no one's view of the monitor is obstructed.

Be sure that you are not blocking anyone's view of your screen, flip chart, or other visual aid.

Complete Guide to Speech, Style and Grammar

Check that glare is not a problem and that the illumination on your visual aid is adequate when the room is lit as it will be throughout your presentation. Will you need someone to dim the lights? Be totally familiar with any equipment you will be using during your presentation, including any sound equipment.

Make Your Presentation

As you face your audience, remember why you are there: You want these people to understand what you are about to present. Look over your audience. Take a deep breath to relax yourself, and begin.

Remember you are in charge. Look at your audience as you give your presentation. Adjustments you make at this point are fine tuning. You may need to speak slightly louder or slower, but your hours of preparation have readied you for this moment.

Evaluate

While the presentation is still fresh in your mind, evaluate your effectiveness. Be specific. Write down your observations. The information you record will be valuable in your future efforts. Use questions like the following:

- Did I maintain the center of attention?
- Did I position myself to be seen and heard?
- Did I use any unfamiliar words or stumble over a sentence that was too complex?
- Did I attempt to cover too much material?
- Did I speak naturally?
- Did I read from my notes too much?
- Did I convey enthusiasm?
- Was each visual aid quickly understood?
- Was any visual aid left on display after serving its purpose?
- Was the setting (seating, sound system, projection system, etc.) adequate to the task?
- Did I communicate effectively to fulfill my purpose?

The Interview

A critical step in obtaining employment is the interview.

In the normal course of events, the job applicant has prepared his or her basic resumé (see page 257), tailored it specifically to the current opening, submitted it with a well-written cover letter (see page 248), possibly had to complete a standardized application form as well, and has been scheduled for an interview. Job applicants who have prepared their resumés properly have examined their skills and experiences and are ready to prepare for the interview itself.

Make a Good Impression

The first few minutes of the job interview are crucial. As you meet the interviewer, smile and greet him or her by name. Let the interviewer determine whether or not you shake hands at meeting, at the close of the interview, or both, but be ready to accept the gesture. This tends to be more a problem for women than for men as women may be carrying both a purse and a portfolio or briefcase. If possible, let the briefcase serve as purse.

Carry extra copies of your resumé with you. For whatever reason, you may find yourself talking to someone who does not have a copy.

Choose your clothing carefully. A man should wear a suit and tie. A woman should avoid the extremes of fashion. The best attire for a woman applicant is also a suit, avoiding high hemlines regardless of current style. Her blouse should soften the image but not reveal her cleavage. Jewelry should be conservative. Avoid the military or "uniformed officer" look unless you are interviewing with a recruiter from a military or law enforcement organization.

Get a good night's sleep before the day of the interview, and arrive at your destination fifteen to thirty minutes early, but do not go to the interview early. Collect your thoughts outside the building or go inside to the restroom and check your appearance.

Use the time to glance over your resumé and tell yourself what a wonderful candidate you are. Review some of your sample responses to the stock questions you practiced with a friend (such questions are included in the pages that follow). Remind yourself of the impression you want to make.

Do not allow your presence to be announced to the interviewer until just two or three minutes before you are due as you do not want to appear to be rushing the interviewer. Then present yourself "on time."

Although for many, interviews are the most fearsome part of finding a job, they are also the best chance to show an employer one's qualifications. Interviews are far more flexible than application forms or tests. Use that flexibility to your advantage. As with tests, you can reduce your anxiety and improve your performance by preparing for your interviews ahead of time.

Begin by considering what interviewers want to know. You represent a risk to the employer. A hiring mistake is expensive in terms of lost productivity, wasted training money, and the cost of finding a replacement. To lessen the risk, interviewers try to select people who are highly motivated, understand what the job entails, and show that their background has prepared them for it.

You show that you are highly motivated by learning about the company before the interview, by dressing appropriately, and by being well mannered—which means that you greet the interviewer by name, you do not chew gum or smoke, you listen attentively, and you thank the interviewer at the end of the session. You also show motivation by expressing interest in the job at the end of the interview.

You show that you understand what the job entails and that you can perform it when you explain how your qualifications prepare you for specific duties as described in the company's job listing and when you ask intelligent questions about the nature of the work and the training provided new workers.

Rehearse Typical Questions

One of the best ways to prepare for an interview is to have some practice sessions with a friend or two. Here is a list of some of the most commonly asked questions to get you started.

- Why did you apply for this job?
- What do you know about this job or company?
- Why did you choose this career?
- Why should I hire you?
- What would you do if . . . (usually filled in with a work-related crisis)?
- How would you describe yourself?
- What would you like to tell me about yourself?
- What are your major strengths?
- What are your major weaknesses?
- What type of work do you like to do best?
- What are your interests outside work?
- What type of work do you like to do least?

- What accomplishment gave you the greatest satisfaction?
- What was your worst mistake?
- What would you change in your past life?
- What courses did you like best or least in school?
- What did you like best or least about your last job?
- Why did you leave your last job?
- Why were you fired?
- How does your education or experience relate to this job?
- What are your goals?
- How do you plan to reach them?
- What do you hope to be doing in five years? ten?
- What salary do you expect?

Many jobhunting books available at libraries discuss ways to answer these questions. Essentially, your strategy should be to concentrate on the job and your ability to do it no matter what the question seems to be asking. If asked for a strength, mention something job related. If asked for a weakness, mention a job-related strength (you work too hard, you worry too much about details, you always have to see the big picture). If asked about a disability or a specific negative factor in your past—a criminal record, a failure in school, being fired—be prepared to stress what you learned from the experience, how you have overcome the shortcoming, and how you are now in a position to do a better job.

Questions for You to Ask

So far, only the interviewer's questions have been discussed. But an interview will be a two-way conversation. You really do need to learn more about the position to find out if you want the job. Given how frustrating it is to look for a job, you do not want to take just any position only to learn after two weeks that you cannot stand the place and have to look for another job right away. Here are some questions for you to ask the interviewer.

- What would a day on this job be like?
- Whom would I report to? May I meet this person?
- Would I supervise anyone? May I meet them?
- How important is this job to the company?
- What training programs are offered?
- What advancement opportunities are offered?

- Why did the last person leave this job?
- What is that person doing now?
- What is the greatest challenge of this position?
- What plans does the company have with regard to . . . ? (Mention some development of which you have read or heard.)
- Is the company growing?

After you ask such questions, listen to the interviewer's answers and then, if at all possible, point to something in your education or experience related to it. You might notice that questions about salary and fringe benefits are not included in the above list. Your focus at a first interview should be the company and what you will do for it, not what it will pay you. The salary range will often be given in the ad or position announcement, and information on the usual fringe benefits will be available from the personnel department. Once you have been offered a position, you can negotiate the salary. The jobhunting guides available in bookstores and at the library give many more hints on this subject.

At the end of the interview, you should know what the next step will be: Whether you should contact the interviewer again, whether you should provide more information, whether more interviews must be conducted, and when a final decision will be reached. Try to end on a positive note by reaffirming your interest in the position and pointing out why you will be a good choice to fill it.

Immediately after the interview, make notes of what went well and what you would like to improve. To show your interest in the position, send a followup letter to the interviewer, providing further information on some point raised in the interview and thanking the interviewer once again. Remember, someone is going to hire you; it might be the person you just talked to.

WRITTEN COMMUNICATION

Written communication, like spoken communication, begins with words. Words and numbers are the symbols that allow us to see beyond ourselves and the present. Written communication allows us, through the mind's eye, access to knowledge, sights, and sounds of times long gone and of places and people only imagined.

Through the writings of others, we can share their visions: we can be enriched by reading the Bible or the works of Greek philosophers, on the one hand, or the famous speeches of twentieth century orators such as President John F. Kennedy and the Rev. Martin Luther King, Jr., on the other hand. We may also learn about a chemical reaction, enjoy a fanciful tale, or be moved to action.

By writing, we may communicate to others our own words of knowledge, concern, or inspiration. We may enlighten, amuse, or challenge. Whereas reading opens up vast possibilities, all that we read is inbound. Writing provides the opportunity to reach out, to share, to send outbound messages.

As with speaking, the easiest and best way to learn about good writing is through reading. Read as much as you can, and take time to evaluate the writing involved. Journalistic writing is different from college textbooks; and textbooks differ from the novels of Nathaniel Hawthorne, Jack London, Agatha Christie, or James Michener.

ACCESSING THE WRITTEN WORD

Reading Skills

It is important for student and nonstudent alike to be able to read well and quickly. Even in this age of audio and video, reading is an essential skill.

Every student must be able to master without undue delay the contents of the textbooks or other materials that form a part of his course. The good student is an efficient reader. He reads rapidly with good comprehension, he is able to read critically, and he retains what he has read.

Complete Guide to Speech, Style and Grammar

Previewing

A good way for a reader to approach a new text is to devote a few minutes to *previewing* the material. This is a useful reading technique by which the reader familiarizes himself with the general contents of the text before he begins the actual reading. To preview a selection:

1. *Read the titles and subtitles.* If the titles have been well prepared, they will indicate the main ideas of the material. The subtitles generally indicate the various points that go logically under the main idea. To read subtitles in order is apt to provide you with a good outline of the material.
2. *Read introductory and summary passages.*
3. *Examine the diagrams, charts, and other illustrations.* These visual aids are included to help explain difficult concepts or to repeat essential points.
4. *Determine the speed you will read* by the complexity and familiarity (or lack of it) of the material. Obviously, reading about topics with which you are unfamiliar must go slower. Unless the author has taken care to define all terms, the reader will need to use a dictionary or glossary. Making mental or written notes will slow the process but, for most readers, increases recall. Speed of reading will also be affected by the reader's goals—whether for entertainment, ideas, or specific information.

It is a good idea to preview everything you read—textbooks, newspapers, magazines, technical journals, essays, and so on. This applies especially to material that has a title, subtitles, and visual aids. The few minutes it will take you will pay off in time saved and greater reading efficiency.

Finding Main Ideas

In presenting factual-type material, the author has set out to convey to you, the reader, in as logical and lucid a manner as possible, the ideas he wishes to impart. In a single paragraph he usually presents the one basic idea; this may be contained in a single sentence, or it may be implied in various sentences in the paragraph. Further, in any given paragraph, most sentences will contain details that explain, illustrate, amplify, or in some way develop the main idea.

You, as the reader, will want to command those skills that will help you to pick out as quickly as possible the central thought of a paragraph. This implies the ability to understand the relationship between the main idea and the supporting details.

Here are some guides to finding the main idea:

1. The main idea may be directly stated in the first sentence of the paragraph. But the first sentence may simply signal a change from the contents of the preceding paragraph. If the central thought is in the first sentence; note how the following sentences amplify the thought.

2. The main idea may be directly stated in the first sentence and repeated, for emphasis, in the last sentence of the paragraph. Again, the remaining sentences *explain* the main idea.

    Often only a *part of a sentence* contains the main thought. Textbook writers, because paragraphs in textbooks are short, often employ this technique.

3. The main thought may be directly stated in a sentence located in the middle of a paragraph.

Of course, not all writers prepare their material in precisely this way. Individual styles of writing and the nature of the material often suggest other ways of presenting one's thoughts.

There may be paragraphs that contain sentences only *implying* the main thought; they do not specifically state it in any one sentence. Other paragraphs may be so short that it becomes difficult to determine the central thought. Or a paragraph may contain two equally important ideas.

To find the main thought in a paragraph, regardless of the type of paragraph construction, ask yourself two questions in regard to the paragraph; then put together the two answers to these questions into a single sentence. This sentence will provide the main idea. Thus:

a. Ask yourself who or what the paragraph is about.

b. Ask yourself what this paragraph says about the subject.

c. Combine the answers to these two questions into a single sentence, and you will have the main idea.

This technique can be applied whether the main idea is definitely stated, or whether it is implied. The same technique can be used in determining the basic theme of an essay, a chapter, or a short story.

In stressing main ideas, you are not to infer that they alone are important, and that the details are useless. The sentences containing the details often furnish the "substance" of the story. Details can provide nuances of meaning; they can involve the reader's imagination.

Critical Reading

Reading quickly with adequate comprehension is not enough. The effective reader must also be able to read critically, to evaluate what he or she reads. Such critical reading is a refinement of skill in reading. It requires that the reader be aware of the sources of the author's information; that he recognize the possible use of propaganda techniques; that he be able to differentiate between fact and opinion.

Once you realize you are reading an opinion, accord it only the value you consider it to be worth. This does not mean that opinion should be arbitrarily dismissed. Not at all. But not all opinion is worth accepting. Before you accept an opinion, evaluate it.

First, consider the author. Is he or she an expert on the subject? You would not be very likely to accept the opinion of your neighbor, a carpenter, if he or she were to write an article on the causes of heart disease. But the chances are that you would give credence to the statements on heart disease made by an eminent cardiologist. The critical reader does not blindly accept what is read without knowing something about the author's qualifications.

Guard against accepting overgeneralizations. Evaluate the reasoning the author has used. Remember, the truth is rarely simple. The same fact can often be used to support conflicting points of view, depending on what other facts are presented or omitted.

These suggestions pertain primarily to the reading of nonfiction: newspapers, magazines, textbooks, professional journals—even pamphlets one may be handed on the street or find on the windshield of a vehicle left in a public parking area. In reading fiction for entertainment, the reader should consciously or unconsciously evaluate the quality of the writing, plot, characterizations, etc., if for no other reason than to determine whether to spend the time reading the remainder of the piece. Well-written, well-edited fiction also offers the reader a pleasant means of improving vocabulary and writing style.

Rate of Reading

Most readers can improve their rate of reading without losing the essential ability to comprehend. (Obviously, there is no value or virtue in speed without comprehension.) Let your rate be determined by the purpose for which you read, and by the difficulty of the material.

For difficult factual reading, your reading rate must, of necessity, be considerably less than your most rapid reading. You may easily race through a popular magazine article or a book of light fiction; in reading *Moby Dick* or *Macbeth,* you will have to go more slowly if you wish to explore the deep meaning of these classics and to enjoy the beauty of the language. Nor should the student try to rush through a chapter of a physics or history text. What you want to do is to absorb and digest, and make a part of your mental make-up, every fact and idea you come upon in your reading.

Some of the more important rate-of-reading skills are skimming, skim-reading, and reading for key words.

Skimming

Skimming and reading are not one and the same. Skimming is a subskill in the reading process. Most readers who claim that they can "read" five or ten thousand words an hour are probably skimming, not reading at all.

In skimming you leave out whole sentences, whole paragraphs, even whole pages. When you glance at the headlines and sub-headlines of your morning newspaper, you are skimming, not reading. The basic rule is to *skim for a definite purpose*. You will skim for a specific answer to a question, and you will skim when you want to get a general idea of the contents of some printed material.

1. SKIMMING FOR AN ANSWER TO A QUESTION. It may be a telephone number, or some general's middle initial, or the birth date of a President. Here is what you do.

   a. *Preview the material* to find the answer you are looking for.
   b. *Use guide words or phrases* to help direct you to the answer. For example, for the date of George Washington's marriage, turn to "Washington, George" in the encyclopedia, almanac, or other source book. Try to locate the words *marriage, married, wedding, wife,* or the like.

    c. In skimming, *let your eyes move rapidly and efficiently over the text*. You will not be moving your eyes from left to right from line to line as you do in ordinary reading; instead, there are two different ways you can let your eyes move. When the printed column is narrow (as in most newspapers, some textbook chapters, some magazine articles, etc.), your eyes can follow a vertical path down the center of the column. They will be able to see words to the left and to the right. As soon as you come upon the guide word or words, stop and read carefully. Another procedure is to let your eyes move in a left-to-right, then a right-to-left progression, taking in two or three lines of print as you go along. You can with this procedure observe words near the center of the zigzag path your eyes are taking.

       In skimming, speed is essential. Go ahead as fast as you can.

2. SKIMMING IN ORDER TO GET A GENERAL IDEA OF THE CONTENTS. This can be a valuable procedure, for most of us just do not have the time to read thoroughly every bit of reading material that comes to our attention. The procedure is simple: First *preview* the article; then *read* the *first paragraph;* next *read* the *first sentence* of each following *paragraph;* last, *read* the *last paragraph* thoroughly.

Skim-Reading

This is a combination of reading and skimming. You read the important sections and skim the less important ones.

You can increase your rate of reading by reading the key words in sentences. Utilizing what may be called the "telegram style," perhaps 50 percent or more of a sentence is left out without the reader's losing the meaning of the sentence. In the following paragraph, the key words have been italicized. By reading them, and them only, the reader will get the sense of the material.

Our *forefathers fought* bloody *wars* and *suffered torture* and *death* for the *right to worship God according* to the varied *dictates* of *conscience*. Complete *religious liberty* has been *accepted* as an unquestioned personal *freedom* since our *Bill of Rights* was *adopted*. We have insisted only that *religious free-*

dom may *not* be pleaded as an *excuse for criminal* or clearly *antisocial conduct*.

A word of caution: Such words as *no, not, only,* and *less* are extremely important; so watch out!

Finally, your attitude when reading is important. Do not be afraid of the printed page! With material that is not especially difficult or technical, read on just as fast as you can without losing comprehension. Enter every reading situation with confidence and enthusiasm, and you will find this frame of mind will be a great help.

For further material on reading skills, refer to the books listed below:

1. Liddle, William, *Reading for Concepts* (New York: McGraw-Hill, 1977). Books "A" through "H" of this series are designed for readers in the seventh through twelfth grades.
2. Pauk, Walter, *How to Read Factual Literature* (Chicago: Science Research Associates, 1970). This book was written for readers in the seventh and eighth grades.
3. Pauk, Walter and Wilson, Josephine M., *How to Read Creative Literature* (Chicago: Science Research Associates, 1970). This book was written for readers in the ninth grade through adult level.

Use of the Dictionary

Few of us value the dictionary for the remarkable tool it is. Not only does the dictionary offer us the meaning and spelling of almost every word, it also provides a guide to pronunciation, use, syllable division, synonyms and antonyms, and derivation. In the dictionary's appended material is a wealth of helpful information in easily accessible form.

Meanings of Words

A word sometimes has as many as fifty or sixty different meanings or shades of meaning. This is not common, but the point to remember is that a word doesn't necessarily have just one meaning. Most words have several meanings, according to the ways they are used in a sentence. Moreover, the same word changes its form, usually its spelling, and often its pronunciation, according to the part of speech it takes. Therefore, never take the definition immediately following an entry as final. You must read—or at least scan—all its definitions. Different meanings are usually numbered. Within a numbered meaning, there may be several related shades of meaning separated by small letters of the alphabet. Often a phrase using the word will be included to aid in understanding a definition. For example, in the entry for *prospective* one might find ⟨a ~ employer⟩ where the ~ represents the word being defined.

Spelling

Occasionally an entry will have two or more different spellings of the same word. This means that all given spellings are in general use. All are acceptable, but the one given first is usually the preferred form. Irregular spellings of the plural form of a word are also given. Regular formations, however, are not given. Thus, when a plural spelling is omitted we can take it for granted that the word forms its plural in the regular way, by adding *s* to the singular and by adding *-es* to words ending in *s, x, z, ch,* and *sh.* Plurals of compound words are also generally omitted when they are formed in the same way as the plurals of the main word. British spelling variations are preceded by the abbreviation *Brit.* Such forms are acceptable in Great Britain, not in the United States.

Inflectional Forms

Often a word is spelled in various ways according to its use; we call these various spellings the *inflectional forms* of the word. For example, plurals of nouns are inflectional forms of the nouns, various tenses of verbs are inflectional forms of the verbs, while comparative and intensive forms of adjectives are their inflectional forms.

A good dictionary lists the inflectional forms that are irregular or that give trouble in spelling. When two inflected forms are listed for a verb, the first is the form for both the past tense and the past participle. When three forms are given, the first is the form for the past tense, the second the past participle, and the third the present participle.

Inflections formed in the regular way are seldom given, even in good dictionaries. In addition to the spelling of plurals, forms regarded as regular inflections include, for verbs, present tenses formed by adding *-s* or *-es,* past tenses and past participles formed by adding *-ed*, and present participles formed by adding *-ing*. Comparatives and superlatives formed in the regular way (by adding -er and -est to the positive form) are also omitted in most entries.

Usage Labels

Various labels signify a word's status in actual usage. These labels are extremely important. They indicate under what circumstances a word may properly be used. The conventional labels are: *colloquial* (used in conversation but not in formal writing), *slang* (restricted to rare occasions in informal conversation and informal writing), *obsolete* (no longer used), *archaic* (used only in special contexts, as in church ritual, but no longer in general use), *poetic* (restricted to poetry), *dialect* (restricted to special geographical areas), and *British* (characteristically British rather than American). Words that have more than one meaning are generally treated as follows: when the label follows the number introducing a definition, it applies to that definition only; when it precedes a number, it applies to all the definitions that follow.

Synonyms and Antonyms

Synonyms, words that have the same or nearly the same meaning, are part of the standard dictionary entry when available. They are usually preceded by the abbreviation *syn*, which may be in bold type or italic to set it off from other parts of the entry.

Synonym lists are very useful to writers as they strive to avoid needless repetition of the same word or phrase. Likewise antonyms are useful in clarifying meaning and as alternative expressions.

Syllable Division

The division of all words into syllables is a universal practice of dictionaries. This is done partly as an aid to pronunciation and word derivation, and partly to show how a word is divided at the end of a line when there is not enough space to write the full word on the same line. Syllable division is indicated by centered dots or small dashes. Some dictionaries divide the word's main entry into syllables, others indicate them in the phonetic respelling (see below) that immediately follows the entry. Many persons confuse the dot (·) or short dash (-) with the longer, heavier dash (–) that indicates a hyphen in compound words. The following is a sample compound word entry in Webster's

Complete Guide to Speech, Style and Grammar

New World Dictionary (note the difference between the syllable dot and the hyphen):

hel·ter–skel·ter

Accent Marks

Dictionary entries also carry accent marks (') to indicate which particular syllable or part of the word should be stressed. Some dictionaries place the accent marks in the entry itself, others in the respelling that follows the entry. The important thing to remember is that the accent mark appears immediately *adjacent to* the syllable to be stressed. When two syllables in a word are to be accented, the syllable that receives the lighter stress is marked by a light accent mark ('). It should be pronounced with less stress than syllables marked with the dark accent mark, but with more stress than syllables that carry no accent mark at all. Words of one syllable have no accent marks. Instead of light and dark marks, some dictionaries use single and double accent marks. Other dictionaries use an ascending single mark above the base line for strong stress and a descending single mark for less stress.

Phonetic "Respelling"

A wide gulf often exists between how words are spelled and how they are pronounced (see page 6). For this reason, all good dictionaries give the phonetic spelling of troublesome words, in addition to the way they are conventionally spelled. The phonetic spelling indicates how to sound out the various parts of a word in actual speech. It is termed the "respelling." Surprisingly few people know how to handle a respelling, but it is very simple.

A word respelling may consist of a simple rearrangement or substitution of vowels and consonants. It may also consist of symbols called "diacritical marks," which appear over the vowels. These marks indicate when a vowel is to be pronounced long, short, etc. It is not necessary to know the names of these marks, and it is not even necessary to memorize how to make the sounds of any particular mark. They appear in a key of all good dictionaries. And next to each mark is a short word that anyone can readily pronounce and that shows just what sound is called for. Sometimes the mark is contained in the short word instead of appearing separately. The marks appear in alphabetical order for ready reference. All you need to pronounce a word is to refer to this key listing. You find the vowel with the diacritical mark that corresponds to the mark in the respelling of the word given in the main entry. You pronounce it just as it is sounded in the short word given in the key.

Suppose that we want to be sure of the proper pronunciation of the name of the composer Wagner. The entry in Webster's *New World Dictionary* (Compact Desk Edition) gives the following respelling after the main entry:

väg′nēr

Now we immediately know that the beginning letter *W* is pronounced as a *V*. But how about the *ä* and the *ē*? These are termed "two-dot *a*" or "umlaut *a*" and "tilde *e*" respectively, but we do not need to know this. At the bottom of the page is the following key list:

fat, āpe, bâre, cär; ten, ēven, ovēr; is, bīte; lot, gō, hôrn, tōōl; look; oil, out; up, ūse, fūr; ə for *a* in *ago; th*in, *th*en; zh, leisure; ŋ, ring; ë, Fr. leur; ö, Fr. feu; Fr. mo*n; ü,* Fr. duc; kh, G. ich, doch. ‡ foreign; ⟨ derived from

We can see that the *a* with the two dots above it is in the short word *cär,* so we know that the *a* in *Wagner* is pronounced as the *a* in *car*. Similarly, the *e* is contained in the short word *over,* which is how the *e* in *Wagner* should be sounded.

A comprehensive version of the phonetic key appears in the front pages of your dictionary. Phonetic alphabets vary somewhat between dictionaries, but when you are acquainted with the markings of one, you will be able to interpret the others easily.

One mark that may give some trouble is the so-called *schwa,* or inverted *e* (ə). Not all dictionaries employ the schwa, but it is coming into increasing use, and you should know about it.

When the schwa (ə) appears in a respelling, it always takes the place of a vowel. It is a sign that the vowel is reduced in strength of stress. It has an enfeebled *uh* sound, as the *a* has in the words *ago* and *about*. The schwa can present difficulties, as you cannot be sure just how to sound it in every case. You will soon get the knack of it, however, after you see it used a number of times in a dictionary. Its purpose, to repeat, is to reduce, almost to ignore, the vowel's stress. The schwa's importance will be apparent when you realize how dull and unpleasant English would sound if every vowel were clearly stressed and enunciated. To relieve the monotony of vowel enunciation, there are times when vowels should lose their force, and the schwa tells us just when to pass quickly over them.

Word Derivation

The chief languages upon which English is founded are Anglo-Saxon, Old Norse, Old French, Middle English, Latin, and Greek. The abbreviations used by dictionaries to specify the language (or languages) from which a word is derived are, in order of their appearance above: AS., ON., OF., ME., L., and Gk. Additional language abbreviations are listed in the front of the dictionary. The symbol ⟨ means "derived from." Generally, word derivation information appears in brackets, either at the beginning or at the end of the entry. A question mark following the derivation signifies that it is only a guess and at best is uncertain.

Appended Material

The preceding paragraphs have described major parts or functions of the dictionary entry, but much can be learned from the introductory material at the front of the dictionary and the supplementary material at the back of the book. Often the opening material includes an introduction to the English language, extensive instruction on use of the dictionary, and a key to its abbreviations and symbols. The appendices (or appendixes, as both are currently correct) usually include a list of colleges and universities, a guide to signs and symbols, and tables of weights and measures. Often dictionaries include brief guides to grammar and punctuation, a list of foreign words and phrases, a list of geographical names, and a list of biographical names. Altogether a good dictionary contains many helps for the communicator beyond definition, spelling, and pronunciation of several thousand citations from A to Z.

Use of the Library

A crucial skill for a literate person is the ability to use the library effectively. Not only is it essential for any organized research project, but it enhances the caliber of all other kinds of writing, and it provides a basis for the fullest enjoyment of pleasure reading.

Librarians are helpful and can direct you to almost any information you seek.

Since the core of the library is the book collection, people need to know how to find and use books most effectively.

Parts of a Book

In addition to the main body of printed matter, each book contains some or all of the following parts. Every book has a *title page,* the right-hand page near the front on which are printed the title, the author, the publisher, and the place of publication. Sometimes there is a subtitle printed beneath the title which is added to give a better idea of the scope of the book.

The date on the title page may merely indicate when the book was printed, so the date on the reverse side of the title page is more important, as it tells the *copyright date,* near the time when the book was actually completed. The listing of more than one copyright date often means that additions or revisions were made to the original book. In a bibliography use the latest copyright date.

The *foreword* and *preface* are very similar. They tell something about the purpose of the book, how it can be used, or they acknowledge people who have helped prepare it. An *introduction,* written by the author or an authority on the subject, can summarize the book or introduce the subject.

The *Table of Contents* appears in the front and lists the chapters in order of their appearance, while the *index* is found on the last few pages and is an alphabetical arrangement listing specific persons, places, and topics with the exact page numbers where they are found.

Lists of maps, illustrations, and *charts* are usually found immediately after the Table of Contents.

Many books have an *appendix* near the back containing material that is not really part of the text but which is closely related to it. A United States history book, for example, may have in its appendix a copy of the Constitution. Many books containing scientific, foreign, or other words that people may not understand have a *glossary* to define these terms.

Types of Books

To help people find books, libraries classify, or arrange, books according to a clearly defined plan so that those which are similar in some way stand together on the shelves. They usually first divide the books into *fiction, biography,* and *non-fiction* categories. Fiction is a made-up story, although it can have much truth in it in the way of factual details, real-life characters, and actual settings. Novels and short stories are fiction.

A *biography* is the account of someone's life, and an *autobiography* is the account of one's own life. *Amos Fortune, Free Man* by Elizabeth Yates is a biography, while *The Story of My Life* by Helen Keller is an autobiography.

All other books in the library are usually designated non-fiction, or factual books, although this also includes such special types as folklore, mythology, poetry, drama, and essays.

Dewey Decimal System

In school and public libraries non-fiction is cataloged by the *Dewey Decimal System,* named for Melvil Dewey who in 1876 divided all knowledge into ten main classes and assigned numbers to each. Here is a listing of the Dewey class numbers:

CLASS NUMBER	MAIN CLASS
000–099	General Works
100–199	Conduct of Life (Philosophy)
200–299	Religion
300–399	Social Sciences
400–499	Language
500–599	Pure Sciences
600–699	Applied Science/Technology
700–799	Fine Arts and Recreation
800–899	Literature
900–999	History, Geography, Biography

Each of the main classes is subdivided into ten subdivisions. For instance, Pure Science is broken down this way:

510—Mathematics
520—Astronomy
530—Physics
540—Chemistry
550—Earth Sciences
560—Fossils

570—Biology
580—Botany
590—Zoology

Each subdivision is further broken down. For example, within the subclass 790–799 (Recreation), there is 796, outdoor sports; 797, water and air sports; 798, horse and other animal racing; and 799, fishing. Further subdivision comes after the decimal. Thus 796.3 is for ball games, while 796.32 is for basketball; 796.33 is for football; 796.34 is for racquet games; 796.35 is for baseball, etc.

Call Numbers

In addition to the class number, each book also has an author designation which is placed under the class number. These two lines make up the call number which appears on the spine of the book and the catalog card or computer listing. The call number for *The Many Faces of the Civil War* by Werstein:

973.7 = Dewey # for U.S. history, Civil War period
W498m = W498 for Werstein, the "m" for first word of title

Reading Shelves

You "read" shelves of books just as you read pages in a book, left to right, line by line (or row by row), with shelf dividers setting off the different "pages." Dewey numbers range from lower numbers on the left to higher on the right, with authors alphabetized within the same number. This is the correct placement of books on a shelf;

155	155.03	155.1	155.1	155.12	155.22
N36g	B42k	M32q	N19h	K14b	A12n

Classifying Fiction/Biography

Although fiction can fall within the 800s of the Dewey system, and biography in the 900s, most school and public libraries pull these books out and arrange them separately. Fiction is arranged alphabetically by the author's last name. If two authors have the same last name, then the first name is alphabetized, so books by Elizabeth Allen come before those by Merritt Allen. Novels by the same author are alphabetized by title, so Stevenson's *Kidnapped* comes before his *Treasure Island*.

Complete Guide to Speech, Style and Grammar

Many libraries give fiction an "F" classification for the first line of the call number, with an author code below it for the second line. A library might have this call number for *Little Women* and *Little Men*, both by Louisa May Alcott:

$$F = Fiction$$
$$Alc = Alcott$$

Biographies are arranged alphabetically by *the person being written about*, so all the books about a person will stand together on the shelf. Often libraries give these books a "B" classification, or sometimes a 92 (part of the Dewey number for biographies.) Thus two biographies of Abraham Lincoln, one by Judson and one by Nolan, would have almost identical call numbers:

B   B   (The only difference is the author designation
L63j   L63n   at the end of the number representing Lincoln)

A collective biography, containing the lives of several people, is placed in the Dewey category for biography, 920–928, and has a regular author number.

Special Collections

Sometimes there are other special collections that are housed separately. Short stories may be pulled out of their regular 800 number and put in a place designated S. C. (for story collection). Reference books are routinely shelved by themselves. The reference book *Twentieth Century Authors* by Kunitz would have the following number:

R
928
K96t

It is interesting how books from all these sections can be brought together for a special use. A teacher of American history preparing for a class unit on colonial life and the Revolution might go to the library and choose books from every single Dewey class number plus the other designations. Here are some books she might pick, with their broad class numbers: (Notice every class number is used.)

SUBJECT	CLASS NUMBER
Schools in colonial times	300
Signers of the Declaration (collected biography)	900
Development of constitutional government	300
Revolutionary war weapons	600
Sports and games in colonial days	700
A biography of George Washington	B
Johnny Tremain, a novel laid in Revolutionary days	F
The poem "Paul Revere's Ride"	800
How to embroider a sampler	700
A U.S. history book	900
Slavery	300
Tools used to build a log cabin	600
Foods and recipes	600
Story behind the song "Yankee Doodle"	700
Indian words adopted into our langauge	400
A description of Monticello, Jefferson's home	900
Colonial costumes	300
The founding of Pennsylvania by Quakers	200
Witchcraft in Salem village	100
Skits from American history	800
An encyclopedia article	000
Native birds painted by Audubon	500

Library of Congress Classification System

A classification system especially suited to very large libraries or those with large collections of books on one subject find that the Library of Congress System suits their needs better because it can be divided into more precise categories than the Dewey Decimal System. Major classes are indicated by letters rather than by numbers, subdivided then by other letters and numbers. A book, *The Loch Ness Monster* by Cooke would have the L.C. number QL89.C65, while its Dewey call number would be:

001.94
C7721

Complete Guide to Speech, Style and Grammar

The Card Catalog

Access to the books and a record of them is combined in the card catalog. This file for the library contains alphabetized cards for every book in the library. For each book there is an author card, a title card, and as many subject cards as are necessary to cover the subjects dealt with in the book. Books of fiction have subject cards only if they contain authentic information about a location, a time period, specific events, or people. Subject cards are distinguished because they are typed either in red or all capital letters. On pages 35 and 36 are examples of catalog cards.

Using the Card Catalog

How do you look up a person in the card catalog? Do it as you do someone in the telephone book, last name first. This is true if the person is the author of a book or if the person is the subject of the book.

To find a title, look up the first word of the title unless the first word is "A," "An," or "The." If the first word is an article, go to the second word.

Numbers and abbreviations are filed as though they were spelled out.

All names beginning with "Mc," "Mac," "M'" are filed as though they were spelled "Mac."

In the following listing, parentheses enclose the first three letters of the word you would seek for these titles: *Mr. Roberts* (Mis); *McGregory Strikes Back* (Mac); *1001 Questions about Birds* (One); *A Moveable Feast* (Mov); *Jane Eyre* (Jan); *The Count of Monte Cristo* (Cou); *And Now Tomorrow* (And because the first word is not "An").

Cards for books by a person come before cards for books about that person: Irving, Washington (author of "Rip Van Winkle") precedes IRVING, WASHINGTON (subject of a biography).

Periods in history are arranged chronologically, factual books first, then fiction.

> U.S.—History
> U.S.—History-Revolution
> U.S.—History-Revolution-Fiction

Author Card

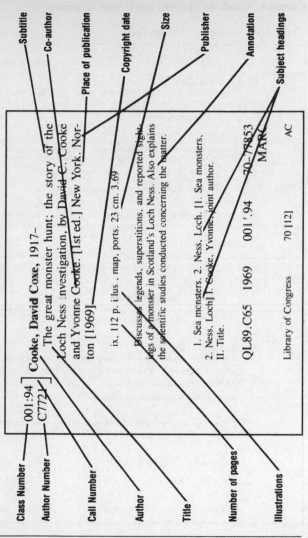

Class Number

Author Number

Call Number

Author

Title

Number of pages

Illustrations

Subtitle

Co-author

Place of publication

Copyright date

Size

Publisher

Annotation

Subject headings

001:94
C772t

Cooke, David Coxe, 1917–
    The great monster hunt; the story of the
Loch Ness investigation, by David C. Cooke
and Yvonne Cooke. [1st ed.] New York. Norton [1969]
    ix, 112 p. ilus . map. ports. 23 cm. 3.69
    Discusses legends, superstitions, and reported sight-
ings of a monster in Scotland's Loch Ness. Also explains
the scientific studies conducted concerning the matter.

    1. Sea monsters. 2. Ness, Loch. [1. Sea monsters.
2. Ness, Loch] I. Cooke, Yvonne, joint author.
II. Title.

QL89.C65   1969   001'.94   70–77853
                                    MARC

Library of Congress   70 [12]   AC

35

Complete Guide to Speech, Style and Grammar

Title Card

The great monster hunt

001:94
C7721
    Cooke, David Coxe, 1917–
        The great monster hunt; the story of the Loch Ness inves-
tigation, by David C. Cooke and Yvonne Cooke. [1st ed.]
New York. Norton [1969]

        ix, 112 p. illus., map, ports. 23 cm. 3.69

        Discusses legends, superstitions, and reported sightings of a monster in Scot-
land's Loch Ness. Also explains the scientific studies conducted concerning the
matter.

        1. Sea monsters. 2. Ness, Loch. [1. Sea monsters, 2. Ness, Loch]
I. Cooke, Yvonne, joint author. II. Title.

QL89.C65 1969   001'.94   70–77853
                                               MARC

Library of Congress   70 [12]   AC

Subject Card

SEA MONSTERS

001:94
C7721
    Cooke, David Coxe, 1917–
        The great monster hunt; the story of the Loch Ness inves-
tigation, by David C. Cooke and Yvonne Cooke. [1st ed.]
New York. Norton [1969]

        ix, 112 p. illus., map, ports. 23 cm. 3.69

        Discusses legends, superstitions, and reported sightings of a monster in Scot-
land's Loch Ness. Also explains the scientific studies conducted concerning the
matter.

        1. Sea monsters. 2. Ness, Loch. [1. Sea monsters, 2. Ness, Loch]
I. Cooke, Yvonne, joint author. II. Title.

QL89.C65 1969   001'.94   70–77853
                                               MARC

Library of Congress   70 [12]   AC

U.S.—History-Civil War
U.S.—History-Civil War-Fiction
U.S.—History-20th Century

Alphabetizing

People may think they know how to arrange in correct alphabetical order, yet they still have trouble finding things in the card catalog. One reason is that there is more than one system of alphabetical arrangement. The library uses the "word-by-word" system, meaning alphabetizing by letters to the end of each word, short words before long words. The other system, used by many encyclopedias and people who index books, is the letter-by-letter system, which is a strict alphabetical arrangement of all letters disregarding the ending of words.

LIBRARY SYSTEM	OTHER SYSTEM
New Amsterdam	New Amsterdam
New Delhi	Newark
New Zealand	New Delhi
Newark	New Zealand

Subject Heading

The most difficult part of library research seems to be establishing the key word or phrase (i.e., subject heading) that will lead you to the information you seek. This is true not only for the card catalog but also for any other index, in books, encyclopedias, the *Reader's Guide*, etc.

One help is the existence of cross references, "See" and "See also" cards. A "See" card means there is nothing here, that you must look elsewhere. A "See also" card means there is something here, but the information you seek may be listed under another heading. For instance, if you look up "Child abuse," you may be told to see the correct subject heading which is "Cruelty to children." Or if you look up "Energy," there may be a "See also" reference which tells you that "Energy" is a valid subject heading (for books about the physics of force and energy), but if you want something about energy as a fuel you should "See also" the alternative heading, "Power resources."

Here are some questions to ask yourself if you are having trouble with subject headings:

Complete Guide to Speech, Style and Grammar

- Is there a larger subject that might include it? (United States—History—Civil War, rather than Gettysburg, Battle of).
- Is there a smaller subject? (American poetry, rather than Poetry).
- Does your subject overlap another? (Are you searching for the entertainment or the electronics aspect of television?)
- Is there another way to spell it or say it? (Cookery, French vs. French cookery; or Balzac, Honoré de vs. de Balzac, Honoré).
- Does it have a prefix? (U.S. Supreme Court instead of just Supreme Court).
- If your topic is a person, where and when did he live? What was he famous for? (For a report on Michelangelo you would probably do much better not reading a full-length biography but using information under Art—History; European history; Painting—History; Renaissance; Sculpture.)

Other Sources

While today's libraries still find books the most useful sources of information, do not overlook the many non-book materials in its collection. Catalog cards will direct you to recordings, tapes, filmstrips, microfilm, microfiche, pictures, etc. The Vertical File contains pamphlets, clippings, maps, and other materials arranged alphabetically by subject matter in a filing cabinet or pamphlet boxes.

Computer Search

Many libraries now have some of their data on computers. Searching for references by means of the computer can save hours of time, but may entail a service charge. Some of the computerized files give only the bibliographic citation; others may include abstracts or even complete texts. Sometimes the files are also available in printed form. Consult with a librarian to find the most efficient method for your research.

Other Information Retrieval Sources

The card catalog is a comprehensive index to materials in the library; however, there are additional useful indexes to help you. Indexes are lists (or catalogs) of subjects, authors, or titles with information about where to find more material.

- Computers, besides storing information, can tell where it is located, both within a library and in other places.
- Indexes to books and to encyclopedias are a useful aid to finding material in a book or encyclopedia. Too many people commonly ignore the index volume of an encyclopedia set (usually the last volume), but it is an invaluable tool, as it locates all the information in the entire set and often pinpoints where material is found that has no separate article in the alphabetical listing. It can save time, also, as different encyclopedias head the same information differently, i.e. Man, Prehistoric; Prehistoric man; Fossil man; Evolution of Man.

Here is a typical index listing:

> Newton, Sir Isaac (English physicist) N:306 with picture
> Aerodynamics A:78-79
> Calculus (History) C:22
> Color Ci:666
> Dynamics D:321
> Gravitation G:320

Specific information about Newton's Theory of Gravity will be found in volume G on page 320.

- Some magazines and newspapers, such as *National Geographic* and the *New York Times* have indexes to back issues of their publications. Larger libraries index the local newspaper and put it on microfilm or microfiche.
- Reference books, such as *Play Index, Short Story Index, Poetry Index* tell in which books specific plays, stories, and poems are located.
- One of the most valuable indexing tools is the *Reader's Guide to Periodical Literature*, which indexes almost two hundred magazines of general interest. Paperback supplements, published twice a month, are combined into three-month supplements. Then a full year's guide is bound in a single hardcover volume. There is also an *Abridged Readers' Guide* covering fewer magazines. This service is especially useful for finding recent, current information. Here is a typical entry, with explanation:

Under "Libraries" there are four sub-heads in one issue: Automation, Circulation, Federal aid, and Fines. Under "Fines" is found this entry:

A librarian throws the book at overdue borrowers. L. Giuliano. il por People Wkly 17:133 Ap 5 '82

This means L. Giuliano has written an article titled "A librarian throws the book at overdue borrowers" which is found in the magazine *People Weekly,* dated April 5, 1982, on page 133. The volume number for that issue is 17. The article also contain pictures (il) and a portrait (por).

A Home Reference Library

Reference books, which are usually expensive, are not intended for straight-through reading but are designed to impart specific information quickly. The reference collection in a library is usually extensive and is not available to be checked out. Everyone should make a survey of what is available at their favorite library, but most people like to build a small home collection which can prove to be very useful at odd times of the day or night. Many of these books can be purchased in paperback so they fit into the average family's budget.

Indispensable in the home is a good *dictionary* which defines words, gives correct spelling and syllable division, and contains a great deal of additional front and back matter. This other material may include such items as a list of colleges and universities, a table of weights and measures, a conversion table for metric measures, and a brief guide to English grammar and usage. An unabridged dictionary contains almost all the words in the language, while an abridged one is shortened.

For anyone who writes anything a *thesaurus* is most helpful. Also available in paperback, it is a dictionary of synonyms, to help the writer find the exact word needed.

Quotation books, again in paperback, allow the reader and writer to identify a quotation, to cite it in full, and to find an apt one on a particular theme.

Also useful in the home is an *atlas,* a book of maps, which is indispensable for planning trips as well as for obtaining information on political divisions, population, climate, resources, etc.

A multi-volume general *encyclopedia* containing information about people, places, things, ideas, and events can be useful. Annual yearbooks keep it up-to-date. While a one-volume encyclopedia is ideal for quick reference, the more comprehensive multi-volume set is naturally better for detailed information such as school reports. However, most high schools today require several original sources for reports, so the greater need in families with school-age children is often for encyclopedias that can be comprehended by elementary-age students.

A handy tool is an *almanac,* such as the *World Almanac,* which is published yearly in paperback and is chock full of lists, tables, statistics, and all kinds of facts and figures.

If a family has special hobbies or students pursuing special interests, there are innumerable single-subject reference books that could be purchased. Your local library or bookstore have personnel to help you identify appropriate materials.

WRITING EFFECTIVELY

Words are the basic building blocks of all writing, but without effective sentences words mean little. Sentences assembled meaningfully into paragraphs comprise the structure of any composition, whether a letter to a friend or a book on physics.

Sentences

A *sentence* is a group of words expressing a complete thought. It may make a statement, ask a question, give a command, or express an exclamation.

>Antarctica is the seventh continent.
>Are Europe and Asia separate continents?
>See America first!
>So this is Africa!

However, a complete thought may be expressed by a single word: the emphatic "Never!"; a man entering an elevator and saying, "Down"; and the answers ("Are you going?") "No," ("Where is it?") "Here," or ("How do you feel?") "Happy." The concept of a *complete thought* is satisfied by such limited sentences as the telegraphic ARRIVING LAGUARDIA FRIDAY. HOME BEFORE SIX. LOVE STANLEY; or the journalistic headline LABOR UNIONS/HIT JOB

LOSSES. But readers expect most sentences to be *grammatically complete*.

Grammatical Completion

The grammatically complete *simple sentence* consists of a subject and a predicate. The *subject* is a noun or a noun equivalent (pronoun, noun clause, gerund, infinitive; for more about the parts of speech, see the section on "Grammar," page 82) naming the person, place, or thing with which the sentence is chiefly concerned. The *predicate* is the verb or verb phrase asserting something about the subject.

> *Children* (subject) *play* (predicate).

This simple sentence may be expanded and made more complicated (or significant) in various ways.

The subject may be modified:

> *Happy* children play.

Or it may be a *compound subject* when two or more subjects attach to a single predicate:

> *Children* and *adults* play.

The predicate may be modified:

> Children play *hard*.

Or the verb may be given a complement:

> Children play *games*.

The sentence has a compound predicate when two or more predicates follow from a single subject:

> Children *play* and *sleep*.

It becomes a *compound sentence* when two or more simple sentences closely related in thought are joined by commas, semicolons, or coordinating conjunctions:

> Children play, men work, and women manage.

However complicated it may become, the sentence rests on the solid base of subject and predicate. This is true in the *declarative sentence* (above), the *interrogative sentence:*

Do children play?

the *exclamatory sentence:*

How happily the children play!

and the *imperative sentence:*

Play, children! (the subject, *you,* is understood)

The sentence may be made more flexible and expressive by the use of phrases and clauses.

Phrases

A *phrase* is a group of words used as a single part of speech (noun, adjective, adverb, or verb). It does not contain a subject and a predicate.

NOUN PHRASE:	It is impossible *not to pity him; trying to help him* is a problem.
ADVERBIAL PHRASE:	*By Monday* they were gone. I hung it *on the wall*.
ADJECTIVE PHRASE:	A man *of honor,* a name *to admire*.
VERB PHRASE:	He *has asked* for you; he *must have forgotten* already.

Phrases may also be classified by form:

A *prepositional phrase* consists of a preposition and its object and any accompanying modifiers. It is used as an adjective or adverb.

At once they left *for the big town*. (prepositional phrases used as adverbs)

The man *with the hoe*. (used as adjective)

He felt lost *in the impersonal clamor* (used as adverb) *of the advertising industry*. (used as adjective)

An *infinitive phrase* consists of an infinitive (and its object, if present) and any accompanying modifiers. It is used as a noun, adjective, or adverb.

I want *to see* (infinitive) *the moon* (object). (infinitive phrase used as noun)

Professor Thomson is the man *to know*. (used as adjective)

A diplomat must be able *to make* (infinitive) *the most* (object) *of the existing situation* (prepositional phrase, adjective modifying *the most*). (infinitive phrase used as adverb)

A *participial phrase* consists of a participle (and its object, if present) and any accompanying modifiers. It is used as an adjective.

Thinking quickly, he regained his poise.

The plane *carrying* (participle) *the serum* (object) arrived in time.

Shirley, *earnestly* (adverb modifying the next word, *talking*) *talking* (participle) *to the group* (prepositional phrase, adverb modifying *talking*), signaled Carrie to wait.

A *gerund phrase* consists of a gerund (and its object, if present) and any accompanying modifiers. It is used as a noun.

Daily *swimming* kept him in trim.

Flying (gerund) *a kite* (object) can be hard work.

His editor advised *writing* (gerund) *on a totally new subject*. (prepositional phrase, adjective modifying *writing*)

A *verb phrase* consists of a verb and its auxiliaries.

I *will have seen* him by then.

The Senate *could* hardly *have foreseen* the result of its action.

Clauses

A *clause* is a group of words containing a subject and a predicate. It may be independent or dependent. An *independent clause* is, essentially, a sentence; it differs only in its capitalization and punctuation. In the following example the independent clause can stand alone by capitalizing *he* and adding a period after *plotters*.

Mindful of his honor, *he avoided every contact with the plotters* while continuing to insist on his innocence.

A *dependent clause* cannot stand alone. It is connected to an independent clause by a relative pronoun, present or implied (*who, which, that*), or by a subordinating conjunction (*after, because, since, while,* etc.) and functions as a part of the sentence—as noun, adjective, or adverb.

> *That everyone was against him* was his constant complaint. (noun clause, subject)

> He estimated *which of the problems he could solve.* (noun clause, object of verb)

> In the afternoon we came to *what was evidently the main road.* (noun clause, object of preposition *to*)

> The man *who fails at everything he tries* may not be trying. (adjective clause, modifying *man;* [*that*] *he tries* is a dependent phrase although part of the larger dependent phrase is also a dependent phrase used as an adjective modifying *everything*)

> He may succeed *if he tries a completely new approach.* (adverbial clause, modifying *succeed*)

A dependent clause need not be so complete as these examples. Often, especially in spoken language and informal writing, the connective between independent clause and dependent adjective clause is merely implied and not expressed.

> The man *he said was coming* never showed up. (*Who* or *that* is understood.)

Sometimes in informal speech or writing a dependent clause contains neither subject nor verb.

> *When crossing,* look both ways. (*When you are crossing* is understood.)

> His clothes were old *though clean.* (*Though they were clean* is understood.)

Constructions such as these are called *elliptical clauses.* When properly related to the main clause, an elliptical clause adds economy and punch to writing. The dependent clause used as an adjective

Complete Guide to Speech, Style and Grammar

(*adjective clause*) is called *restrictive* if it adds information necessary to identify the subject or restricts it to a special case.

> The boy *you met last Friday* telephoned again.

> The man *who can plan ahead* is automatically at an advantage.

> Rebellions *that are successful* are recorded as revolutions.

If the subject requires no further identification after being named, the clause is *nonrestrictive* and simply adds additional information.

> Jaspar, *who never gave up,* finally hit on a way to catch the chipmunk.

There is only one Jaspar being discussed, and the reader presumably knows who he is; the nonrestrictive clause is not essential to the meaning of the sentence, though it enriches it. Additional examples of nonrestrictive clauses follow.

> He sat on the table, *which could barely support him*.

> She was sure that the man, *whom she had not met,* must be her long-lost brother.

Who (whom) and *which* may introduce either restrictive or nonrestrictive clauses, but *that* introduces only restrictive clauses. Relative pronouns may be omitted only in restrictive clauses.

> The man *we hoped to see* has left. (Restrictive *who* is understood.)

> We all liked the pie *she baked*. (Restrictive *that* is understood.)

Nonrestrictive clauses are set off by commas, and often the various choices of punctuation can give the sentence radically different meanings.

RESTRICTIVE
CLAUSE: Engineers who have little understanding of theory are rarely put in charge of a program.

NON-
RESTRICTIVE
CLAUSE: Engineers, who have little understanding of
                      theory, are rarely put in charge of a program.

The first is a warning; the second is a sneer. (For the specific rules
on punctuating restrictive and nonrestrictive clauses, see page 136.)

Kinds of Sentences

A *simple sentence* contains only one independent clause, however
modified.

> In times of economic expansion, almost any investor may
> seem a financial wizard by his luck on the stock market.

Stripped of the adverbial prepositional phrases *in times of eco-
nomic expansion* and *by his luck,* the adjective phrase *on the stock
market,* the adverb *almost,* the adjective *financial,* this example re-
veals itself as basically the simple sentence *(almost any) investor may
seem a wizard.*

A *compound sentence* contains two or more coordinate independent clauses, joined by a coordinating conjunction:

> He tried hard, but he simply had no talent.

or by a conjunctive adverb preceded by a semicolon:

> It had begun to rain; however, they had brought umbrellas.

or by a semicolon (or colon) alone:

> He was tired of life; he was afraid to die.

> The Greeks made their decision: They would resist the Per-
> sian invasion.

A *complex sentence* contains one independent clause and one or
more dependent clauses.

> However fast we ran, the ball ran faster.

> He whispered that he was sure (that) he had recognized one
> of the men who had come in. (three dependent clauses, the
> second with *that* understood)

Complete Guide to Speech, Style and Grammar

A *compound-complex* sentence contains two or more independent clauses, and one or more dependent clauses.

> Although the weather forecast promised rain, the sky was cloudless, and the dry spell continued.

Effective Sentences

To write effective sentences, you must learn not only to avoid certain basic errors but also how to employ the tools of good writing. Often the "tool" to be used is simply on the other side of the coin from the error to be avoided. For example, to correct a *wordy* sentence, you take all unnecessary words out of the sentence; however, you should try to avoid wordiness by writing concisely, by writing no unnecessary words in the first place. Below you will find some constructive suggestions on how to write effective sentences.

Note the word *effective*. It carries the implication that, in writing, we wish to *do* something to our readers, to have an "effect" on them. If we fail to determine what this effect is to be, our sentences will be ineffective. On the other hand, if we do assign a purpose to everything we write—something specific that we want to say—we will have found one pathway toward effective writing.

Making Sentences Effective

Use Concrete Language

A good writer uses concrete and definite words frequently, and avoids vague or abstract words. Concrete language gives the reader a specific picture rather than a general statement. It builds images that the reader can readily grasp.

General   The lovely sounds of nature woke me.

Specific   The wind in the trees and a bird's chirping woke me.

Be Positive

Good writing makes direct, positive statements. Use the word "not" only when the negative idea is emphatic; otherwise express what you want to say in the positive form.

Written Communication

Indirect   He did not like Mr. Harvey's approach to grammar.

Direct   He disliked Mr. Harvey's approach to grammar.

Indirect   I did not think the trip would be very interesting.

Direct   I thought the trip would be a bore.

Indirect   Mr. Alexander was perhaps our best committee chairman. He was not long-winded, he was never biased, and he never failed to get the business before us covered.

Direct   Mr. Alexander was the best committee chairman we ever had. He was direct, unbiased, and efficient.

Use the Active Voice

Use the passive voice only when the subject is unknown or when the fact that something was *done to* the subject is of primary importance. Otherwise use the active voice.

Vary Your Sentences

Avoid monotonous writing by keeping sentences varied in both structure and length. Check that sentences begin with the various parts of speech. Note that appropriate use of compounds and series can make your writing more concise as well as more varied. (See *Basic Sentence Errors: Monotony,* page 56.)

Use the Important Positions

Gain emphasis by placing important words or ideas at the important positions in the sentence—at the beginning or at the end, especially at the end. Either kind of sentence is effective, but a preponderance of one or the other is decidedly ineffective and artificial. Whatever kind of sentence you select to express an idea, be sure to tuck away illustrative details and parenthetical expressions in the middle of the sentence.

Euphony and Rhythm

Euphony is the smooth, pleasant flow of agreeable sounds. An experienced writer chooses and arranges his words so that they form patterns of sound that are rhythmical and euphonious when read

49

aloud. The more experienced and skillful the writer, the more pleasant are the sounds he produces. The ability to produce these sound effects comes only from experience.

Do not repeat words that have the same sound. Do not alliterate. Do not confuse rhythm with rhyme. An alliteration is the repetition of an initial sound in two or more words in the same phrase or clause. It is an eye-catching device used by advertising copy and newspaper headline writers, but it has no place in formal prose writing. Rhyme, the repetition of end sounds, is a device of verse, not of prose. The first example below illustrates how euphony can be destroyed by alliteration; the second, by rhyme.

Alliteration   In a fury I flew into the fray.

Rhyme   I yearn to learn who she is.

Figures of Speech

A prevalent belief among students is that figures of speech are old-fashioned and should be confined to rhetoric and poetry. This is a false belief. We all use figurative language every day, and more often than not, without realizing it. *Hungry as a bear, quick as lightning, time flies, drive a bargain*—these are common figurative expressions. A figure of speech is any deviation from the literal meaning or ordinary use of words that is designed to make a thought clearer or more forceful.

Suppose we express how a girl sings by comparing her with a nightingale. *May sings like a nightingale.* We do not say literally how May sings. We suggest the image of the nightingale and leave it to the reader's imagination to know the quality of May's voice. This is communication in figurative language. The example of May's voice is a figure of speech known as a *simile*. The simile expresses a figurative resemblance or comparison between essentially different things. One thing is said to be like another, and the resemblance is usually introduced by *like* or *as*. *Hungry as a bear* and *quick as lightning* are also similes. Actually, the best similes compare things which are in most respects unlike, but which have at least one point of striking resemblance.

Let us go one step further. We don't simply say that May has a voice *like* a nightingale, but we say that her voice *is* the voice of a nightingale. *May has the voice of a nightingale.* The two voices are equated. This is a *metaphor*. It is simply an expanded simile. A simile states that one thing is *like* another; a metaphor, that one thing *is* another.

Simile He mouths a sentence as curs mouth a bone.

Metaphor All the world's a stage,
And all the men and women merely players.

Similes and metaphors are the most common figures of speech. Other figures of speech also are common: *hyperbole* (extravagant but deliberate and fanciful exaggeration), *litotes* (deliberate understatement), *personification* (infusing life into inanimate things), and *metonymy* (naming one thing in terms of another which is part of it or associated with it).

Hyperbole Thanks a million.

Litotes Faulkner is not a bad writer (meaning he is a great writer).

Personification Time flies.

Metonymy She set a good table (meaning she prepared a good meal).

The "Intentional Fragment"

The grammatical structure of the sentence has been analyzed. We have already stated that a sentence need not necessarily contain a subject and a verb, although by far the majority of our written sentences do. Expressions such as "Why not?" or a conversational colloquialism such as "Me, too" are considered to be sentences. In writing, the sentence that intentionally lacks a subject or a verb is called an "intentional fragment." Professional writers use intentional fragments for stylistic effect. Beginning writers, however, are best advised not to use fragments of any kind.

Idioms

In every language, combinations of words have developed which appear completely proper to the natives of the country where the language is spoken, but which sound peculiar to a foreign visitor. Such expressions are known as *idioms*.

Complete Guide to Speech, Style and Grammar

Sometimes idioms conform to grammatical rules, and at other times they may conflict with such rules, but idiomatic usage has established the expression as proper.

The prepositional idiom is a type of expression that gives even the native some difficulty. A seemingly well-written sentence will be ruined by a careless use of a prepositional idiom. The trouble sometimes arises in determining the correct preposition. For example: It is *dependent on* and *independent of.* To determine which preposition an idiom takes, see a good dictionary. Some idioms require using words as adverbs that more frequently are used as prepositions. When combining two or more idioms, we must be careful not to drop part of one idiom.

Wrong   Laura had no desire nor need *of* Sam's approval.

Right   Laura had no desire *for* nor need *of* Sam's approval.

Synonyms

Synonyms are good words to become familiar with. They help give variety to sentences, and their proper use avoids repetitious phrases. A *synonym* actually is a word that means the same or nearly the same as another word. Practical students often resort to synonyms as a device to avoid using words they do not know how to spell. A student may wish to use *lugubrious* on his essay examination but, unsure of the spelling, resorts to the word *dismal.* Careless substitution can change the subtle meaning of a sentence, even if it would appear that the two words are almost identical. To *plagiarize* and to *copy* often mean the same thing; there is, however, a distinct difference. To *plagiarize* definitely means to steal another person's literary effort and pass it off as one's own, whereas one may *copy* another person's work, with or without intent to steal it.

Antonyms

This is a word that means the opposite of another word. But even antonyms can be useful in giving sentences a greater variety if properly used. *Happy* and *sad* are antonyms. Seemingly, it would appear they are not interchangeable in a sentence, yet the writer may feel that the word *happy* is too strong, and he may decide, despite the admonition against the use of the negative, that *not sad* is just the right state he is trying to describe.

Basic Sentence Errors

The Fragment

The *fragment* is a statement that fails to state a complete thought; it is an incomplete sentence. Generally, the error can be corrected by simply attaching the fragment to the sentence before or after it, as in each of the corrections below. Unintentional fragments used as complete sentences generally consist of phrases, appositives, or dependent clauses.

> **Fragment** The soldiers stood stoically in the rain. *Cursing quietly over their wretched luck.* (verbal phrase incorrectly used as a complete sentence)

> **Complete** The soldiers stood stoically in the rain, cursing quietly over their wretched luck.

> **Fragment** He was an unbelievable person. *A man as well read and as outspoken as any I've ever met.* (an appositive incorrectly used as a complete sentence)

> **Complete** He was an unbelievable person, a man as well read and as outspoken as any I've ever met.

> **Fragment** The soldiers were careful to place twenty-four-hour guards around the encampment. *So that they would not be caught off guard by an attack at any time.* (dependent clause used incorrectly as a complete sentence)

> **Complete** The soldiers were careful to place twenty-four-hour guards around the encampment, so that they would not be caught off guard by an attack at any time.

The Run-on Sentence

The *run-on sentence* occurs when the writer has failed to separate properly two sentences or independent clauses, with the result that the two "run into" each other. Two major types of run-on sentences occur. The first type contains no punctuation at all between the sentences. Such sentences are known as "fused sentences" or "stringiness." The second type of run-on sentence is one in which a comma has been improperly used. This is often called a "comma splice."

Complete Guide to Speech, Style and Grammar

Run-on Let us be wary but let us not fall prey to fear. (fused: failure to use punctuation between independent clauses)

Improved Let us be wary, but let us not fall prey to fear.

Run-on A soft answer turns away wrath, grievous words stir up anger. (comma splice: comma incorrectly used to separate independent clauses)

Improved A soft answer turns away wrath; grievous words stir up anger.

To avoid writing run-on sentences, one must know the four possible ways of connecting independent clauses. (See also *Punctuation: The Comma*.) As a general rule, if the ideas are to receive equal emphasis, use the period and place the ideas in different sentences, or use the semicolon alone. If one idea is more important than the other, use the comma and a coordinating conjunction, or the semicolon and a conjunctive adverb.

Mixed Constructions

A *mixed construction* results when one part of a sentence does not agree grammatically with another part of the sentence. The two major types of mixed construction involve subject and verb disagreement, and pronoun and antecedent disagreement.

Wrong A series of lectures were given by Mr. Olsen. (Plural verb *were* does not agree with singular subject *series*.)

Right A series of lectures was given by Mr. Olsen. (Verb agrees with subject.)

Wrong Sometimes circumstantial evidence will convict a person of a crime they did not commit. (Plural pronoun *they* does not agree with singular antecedent *person*.)

Right Sometimes circumstantial evidence will convict a person of a crime he or she did not commit. (Pronoun agrees with antecedent.)

Dangling Modifiers

The *dangling modifier* is a verbal phrase that either has no word in the sentence to modify or is placed in such a way that it appears to modify unintended words in the same sentence.

Dangling   Making a flying tackle, Sam's shoe came off. (The participial phrase is *Making a flying tackle,* but the subject of the clause that follows is *shoe. Making a flying tackle* cannot possibly refer to a shoe.)

Improved   Making a flying tackle, Sam lost his shoe. (*Sam* is now the subject to which the participial phrase properly refers.)

Dangling   To be sure of a good seat, your tickets must be bought far in advance. (The understood subject of the infinitive phrase *To be sure* is not the same as the subject of the clause that follows.)

Improved   To be sure of a good seat, you must buy your tickets far in advance. (The infinitive phrase modifies *you,* the subject of the sentence.)

Dangling   After waiting an hour, the train finally came. (The train waited an hour? Obviously not. *After waiting an hour* has no word in this sentence to modify.)

Improved   After waiting an hour, we finally caught our train. (*After waiting an hour* refers to *we,* the subject of the sentence.)

Squinting Modifiers

A *squinting modifier* is one that is carelessly placed so that it appears to modify both the words preceding and the words following it. The reader has to stop reading to figure out what is being modified.

Squinting   The man who shoved his way to the platform angrily addressed the crowd. (What does *angrily* modify? The way the man made his way to the platform? Or the way he addressed the crowd?)

Improved   The man who angrily shoved his way to the platform addressed the crowd. *OR* The man who shoved his way to the platform addressed the crowd angrily.

Complete Guide to Speech, Style and Grammar

There are two types of verbal phrase constructions that are independent of the rest of the sentence and that need not modify the subject of the clause that follows it. The first type is the *absolute phrase* consisting of a noun or pronoun followed by a participle.

The play having finished, the audience left.

The second type of verbal phrase that can be independent of the rest of the sentence is a phrase that states a general truth. A general truth does not refer to the action of a specific person or thing. Such expressions as *taking everything into consideration* and *to put it another way* are verbal phrases that can stand apart from the rest of the sentence.

Monotony

The most common form of this fault is the dull repetition of a subject-verb sentence pattern. Monotony also occurs when the writer fails to vary the length of his sentences. Monotony results, in fact, from any continued, dull repetition of sentence structure or length.

> **Not Varied** He opened the car door. He stepped out. He walked toward the store. He tried to remember all the things his wife had told him to buy. He hated shopping!

> **Varied** Opening the car door, he stepped out and walked toward the store, trying to remember all the things his wife had told him to buy. How he hated shopping!

Faulty Parallelism

A series of related ideas of equal importance can often be most effectively expressed by writing them in what is called "parallel form." Parallelism, which treats like ideas in like form, balances words, phrases, and clauses against one another. In a series, for example, words should be in the same class and in the same parts of speech. One may begin a series of parallel forms, then lose the parallelism, and thus commit the error known as "faulty parallelism."

> **Not Parallel** Although very good-looking, Ted was modest, shy, and didn't talk much. (The parallel adjectives *modest* and *shy* demand a third adjective rather than a clause to

follow them, in order that the sentence should read smoothly and clearly.)

Parallel   Although very good-looking, Ted was modest, shy, and quiet.

Not Parallel   The man at the desk ordered me to be silent, to sit down, and that I should wait until I was spoken to. (The two infinitives and the phrase beginning *and that* constitute unparallel form.)

Parallel   The man at the desk ordered me to be silent, to sit down, and to wait until I was spoken to. (A third infinitive has been added to complete the parallelism begun by the first two.)

Correlative Conjunctions and Parallelism

The use of the correlative conjunctions can lead the writer to make mistakes in parallelism. These conjunctions—*either . . . or, neither . . . nor, not only . . . but also*—help tighten sentence structure and strengthen expression, but they must be used logically. That is, the same kinds of words and the same grammatical structure must appear on both sides of the correlatives, otherwise, parallelism and sense and effectiveness will be lost.

Not Parallel   Al is both a marvelous athlete and he dresses very well. (A modifying phrase on one side and an independent clause on the other.)

Parallel   Al is both a marvelous athlete and a fine dresser. (Modifying phrase on either side.)

Not Parallel   Your grandmother has not only a sharp mind but also her humor is lively.

Parallel   Your grandmother has not only a sharp mind but also a lively humor.

Mixed Metaphor

Combining two different comparisons or figures of speech that are inconsistent or incongruous with each other, produces the "mixed metaphor." The writer must be careful to maintain logic as he adds

Complete Guide to Speech, Style and Grammar

color with images and comparisons; he must make sure his comparisons "fit" one another. A "ship of state" cannot get "lost in the woods of diplomatic entanglements" (ships do not sail in the woods); "her eyes" could not be "glistening pebbles in the twilight sky" (pebbles do not glisten in the sky).

> **Mixed** With determination Ellen dug into the sea of work before her.

> **Logical** With determination Ellen dug into the pile of work before her. *OR* With determination Ellen plunged into the sea of work before her.

> **Mixed** Now, friend, chew upon this branch of my thoughts: all good looks are a snare that no man should let himself be drowned in.

> **Logical** Now, friend, chew upon this morsel of my thoughts: all good looks are a snare that no man should let himself be trapped in.

Inadequate Subordination

Immature minds seldom use subordination. It takes maturity to select a lesser idea and to subordinate it to the important one. A child, for example, is likely to give new facts equal importance. Learning about Columbus, the child is likely to say: "Columbus was born in Portugal. He was given three ships by the Queen of Spain. He became famous as the discoverer of America. He died in poverty and neglect." A more mature version of these facts would be: "Columbus, who was born in Portugal, was given three ships by the Queen of Spain. He became famous as the discoverer of America; however, he died in poverty and neglect." Two simple words, the relative pronoun *who* and the conjunctive adverb *however,* place the facts about Columbus in truer perspective by subordinating the less important facts to the more important ones.

Inadequate subordination is the sign not only of immaturity but of ineffective writing. It results in short, choppy sentences. The writer who combines ideas in sentences without proper subordination inevitably is guilty of an excessive number of *and* and *so* clauses. The rule to remember is: Put subordinate ideas in subordinate (dependent) clauses (or phrases) and main ideas in main (independent) clauses.

Inadequate Subordination Tom was tired of listening to the lecture, and no one could see him, and so he slipped quietly out of the room. (Three ideas are placed in independent clauses, thereby giving each idea equal importance and resulting in no subordination at all.)

Improved Tom was tired of listening to the lecture, and since no one could see him, he slipped quietly out of the room. (One idea has been made subordinate to the other two, by putting it in a dependent clause). *OR* Since Tom was tired of listening to the lecture and as no one could see him, he slipped quietly out of the room. (Two ideas made subordinate.)

Faulty Subordination

When combining several ideas in one sentence, be sure not to make the mistake of subordinating the main idea. The less important of two ideas should always be in a dependent clause or phrase. Never introduce the main idea of a sentence with a conjunctive adverb.

Weak Although he easily won the club tennis championship, he showed some signs of fatigue. (The main idea of the sentence is weakly introduced by the subordinating conjunction *although*. The subordinate idea is in an independent clause.)

Improved Although he showed some signs of fatigue, he easily won the club tennis championship. (The subordinate idea is properly placed in a subordinate clause, and the main idea is properly placed in the independent clause.)

"Fine" Writing

"Fine" writing is a ruse to cover up absence of knowledge. It is the use of big, pretentious words for simple, direct words. It is word exhibitionism at its worst. Students often resort to "fine" writing to impress, to make the reader think that they know what they are talking about. "Fine" writing is a puerile, sophomoric device, and it impresses nobody. Of course, writers often inject pretentious words into the speech of teenage delinquents, race track touts, and hoodlums of diverse sorts. This they do for comic irony, and the results can be hilarious. But it is pathetic to hear the same words uttered by high school and college students.

There is nothing wrong with big words, but they should normally be used only to express meanings and shades of meaning for which simpler words do not exist.

Split Infinitives

To split an infinitive is to insert an expression between the *to* and the verb. The inserted expression is usually an adverb (to *entirely* comprehend). Grammarians at one time insisted that a preposition should never be separated from its object by any other words. The rule now generally accepted sanctions the split infinitive when it results in a clearer meaning or a pleasanter sound. In the illustrations of acceptable split infinitives below, note how a transposition of the *to* would affect the meaning and the rhythm of the sentences.

> Do you want us to really enjoy ourselves?
> The judge refused to summarily dismiss the case.
> He failed to entirely comprehend the charge.

The Double Negative

Avoid the double negative because a double negative makes a positive. Use a single negative to express a negative idea.

Wrong   I haven't no money left.

Right   I have no money left.

The following are troublesome words. They are all negative, or negative by implication, so they should not be accompanied by a second negative word.

barely	no one
hardly	none
neither	nonesuch
never	not
no	nothing
nobody	only

Unneeded Words

Beware of repeating ideas already expressed.

Repetitious   Repeat what you said again.

Concise   Repeat what you said.

Repetitious   The reason I didn't do my homework was on account of the fact that I forgot the assignment.

Better   The reason I didn't do my homework was that I forgot the assignment.

Concise   I didn't do my homework because I forgot the assignment.

Weak Words

The weakest words in the English language are the intensives *very, little, rather,* and *pretty*. An *intensive* is a word that supposedly makes another word more forceful and emphatic. But the use of an adjective (as an adverb) to intensify another adjective often has the opposite effect. This is especially true of adjectives that have been used so often with so little regard for their true meanings that they have lost all the force they once had. Take the words *awful, dreadful, fearful,* and *horrible*. These are potent words when used to mean "to inspire awe" *(awful),* "to inspire dread" *(dreadful),* "to instill fear" *(fearful),* and "to excite horror" *(horrible)*. However, when these words are loosely used as intensives, they languish into impotence. They are especially absurd when they intensify words that contradict their own meanings. Expressions such as *awfully nice* and *horribly sorry* are not only feeble and placid but absurdly contradictory. The following is a list of words that should not be used as intensives. Unless you know the true meanings of these words, do not use them at all.

amazing	gorgeous	splendid
awful	grand	stunning
colossal	horrible	stupendous
devastating	huge	superb
dreadful	little	terrible
enormous	magnificent	terrific
fabulous	marvelous	tremendous
fearful	pretty	very
frightful	rather	wonderful

Complete Guide to Speech, Style and Grammar

Slang

Slang is unacceptable in either ordinary conversation or formal writing. If it belongs anywhere, it is in light banter in an informal setting—but only if it is original and lively. Effective slang usually is a cleverly humorous or dramatically surprising play on words, achieved by taking words out of context, juxtaposing unexpected words, using very compressed metaphors, and the like. Unfortunately, slang ages quickly and becomes stale.

Why, then, is it so popular? Its chief attraction is that it makes a single word do so much. In an instant, a word of slang can communicate a reasonably exact meaning, suggest a humorous comparison, arouse emotion, and suggest personality. Think of how much more is said in the single word "Scram!" than in the sentence, "You may go now." In this very flexibility of slang lies one of its chief dangers: It may be used for so many things that it becomes a crutch for one's vocabulary. One may, for example, use the slang word "dig" in a variety of contexts: "I don't dig (understand) this equation"; "I dig (feel satisfied with) the mark I got in English"; "Baby, I dig (am attracted to) you." With so handy a word available, the lazy or obtuse person will overuse it, quite failing to make distinct the various meanings he or she actually intends. Such dependence on slang prevents the development of a good vocabulary.

In sum, therefore, if you wish to inject slang into the dialogue of your fictional characters, by all means do so—with care and with a sparing hand. Incidentally, never enclose slang words within quotation marks, either single or double.

Solecisms

A *solecism* is the violation of correct grammatical structure. It is considered a blunder, not an illiteracy or a barbarism, and is usually the result of carelessness.

Colloquialisms

Most students confuse colloquialisms with provincialisms or localisms and think they refer to sectional peculiarities of speech. Most students also attach some sort of stigma to the word and try to avoid using words or expressions that are labeled colloquial in the dictionary. A colloquialism really has nothing to do with sectional peculiarities, and there is nothing wrong or improper about using it under certain circumstances. The word simply labels expressions that are more acceptable in familiar or ordinary conversation than in formal speech and writing. For example, the president of a college, when talking with his colleagues, may quite properly use colloquialisms. However, when he dons cap and gown to deliver an address at the annual commencement exercises, he scrupulously avoids colloquialisms. The difference is in the setting.

Using colloquialisms is all right when you are talking with members of your family or friends and when you are writing friendly letters or informal reports. An example of a colloquialism and its equivalent formal form is given below.

> **Colloquialism** What a close shave!

> **Formal** What a narrow escape!

Jargon

Dictionaries define *jargon* as language that is "unintelligible." This is an unfortunately broad definition. We usually associate the term with the "bureaucratic jargon" of officialdom, also referred to as *governmentese*. In this sense *jargon* has partly derisive, partly humorous connotations.

In a stricter sense, *jargon* is the specialized vocabulary of persons who are engaged in the same trade or profession. The intelligibility of the specialized vocabulary naturally excludes the outsider, but for the insider it is loaded with meaning. A single expression can stand for a thought or idea that might otherwise take ten, twenty, or even a hundred words to express with a standard vocabulary. As long as the expression is kept within the specialized group, its use is perfectly necessary and legitimate. When the expression is employed outside the field in contexts where other vocabulary is available, it becomes jargon in the commonly accepted sense of the term. Thus, the expression "relate to" is a favorite in the vocabulary of psychologists. Employed by a psychologist outside his professional setting, or by the layman, this same expression loses its specialized meaning and becomes absurd jargon.

Trite Expressions and Clichés

A trite expression is an overused expression. It has been used so much that when the reader sees the first word or two, he can anticipate what follows. And when the reader can anticipate your words, you cannot hold his attention. "A good time was had by all" is a trite expression. A cliché is a figure of speech or turn of words that may have been original and clever once upon a time but that has become trite and stale through overuse. Like an oft-repeated joke, *it wears its welcome thin* (the expression in italics is a cliché). How do you tell when a cliché is a cliché? As happens with jokes, you hear one and you think it is original, or you think one up yourself. You hasten to tell it to your friends. But they have already heard it countless times. So it is with clichés. You must consciously be on the lookout for them in whatever you read or hear. Whenever you spot a cliché, make a mental note not to use it in your own writing.

Provincialisms and Localisms

A *provincialism* is a word, phrase, or idiom peculiar to a major geographical section or region. A *localism* is peculiar to a limited locality. They are legitimate and proper when used in speech by persons who live in a particular section or locality. Since provincialisms and localisms are not in national usage, however, they do not appear in formal, expository writing. Obviously, both are essential to the speech of characters in fiction.

Barbarisms

Barbarism is the name grammarians give to the gross misuse of words. To use *eats* for *food*, as in "Pass me the eats," would be termed a barbarism. Another example of a barbarism is the use of *learn* for *teach*, as in "That will learn you a lesson."

Effective Paragraphs

Any reader is aware that an indented sentence means a new paragraph. In dialogue, such indentation shows merely that a new speaker is being quoted. But the indentation at the beginning of the paragraph always indicates some change of subject or approach—in the description, the narration, the argument—whatever the type of the writing may be.

The new paragraph, however, does more for us than indicate a change in thought. For the paragraph is the real building block of any prose writing. The casual letter-writer, the student, the professional journalist, the novelist—all use paragraphing in their letters, essays, articles, or novels. In order to function correctly, that is, to fit neatly among the other blocks as well as help to hold them up, the paragraph must, itself, be a carefully completed and finely shaped unit. Perhaps the best definition of a *paragraph* might be this: *the carefully rounded development of a single impression or idea*.

The reader should bear in mind that no absolute criteria exist for determining a good paragraph. There is agreement that a paragraph should contain the stylistic elements which effectively convey the writer's idea or purpose. Such a paragraph is effective—it is good.

Paragraphs may be purely descriptive, narrative, or expository; or they may include any mixture of these major types of writing. The principles of good paragraph-writing discussed below can be applied to all types of paragraphs.

Principles

The Topic Idea

A good writer knows exactly why he or she is starting a new paragraph and why he or she is ending it. Within that one paragraph *one thing* is being said as clearly and as completely as possible. That one thing we call the topic idea of a paragraph. Often this topic idea is expressed in a *topic sentence* that generally comes at or near the beginning of the paragraph. The topic sentence, however, need not come at the beginning, nor does the paragraph have to have a topic sentence, so long as the single idea is clear.

Adequate Development

The topic idea can be conveyed only if the writer makes sufficient effort to show what is meant to the reader. The different methods of "showing" are enumerated below, but it is important to remember that no matter how you construct your paragraph, it must give enough details, facts, examples, or reasons to hold and convince the reader.

> **Inadequate** Everyone should play some sport from which he gets both enjoyment and physical toughening. Sports have always been considered important. They make you strong and you can have a lot of fun with them. Further-

more, friendships can be made through sports. Nobody can deny that for many reasons, sports are a "must."

In the above paragraph, note that most of the sentences are mere restatements of the topic sentence or of each other and that they are extremely general. The way to construct your paragraphs well consists of your ability to give details, facts, and specifics in concise and *concrete* language.

Unity

The well-written paragraph sticks relentlessly to its topic idea and departs from that idea only to bring in closely related material. A careless writer, on the other hand, wanders from the topic, and thereby loses the concentrated focus or unity that writing must have if it is to be effective. The best way to keep each paragraph unified is to make the subject of most of your sentences the same as the subject of your topic sentence; hold on to your subject, and you will hold on to your topic idea.

Transition

Transition is "going across" or—in writing—getting the reader smoothly from one thought to another, one image to another, one sentence to the next. You can achieve good transition by practicing these two important principles:

1. *Arrange the sentences of each paragraph in logical order so that each follows the one before it as naturally as possible.*

   Failure to build the paragraph on such a predetermined order can result in confusion and lack of transition. Presenting images or events simply in their *order of occurrence in time* or in their "narrative order" is one of the most common methods of developing a paragraph logically.

   You could also arrange the ideas or arguments in a predetermined order of importance.

2. *Wherever necessary, use words and phrases that tie your ideas together as closely as possible.*

   These words and phrases, sometimes called "transitional devices," can be categorized under three headings: pronouns, echo words, and connectives.

a. Pronouns

Using pronouns whose antecedents are the subject of the paragraph makes transition stronger. The most useful of these for transitional purposes are the demonstratives: *this, that, these, those.*

Nothing in the way of equipment was overlooked. It was because of *this* preparation that the expedition was so successful.

b. Echo words

These are words that relate to or echo the topic idea, and their inclusion holds the paragraph—and the reader—to the subject.

The men fought the *fire* mightily for three days. However, the *blaze* was too much for them; the *flames* would not be extinguished. Such *holocausts* cost Americans millions of acres in valuable forest every year.

c. Connective words and phrases

This group of transitional devices is extensive, and we use many of them quite naturally in our everyday speech. The group includes all conjunctions—subordinate, correlative, and coordinate (see *Grammar: Conjunctions*, page 118)—plus a large number of "connective" adverbs and adverb phrases.

The following paragraph has employed transitional words and phrases. Note that the flow is smooth and its thought easy to follow.

My black, furry poodle, Totor, is a real problem to me. *Ever since* I bought him from a pet shop, he has caused me nothing but trouble. *However,* I do like him *because* he has such a charming, lively personality. *But* this liveliness is also the source of my problem, *for* it leads him to do the most dreadful things. *For instance,* he hops up on the kitchen table and eats a whole ham. *Then* he chews the caps off the milk bottles and drinks all the cream. *And* he is always stealing shoes and chewing them apart. *Nevertheless,* he is worth it *because* I have learned how to outfox him—much of the time.

Necessary Design

The good paragraph is organically dependent upon its topic sentence or topic idea for its overall construction. It has a logical design that arises out of the purpose of the paragraph. Thus, if your purpose is to describe a room, your details would be arranged in an order in which they might be seen if the reader were standing in the room. If, in another paragraph, your purpose is to convince your reader of a certain fact, you would list your points in such a way that they would have maximum effect on him or her (perhaps in an ascending or climactic order of importance).

Developing a Paragraph

The way the writer develops a topic idea in any single paragraph must always be determined by the topic idea and the purpose that the writer has in mind for the paragraph. The six major ways in which a writer can develop a topic idea within any paragraph are described below:

Examples or Illustrations

Sometimes we may be saying something that we cannot explain clearly, and our listener may suggest, "Well, suppose you give me an example." Examples, or illustrations, provide us with ways of putting something abstract and perhaps difficult to comprehend into images or pictures that are easy to understand. You give an example of something; you put forth an illustration of a point. Hence, this method of developing a paragraph is especially useful in *expository* and *argumentative* writing.

Develop a Single Illustration

Often the easiest way to say what you mean is to tell a simple story that says it for you. Such a method of developing a topic idea can help you define a word, make a point clear, or explain an idea. Hence, the "single-illustration paragraph" is used most frequently in *expository* and *argumentative* writing.

Explain by Definition

In *expository* writing, we can sometimes more clearly discuss an idea or concept by *defining* the word that embodies the idea. The definition should expand the basic idea by presenting other ideas with which the reader is already familiar.

Explain by Analogy

An *analogy* is a single illustration that describes or explains one thing by describing something quite different but at the same time similar, so that there is a clear parallel between the two. George Orwell's much-discussed novel *Animal Farm* is an analogy in the form of a novel. In this book, Orwell presents his attitude toward the aftermath of the Russian Revolution by telling a story of a group of very human animals on a farm. The analogy is often more dramatic than a simple illustration because of its suggestive powers. Thus, for example, Orwell's use of animals immediately suggests that the historical figures whom they represent were somewhat less than human in their behavior.

Illustrate by Comparison and Contrast

Comparison and contrast as a method of developing a paragraph can take one of three forms, depending on the topic idea and the purpose of the writer:

1. Showing comparisons or similarities
2. Showing contrasts or dissimilarities
3. Showing both comparisons and contrasts

As you can see, the third is a combination of the first two methods. This approach is especially useful when describing abstract ideas.

Give Reasons

The paragraph that uses reasons to develop its topic idea will be more effective if the reasons are listed in some logical or dramatic order, not haphazardly. The reasons are listed in increasing order of importance. Since the end of the paragraph—like the end of a sentence, an essay, or a speech—is a high point of emphasis, this order is commonly used and is very effective. A "clincher" sentence is used at the end of the paragraph to restate the topic sentence for greater emphasis.

Complete Guide to Speech, Style and Grammar

The Total Composition

Begin every composition by clarifying for yourself the purpose of this communication. Is it to inform, to obtain some action on the leader's part, to . . .

Every composition has a clearly defined introduction, body, and conclusion, but these are not labeled as such or set apart when the paper is written.

The introduction should (1) arouse the reader's interest; (2) state the main idea of the composition; and (3) possibly preview the main topics. It contains your thesis statement (see "The Research Paper") and a number of other sentences designed to introduce your topic and let the reader know what the paper is about. This is your road map, guiding you through the rest of your paper until you reach your destination.

The body of the composition must develop, support, and explain the main ideas stated in your introduction or thesis paragraph. It should include appropriate, specific examples and details to back up your thesis. An outline is essential for a well-constructed paper.

The conclusion of the paper should clinch the main points made in the body of the composition. It pulls together the details of the paper into a final statement, giving a feeling of completeness. It should not contain any new evidence. Depending on your objective, the conclusion may simply summarize your position, emphasize a main point, draw a conclusion, or even spur the reader to action.

Writing the composition entails three steps: planning, drafting, and revising. Be sure to allow enough time for each step, and do not try to take a shortcut by skipping one phase. Even under the constraints of an examination, take a moment to plan the answer to an essay question, then write the answer, and finally check over the answer to be sure you have covered all the necessary points and used correct dates, spellings, etc.

The best ideas and the most detailed research are all to no avail if the end product, the written paper, is not *well* written—if it does not communicate effectively to the reader. Therefore, the mechanics of composition are of paramount importance to you. The three key words to consider in writing are *unity, coherence,* and *emphasis.*

Unity

The principle of unity applies to all components of the paper, to the paragraphs which are the building blocks of the paper, and to the paper as a whole. Each paragraph should contain only one thought, with the topic sentence controlling the idea of the whole paragraph. By the same token, each paragraph should develop, explain, or expand on the main point of the composition. Do not wander off on tangents; eliminate anything that does not fulfill your thesis statement.

Coherence

Following the principle of coherence makes the paper understandable. It requires arranging your ideas in a clear order according to a definite plan, with the ideas linked together clearly and expressed in vivid, interesting language. Paragraphs should flow naturally from one to another with ideas arranged in logical order. Smooth transitions from one paragraph to the next are essential for the reader to understand the relationship between the ideas expressed in the individual paragraphs. Therefore, transitions could be likened to the mortar holding together the separate building blocks of a wall.

Here are some linking expressions to bridge gaps between paragraphs:

1. To go from one point to another: finally, moreover, besides, in addition to, another, in the next place, also, furthermore, to sum up
2. To indicate another time: next, soon, meanwhile, then, later, finally
3. To indicate results: therefore, thus, consequently, as a result
4. To show contrast: nevertheless, however, on the other hand, instead, in spite of
5. To show relationships: accordingly, similarly, likewise
6. To introduce examples: for instance, for example

Style, the way words are put together, is extremely important in getting ideas from your mind to your reader's mind. We all use our language in different ways. In everyday conversation we use contractions, slang, colloquialisms, even dialect. This is fine. In addition to our spoken language, we have our written language. When we write letters to friends, or even informal papers, we write in a chatty, informal style. This is fine, too. Then there is formal written language. For serious papers, informality is totally out of place, so do not use contractions, slang, or colloquial expressions. While avoiding being stodgy or flowery, do be formal or objective in expression, and refrain from using second person (you) or first person (I).

A writer must also be very careful not to be guilty of plagiarism, which is using another person's ideas, words, or sentence structure (wording) as one's own without giving proper credit to the original author.

Emphasis

The third principle of writing concerns emphasis. This means devoting more space to the more important points and explaining what needs to be explained fully. Put yourself in the reader's place, and try to see if another person would have any unanswered questions after reading the paper. Would they really understand what you are trying to say?

It has been said that there is no such thing as good writing, only rewriting. All really great authors polish their works many times. After you have gotten your thoughts down on paper the first time, go through the composition, applying all that you have learned about effective written communication. Then read it aloud to yourself, listening to what it has to say. Get another person to read it to see if it is understandable to an outsider. After you have reworked the paper for sense and style of writing, go over it again checking your grammar and punctuation. Make a third check just for spelling. When you believe you have your paper in its final form, always go over it again to make certain it is free of errors.

For information on the proper ways to type or write your manuscript, see *Academic Assignments: Mechanical Details,* page 228.

Types of Writing

Written communication falls into four kinds of writing: exposition, argument, description, and narration. Expository writing is to inform or explain. Argument is used to persuade by reason and emotion. Description paints a picture appealing to the five senses. Narration gives an account of action or events.

Probably more than 95 percent of contemporary writing is expository for it includes most scientific and technical books, textbooks, philosophical and political tracts (when not contentious), much of biography and history, the bulk of magazine writing, recipes and formulas, essays and editorials, and reviews and criticism, whether of art, music, or literature. Patches of exposition may be found also in argumentation, narration, and description. When a debater pauses to explain or clarify a situation, the temporary digression may serve to strengthen his or her case. He or she is then no longer contending for a point but is engaging in exposition. If the author of a detective story pauses to discuss the layout of the apartment in which the crime occurs, he or she is similarly engaged in exposition, but if the writer simply describes the apartment, leaving consideration of the implications to the reader's minds, the author has used description. In a book like Rachel Carson's *The Sea Around Us,* the text is about evenly divided among narration, description, and exposition.

Expository Writing

Exposition might be called explanatory writing, for it may explain a process or an idea. It may define terms or give reasons. Much of the writing students do fits this broad category, as does much business and technical writing.

Often, expository writing is interwoven with the other forms. Argumentative writing frequently requires the definition of terms early in the process of building a case. A fictional narrative uses expository writing to bridge time and to allow the omission of tedious detail. Descriptive writing may include expository writing, or expository writing may include description as in the description of equipment and methods included in reports on scientific experiments.

Exposition That Defines

Many expository compositions begin with or include writing that defines something. This may be accomplished in several ways, and these ways may be combined. For example, a writer might include the dictionary definition of one or more terms and follow that with examples. In defining a concept or a doctrine, the writer might compare and contrast similar ideas or beliefs. A term or practice may be defined by tracing its origins, that is to say by giving a brief account of its history. In other circumstances a definition may be drawn by recounting connotations.

Definitions may be arrived at by a negative route. A term or thing may be defined by stating what they are not. A word may be defined by listing inappropriate understandings of its meaning.

The How-To Article

Any step-by-step account of—or directions for—a procedure is also exposition. Before Thanksgiving, the food sections of newspapers and magazines tell how to cook a turkey; and each January, the Internal Revenue Service sends every taxpayer forms that include detailed instructions to be followed in supplying the required income tax information. Both kinds of instruction are written using the expository style, as are directions in a home carpentry project.

In this "how-to" form of expository writing, not only is the order critical, but the writer must start at the very beginning and end with the final step in the process. This is not to say, however, that there is no introductory material. On the contrary, there often is. Not only does the writer want to interest the reader in the product or outcome of the procedure about to be explained, but the author also has the responsibility of acquainting the reader with the specifications of the product. (Will the bookcase be too tall for the room? Will the recipe make enough cookies for the party, or should it be doubled?) The writer may also list at the beginning all the materials needed.

Once the instructions are begun, they should be written as simply and clearly as possible. With how-to writing, the possibility of omitting one or more steps constitutes the greatest danger. Consequently, the best practice requires keeping the purpose firmly in mind and revising ruthlessly.

Other Forms of Exposition

Expository writing is the core of most academic and business writing.

For detailed suggestions on writing the research paper, book report, précis, and scientific project report, see the section titled "Academic Assignments," which follows this section.

Résumés and their cover letters are another special form of expository writing. For more information on these forms, see the section titled "Writing an Effective Resumé."

Argumentative Writing

That category of writing which attempts to strengthen a view already held, to weaken or undermine such a view, or to persuade the reader to adopt another is called argumentation. The name, though well established, is unfortunate, for one immediately infers that it involves a contentious type of discussion. Persuasion would be a better name, for the aim is to incline another's will to one's own view rather than to controvert it or break it. The writer who strives to persuade must also assume (even though the contrary may be true) that the reader has not taken a firm position, and, as a reasonable person, would be delighted to follow the writer's lead.

Analysis of the Question

1. DEFINITION OF TERMS

Should a writer wish to contend that New York City is the true capital of America, he would have to define what he means by his terms. Does he mean "Greater New York," or does he mean the financial district? Does "true" have the same sense as "real"? Is "capital" used as "the governing political center" or the "dominant financial center"? By "America" does he mean the United States, North America, or the Western Hemisphere? It will be observed that until these terms are clarified the issue is confused. The process of clarification which must be undertaken by the writer at the outset is known as "defining the terms."

2. HISTORY OF THE QUESTION

Many issues are of long standing and have been discussed previously. Giving this background information and citing previous experts helps the reader to understand the issue and see the logic of your position.

3. DETERMINING THE ISSUES

Whenever there is a difference of opinion, the holders of opposing views frequently find themselves separated on a multiplicity of issues, many of which may be extremely trivial. It is best to dismiss trivial issues and to concentrate only on major issues. The best way to determine the major issues is to list the chief issues for each side and to select the ones that collide most sharply; these are the major issues.

Planning Persuasive Measures

Once the issues have been determined, the writer plans the order in which to present them. If the matter seems obvious, the writer should present the strongest point first. If the reader may be difficult to persuade—perhaps because of strong arguments on both sides of the issue—the writer might begin with a somewhat neutral fact, then mount the argument, placing the most important or persuasive fact at the end of the argument.

Generalizing Processes

Argumentative or persuasive writing needs to be logical. Reasoning is either by induction or deduction.

1. INDUCTION

When a scientist draws a conclusion from a reasonable number of cases, it is called an *induction*. We must remember, however, that there are few perfect inductions, that is, not *all* cases have been surveyed or could be surveyed.

There are four tests that an induction may be subjected to: Is the relative number of the instances observed, as compared with those unobserved, sufficiently large? Are the observed instances fair examples? Are there no invalidating exceptions? Is there an initial probability that the generalization is true?

2. DEDUCTION

It is a general assumption that all science is a product of the inductive method, but scientists frequently imply that the discovery or law was a "hunch" or generalization for which the proof had later to be found by laborious investigation. Be that as it may, there is an almost equal tendency to assume generalizations and to find the assumed law operating in the instance under discussion. This process is called deduction. It is possible to state all deductions in this form, known as a *syllogism:*

> All iron objects are subject to oxidation.
> A steel rail is an iron object.
> Therefore, a steel rail is subject to oxidation.

In the above syllogism, the statement "All iron objects are subject to oxidation" is called *the major premise;* "A steel rail is an iron object," *the minor premise;* and "Therefore, a steel rail is subject to oxidation," *the conclusion*. Mere ability to put a deduction in syllogistic form, however, does not guarantee its validity. Thus, for example:

All men are tall *(major premise)*.
Green is a man *(minor premise)*.
Therefore, Green is tall *(conclusion)*.

This syllogism is completely correct *if* we accept the major premise. But the major premise is the result of a previous faulty induction.

The Common Fallacies

Thus far we have examined errors which occur in logical processes of reasoning, but a person engaged in the process of persuasion may adopt one of two illogical processes of reasoning and be quite unaware that they are illogical processes. Indeed, in practice they may each prove quite effective until an opponent exposes them. They are the common fallacies of *ignoring the question* and of *begging the question*.

1. IGNORING THE QUESTION

A writer ignores the question by substituting an issue which appears to be the same as the one under discussion. This is more immediately apparent in television interviews and political debates.

2. BEGGING THE QUESTION

Whenever a reasoner assumes as true the thing which he or she is trying to establish, this person is said to beg the question.

Refutation

In normal debate, replying to an opponent is usually left to the rebuttal speeches, though in presenting his case the debater may anticipate counterarguments. In a persuasive article there is no opportunity for rebuttal; hence the anticipation must be complete. Experienced writers know, as a rule, what may be offered in opposition to their views. Yielding an unimportant issue creates an impression of a judicious, a reasonable mind. It is in refutation that the reasoner probably should be most conscious, not of his ability to contend, but of his ability to persuade. Even if there is no chance of this with a dogmatic opponent, the persuasive attitude may win over more undecided listeners and readers than the dogmatism of the opponent. The successful reasoner treats his opponent with respect.

Description

That form of writing which depicts objects, living things, and the static elements in fantasies is called *description*. It is the vehicle through which we become acquainted with the world, its animals and machines, and the furnishings of its dreams and visions.

Independent Description

Required to write a description of a given thing, the writer should ask for whom the description is meant. If a professional writer is preparing material for a wholesale hardware magazine distributed to retailers, he or she may assume some knowledge of the object or device; but if the same writer is describing the same device for the general catalog of a mail order house, he or she can assume very little. The writer also has the limitation of space since so many objects are presented through this medium. The amount of description will be further reduced if the catalog uses illustrations and formulas, but the author must know about these to compensate for what is not depicted or formularized.

The householder without experience may write as good an advertisement of the home he or she wishes to sell as would the real estate agent (the owner should, knowing it better), but owners rarely know so well the purchaser or what will appeal to that purchaser.

Contributory Description

Skill in descriptive writing makes for interest in horticultural books, pleas for the preservation of wildlife, travel literature, and adventure stories, though these works may be chiefly narrative or persuasive. As with independent description, it is helpful to readers to discover, in an involved description, a familiar image that will help them to envision the scene.

Long descriptive passages in fictional narrative are not so frequent today as they once were. The fiction writer manages to weave more descriptive detail into the narrative as it proceeds. The device is an old one; it is merely utilized more commonly now.

Narrative Writing

That form of writing which presents an event or a sequence of events involving animate beings is called narrative writing. While usually the actors in such a narrative are human beings, narrative writing is not restricted to their participation. The range of actors may be from insects and animals to trolls and fairies, to mechanical creatures and visitors from other planets. One thinks of the fat spider which disturbed little Miss Muffet, an android named Data (and a host of other characters from *Star Trek* and *Star Trek: The Next Generation*); Br'er Rabbit, Donald Duck, the Three Bears, the Snow Princess, Superman, the Little Train that Could, Frankenstein, Kermit the Frog, and the Man from Mars, whose antics may, or may not, bear some resemblance to human behavior. They do, however, have the capacity to carry the reader through an event or series of episodes, a characteristic which represents the primary function of characters in narrative writing.

Nonfictional Narrative

The simplest event that can occur presents a person acting in a role that is to some slight degree worth remarking. The commonest form of this narrative is the anecdote; the more familiar the actor, the less the writer has to supply by way of characterization. In repeating the legend of Newton's discovery of the law of gravitation from the falling apple which struck him on the head, the writer can count on people generally knowing who Newton was. Elaboration turns an anecdote into a narrative allusion or after-dinner story. A narrative anecdote—it need not be true—that strikes at some foible in human behavior or belief is usually well received.

Narratives usually follow chronological order. Such narratives are found in oral histories, accident reports, and case studies.

The news-reporting type of nonfictional narrative, on the other hand, often begins at another point in the action. This is done to capture the reader's interest. Often the outcome or end of the action holds the most reader interest and is, therefore, the appropriate starting point for the article. Sometimes the opening statements relate to some midpoint in the action. In both cases, the writer must carefully make the reader aware of the time relationships.

The tests of effective nonfictional narrative writing vary with the purpose. The news reporter must use enough detail to be credible and must know when to employ the other forms of nonfictional writing. Too much detail will kill the reader's interest. Slavish adherence to the narrative form can be extremely boring.

Complete Guide to Speech, Style and Grammar

Fictional Narrative

Characters

To assure plausibility in a fictional narrative, start with the people to be involved in the action. Ivan Turgenev, the Russian novelist, told the young Henry James that his fictions began *"always* with the vision of some person or persons, who hovered before him, soliciting him, as the active or passive figure, interesting him and appealing to him *just as they were and by what they were"* [italics ours]. That is, Turgenev started with a real person and transferred that person with his or her potentialities to his book. No procedure more surely guarantees plausibility than this one, for once the character is established he or she can do nothing "out of character"—both the writer and the reader would be instantly aware of the inconsistency. An axiomatic statement in fiction is, "Character governs action."

Plot

The persons in a work of fiction should determine the action; if they do not, it will not move. If three persons are placed together and two of them have traits that clash, the third is either bound to take sides or disintegrate, either through his effort to remain neutral or shift sides—and a plot is born. Imposing a plot on characters already assembled leads to distortion, unnaturalness, and eventually to implausibility.

Increasing the number of characters usually multiplies the possibility of plot intricacy because of the alignment of loyalties. There are only two restrictions on the ramifications of plot: (1) The behavior of the characters must be wholly consistent with their natures, and (2) the high cost of typesetting limits the extent of any story. For the latter reason, three-volume novels and twenty-thousand-word short stories are not the fashion of the twentieth century, though they were common enough in the nineteenth.

All conflicts in life move toward either stalemate or some sort of resolution, but in fiction they must move toward resolution. The ultimate clash of forces we term the *climax* of the tale; the results or consequences of this collision we call the *dénouement*. It is the highest art to make this as brief as possible.

Setting

The leisurely novel of the nineteenth century took pains to set the stage fully for the action of its story. Frequently these novels began with a descriptive passage on which the author expended much conscious art.

But few writers could afford it today. Forced to economize, they have done so by eliminating extended descriptions of their stages. Instead they give the details of their settings as they proceed with their narratives. Scattering graphic bits of description through the narrative seems the best way to impress upon the reader with the greatest economy of means the setting for modern narrative. In order to impart a real sense of the scene, the writer should prepare a good many notes on his setting in order to select from among them.

Point of View

After a writer has chosen the characters, determined the nature of the conflict among them (even perhaps imagined the course of the plot), and determined where the events of this narrative will take place, he or she still must ask an important question: From what point of view shall I tell this story? As the writer, you must follow this by other questions: Should the narrator be outside the tale? Should he know everything that takes place? Should she be a participant in the action? Should he be a major figure or a minor figure? Should she be a limited or prejudiced observer?

If the narrator is to be outside the tale, he or she may definitely be identified with the author. Both Fielding and Thackeray do this and are frankly partisan in the conflicts which they imagine. The advantage of this point of view is that converts are more readily made to the author's views; but the limitations are those of partisanship—the intruding voice and the sense of manipulated characters. Because of these intrusions the narrative is always fiction—it loses a degree of verisimilitude; it becomes something less than life, whereas, if art is selective, it should be something more than life. Another choice from outside the action is to adopt what is known as the "omniscient" point of view. Still another choice remains—to plant a spectator on the periphery of the tale to report what goes on.

The recent tendency of writers of fiction seems to be to locate the point of view "in" one of the participants in action in the tale, either a major or a minor character. The author may identify with the hero or heroine of the tale and become this "I" narrator of the adventure. The merit of this is its immediacy; it has, however, the grave limitation of cutting off the reader from emotions and thoughts (save as they are overt) of other characters in the tale. And what is more boring than one who talks all the time?

Dialogue

Just as character determines the action in a narrative, so also character determines the dialogue. Relations between characters define what they will express and what they will repress. The talk must advance the story, and it does this either by revealing hidden motives or by suggesting aims and devices.

The author has to remember also that a character can divine more than is said from what is unskillfully repressed. To expose the play of mind on mind is one of the most exciting challenges of a writer's career. In good narrative, no bit of dialogue should be pointless.

THE TOOLS OF WRITING

Grammar

Parts of Speech

Words, the basic units for speaking and writing, are classified as parts of speech in the English language. These eight classifications bear the following names:

noun	pronoun	verb
adjective	adverb	conjunction
preposition	interjection	

Few words, however, can be classified absolutely as one or another of the eight parts of speech traditionally distinguished in our language. Most of us would automatically say that *swim* is a verb; yet in the sentence *He went for a swim,* it is clearly a noun. An even more confusing example is *up:*

The proposal was on the *up* and up. (noun)
The auctioneer encouraged us to *up* our bid. (verb)

His time was *up*. (adjective, modifying *time*)
We flew *up* and over the clouds. (adverb, modifying *flew*)
He went *up* the stairs. (preposition)

We may assign a word to grammatical class only by considering its use, or *function,* in its context. Grammar is a way of talking about the relationship of words; or, more specifically grammar is a way of talking about the relationships of word functions.

Nouns

A *noun* is a name. It indicates a person, place, or thing.

The *fireman* climbed to the *top* of the *ladder*.

Not all "things" are concrete objects. A noun may also name a quality, an action, or a concept.

The *brutality* of the *murder* underlined its *injustice*.

Nouns may be further classified according to five types:

1. A *common* noun names a class or group of persons, places, or things. A title is ordinarily treated as a common noun.

   My *father* is a *history professor*.

   But if it used as a specific name or as part of one it is considered a proper noun.

   I introduced *Father* to *Professor White* of the *Department of History*.

2. A *concrete* noun names a particular or specific member of a class or group that can be seen, heard, touched, smelled, or tasted—one that can be perceived by the senses.

   Naomi Swift, the famous contralto, sang a fourth *aria*. In her *hair* the *rose* glowed as red as *wine*.

3. An *abstract noun* names a quality or concept.

   Continued *apathy* will compromise the *freedom* we enjoy under *democracy*.

4. A *proper* noun names a specific person, place or thing; it is capitalized.

Complete Guide to Speech, Style and Grammar

> After *President Jefferson* returned from *Monticello* he addressed *Congress*.

5. A *collective* noun is a proper or common noun which names a group of persons or things.

> The *crowd* edged closer.
>
> the Chicago *Bears*

Note: Nouns can belong to more than one type.

> Concrete, common, and collective: He joined a *brotherhood* to meet friends.
>
> Concrete, proper, and collective: He was a member of the *Brotherhood* of RR Engineers.
>
> Abstract, common, and collective: He believed in the *brotherhood* of man.

A noun may be a single word:

> The *attorney* is Adams.

A noun may be a compound word:

> *Richard Adams* became *attorney general*.

A noun may be a phrase:

> *Hunting the elusive fox* was strenuous sport.

A noun may be a clause:

> *That he could have been lying* was out of the question.

Gender

The *gender* of a noun presents no problem in English. *Masculine nouns* refer to males (boy, father), *feminine* to females (woman, girl). All others are *neuter*. A number of nouns have masculine and feminine forms clearly marked by differences of pronunciation or of spelling (aviator, aviatrix; alumnus, alumna; fiancé, fiancée). Except in the case of the last example, the tendency seems to be toward using masculine forms for everyone. This does not apply to pronouns, however, where the reverse is true.

Number

The *number* of a noun is a way of indicating how many persons, places, and things it refers to. A noun is *singular* if it names one and *plural* if it names two or more.

Case

The *case* of a noun is determined by what it does in a sentence. If it is *doing* something, it is in the nominative (or subjective) case, as in "The *teacher* graded my paper." If something is *being done to it*, the noun is usually in the objective (or accusative) case, as in "The teacher graded my *paper*." If the noun is said to own something, it is in the possessive (or genitive) case, as in "the *dog's* tail."

Since the forms of nominative and objective nouns are identical, writing them correctly is no problem in English. Even the possessive case causes little difficulty in its grammatical relationships.

Use of Nouns

Nouns may be used in a variety of ways.

1. As *subject* (nominative case): The subject of a sentence is the person, place, or thing about which the statement is made or question asked.

   The *girl* enjoyed dancing.
   Didn't the *boy* know how to dance?

2. As *object,* both direct and indirect (objective, or accusative, case): The *direct object* of a sentence is the person, place, or thing directly affected by the action of a transitive verb.

   The car crossed the *bridge*.

   The college announced *that tuition would go up again*.
     (clause as object)

The *indirect object* is indirectly affected by the action of a transitive verb. It precedes the direct object, unless it is a prepositional phrase.

   He sent *his mother* a birthday present.
   He sent a birthday present *to his mother*.

Complete Guide to Speech, Style and Grammar

3. As *subjective complement* (nominative case), also called the *predicate nominative:* The complement is a noun related directly to the subject, not the verb.

   He is the heaviest *player* on the team.

   Jenny seemed the last *person* you'd expect to get into trouble.

   A linking verb (see page 97) connects subject and subject complement.

4. As *objective complement* (objective case): The objective complement completes the sense of a transitive verb, related directly to the direct object, not the verb.

   She called her best friend a green-eyed *monster*.
   Linus considers Beethoven the only *composer*.

5. As *appositive:* An appositive is a noun that usually follows another noun with the same meaning. It must be the same in number and case as the noun with which it is in apposition.

   Our next-door neighbor, a *veteran* of World War II, refuses to join the American Legion. (*Veteran* is in apposition with *neighbor;* both are singular and nominative.)

   He finally joined the VFW, a livelier *organization*. (*Organization* is in apposition with *VFW*, both are singular and objective.)

6. In direct *address:*

   Darling, I agree.
   Be good, my *dear*, and let who will be clever.

Pronouns

A *pronoun* refers to a person, place, or thing without naming it. Pronouns substitute for nouns.

> *She* bit *his* arm. Wash *it* with *this*.
> *Everyone who* wants to come is welcome.
> There are *four*, you say?

The noun (or pronoun) for which a pronoun substitutes is called its *antecedent*. Thus, in the first example above, *arm* is the antecedent of *it*. The antecedents of *she, his,* and *this* are implied; both speaker and hearer (or writer and reader) know who *she* and *he* are, and *this* refers to an object physically present. The antecedent of *who* in the second example, is *everyone*. Pronouns may be classified according to seven types:

1. *Personal* pronouns substitute for the name of a person or object. Personal pronouns can be troublesome because, unlike nouns (which rarely change their forms except in the possessive case), most pronouns take a different form of each of the three cases: nominative, objective, and possessive.

	NOMINATIVE	OBJECTIVE	POSSESSIVE
1ST PERSON			
singular	I	me	my, mine
plural	we	us	our, ours
2ND PERSON			
singular	you	you	your, yours
plural	you	you	your, yours
3RD PERSON			
singular			
masculine	he	him	his
feminine	she	her	her, hers
neuter	it	it	its, of it
either gender	one	one	one's
plural	they	them	their, theirs

2. *Relative* pronouns link a subordinate clause with their own antecedents. The antecedent is always part of an independent clause.

   We smiled at the clerk *who* had been so pleasant.
   The batter hit a line drive *which* sent two men home.

   There is no difficulty of declension with most relative pronouns: only *who* and *whom* (and their related compound forms) present problems. The distinction between these has virtually disappeared in speech, but is still maintained in writing.

Complete Guide to Speech, Style and Grammar

NOMINATIVE	OBJECTIVE	POSSESSIVE
who	whom	whose
whoever	whomever	whosoever
which	which	of which
that	that	whose
what	what	———
as	as	———

Who and its related forms refer to people, *which* to other living creatures and to things; *that* may be used for either persons or things. *What* is the equivalent of *that which* when used as a relative pronoun.

Note: Except for the word *one's,* the possessive case of both personal and relative pronouns has no apostrophe.

3. *Interrogative* pronouns introduce questions. They include *who* (objective, *whom;* possessive, *whose*), *which,* and *what.*

> *Who* saw him leave?
> *Whom* do you mean?
> *Which* are the best roads from here?
> *What* is the direction you want to take?

Who (and its related forms) inquires about a person, *which* about a person or thing in a group, *what* about anything.

Note: Remember that the objective form *(whom)* is the object of a verb or a preposition.

> *Whom* did Petrarch love?

Whose, which, and *what* also function as interrogative adjectives when instead of substituting for a noun they modify it.

> *Which roads* are best?
> *What direction* are you taking?

4. *Demonstrative* pronouns point out specific persons or things. Principal ones are *this* (plural, *these*) and *that* (plural, *those*).

> *This* is the least flattering of all the photos.
> Have you seen *those?*

Note: Demonstrative pronouns may also function as demonstrative adjectives.

This photo is more flattering than *those others*.

5. *Indefinite* pronouns point out persons or things, but less specifically than demonstrative pronouns. A great number in this classification include the following:

SINGULAR INDEFINITE PRONOUNS

another	everything
anyone	somebody
each	such
either	

PLURAL INDEFINITE PRONOUNS

both	many
few	several

SINGULAR OR PLURAL INDEFINITE PRONOUNS

all	most
any	none
more	some

The only problem likely to arise with the use of the indefinite pronoun is that of number; see *Agreement*, page 92.

Note: Except for the words *none* and *plenty,* indefinite pronouns can function as adjectives as well.

6. *Reflexive* pronouns refer back to the subject. A reflexive pronoun is usually the direct object of a verb.

We dressed *ourselves* hastily.

Reflexive pronouns may also be used for emphasis.

Many feared the Senate *itself* was discredited.

In formal English the reflexive form is not used as a substitute for either subject or object; this is likely to be a practical problem only in the first person.

Myrna and I (not *myself*) made all the arrangements.

Complete Guide to Speech, Style and Grammar

They asked Myrna and *me* (not *myself*) to chaperone the dance.

7. *Reciprocal* pronouns are compound indefinite pronouns which indicate some mutual relationship between two or more persons and things.

The lovers lived only for *each other*.
All members of the company saw *one another* every day.

Case of Pronouns

The case rules that apply to nouns apply also to pronouns. Unlike nouns, however, pronouns frequently change their form according to whether they are in the nominative, objective, or possessive case. For this reason the case rules for pronouns are given separately below. A pronoun used as the subject of a verb takes the nominative case.

Right John and *I* are invited, aren't *we*?

When a verb is omitted but understood, be sure to supply it mentally in order to determine whether the pronoun is used as its subject.

Wrong John knows more than *her*.
You are as good a player as *me*.

Right John knows more than *she* (does). (*She* is the subject of the omitted verb *does*.)

Right You are as good a player as *I* (am).

A pronoun used as a predicate nominative takes the nominative case. A predicate nominative is a noun or pronoun that follows *am, is, are, was, were, be,* or *been* and that refers back to the subject.

Wrong Knock. Knock. Who's there? It's *me*.
Could that be *her* already?
It might have been *him*.

Right Knock. Knock. Who's there? It's *I*. (*I* is the predicate nominative after the verb *is*.)
Could that be *she* already?
It might have been *he*.

Written Communication

Do not permit such interrupting expressions as *do you suppose, believe, think,* or *say,* to affect the case of *who* and *whom.*

Wrong *Whom* do you believe was the guilty person?

Right *Who* do you believe was the guilty person? (*Who* is the subject of *was*, not the object of *believe*.)

Be careful not to confuse the subject of a verb with the object of a preposition.

Wrong I will vote for *whomever* is the best candidate.

Right I will vote for *whoever* is the best candidate. (*Whoever* is the subject of *is*. The object of the preposition *for* is the whole clause *whoever is the best candidate*.)

A pronoun that is the subject of an infinitive takes the objective case. The infinitive is the form of the verb preceded by *to: to be, to dance,* etc.

Wrong Do you expect John and *I* to be ready?

Right Do you expect John and *me* to be ready? (*Me* is the subject together with *John* of the infinitive *to be*.)

A pronoun that follows the infinitive *to be* takes the objective case.

Wrong Mary took John to be *I*.

Right Mary took John to be *me*.

A pronoun used as the object of a verb, of an infinitive, or of a preposition, or as the indirect object, takes the objective case.

Wrong *Who* did you ask to the party?

Right *Whom* did you ask to the party? (*Whom* is the object of the verb *ask*.)

Wrong The coach gave John and *I* a briefing.

Right The coach gave John and *me* a briefing. (*John* and *me* are the indirect objects of the verb *gave*.)

A pronoun used in apposition with a noun takes the same case as the noun.

Complete Guide to Speech, Style and Grammar

Wrong The instructor wants us all—Harry, Sam, and *I*—to stay after class.

Right The instructor wants us all—Harry, Sam and *me*—to stay after class. (*Harry, Sam,* and *me* are in apposition with *us* and therefore take the same case.)

A pronoun used before a gerund takes the possessive case. A *gerund* is a verbal used as a noun. It has the same form as the verb's present or perfect participle.

Wrong I was sure of *him* winning the prize.

Right I was sure of *his* winning the prize. (*Winning* is the gerund. It is the object of the preposition *of*.)

The case form of the relative pronouns *who* and *whoever* depends upon how the pronoun is used in the clause it introduces.

Right I already know *who* will come to the party. (*Who* is the subject of the verb *come* and is therefore in the nominative case.)

The captain, *whom* I have never met, has asked to see me. (*Whom* is the direct object of the verb *met* and is therefore in the objective case.)

Agreement

Although the case of a pronoun varies with its use, a pronoun must agree with its antecedent in person, number, and gender. This appears to be a straightforward task, but there are problems that sometimes arise with gender and number.

The standard practice in English grammar has been to use the masculine pronoun to refer to singular nouns and pronouns that were of unknown or mixed gender. Now, however, people prefer to use the phrases *he or she, him or her,* and *his or hers* to avoid what they consider to be sexist language. Others substitute plural pronouns, but this is not correct unless the antecedent is also made plural.

Traditional The employee will wear his uniform at all times.

Also Right The employee will wear his or her uniform at all times.

Also Right Employees will wear their uniforms at all times.

Wrong Every man, woman, and child should wear *their* life jacket.

Traditional Every man, woman, and child should wear *his* life jacket.

Also Right Every man, woman, and child should wear *his or her* life jacket.

Determining the number of an antecedent is sometimes a problem with indefinite pronouns:

another	anyone	someone
one	no one	anything
either	neither	each
everyone	anybody	every
everybody	somebody	nobody

In informal speech, we generally treat these words as collectives, and we make the pronouns that refer to them singular or plural according to sound or whim. In formal writing, these words are treated as singular; therefore, a pronoun that has any one of these words as an antecedent should also be singular.

Wrong Will everyone please open *their* book to page 56.

Right Will everyone please open *his* book to page 56.

Also Right Will everyone please open *his or her* book to page 56.

Wrong Every city had a large increase in *their* population.

Right Every city had a large increase in *its* population.

When two singular antecedents are joined by *or* or *nor,* a singular pronoun is required, but care should be taken to avoid awkward repetitions.

Traditional Either John or Mary left his homework.

Complete Guide to Speech, Style and Grammar

Awkward Either John or Mary left his or her homework.

Also Right John's or Mary's homework was left behind.

When two antecedents are joined by *or* or *nor,* the pronoun should agree with the nearer antecedent.

Wrong Neither the President nor the members of the Cabinet could foresee *his* fate.

Right Neither the President nor the members of the Cabinet could foresee *their* fate.

Use the pronoun *who* to refer to people, *which* to animals other than humans and to things, and *that* for either persons or things.

Wrong *Which* is that person?

Right *Who* is that person?

There are two exceptions to the above rule. *Which* may be used to refer to persons considered as a group. Also, when a reference to an animal results in the awkward *of which* construction, the acceptable alternative is *whose.*

Right Anthropologists believe that the race *which* gave America its first settlers was Mongoloid.

Awkward I claim that the cheetah, the speed *of which* has been timed at seventy miles an hour, is the world's fastest four-legged animal.

Right I claim that the cheetah, *whose* speed has been timed at seventy miles an hour, is the world's fastest four-legged animal.

Reference

A pronoun may be grammatically correct. It may agree in every way—in person, number, and gender—with its antecedent, and it may have just the right case form. Yet if the antecedent is not immediately clear, all the effort will be wasted. An ambiguous or misplaced pronoun may force the reader to reread the sentence or refer back to a previous sentence to find the meaning. A pronoun should have a clearly defined antecedent and should be placed as near the antecedent as possible.

> **Wrong** I had a fascinating time in Mexico. *They* are a color-ful people. (The antecedent of the pronoun *They* may be obvious to the writer, but not to the reader. Who are *They?*)

> **Right** I had a fascinating time on my trip to Mexico. Mexi-cans are a colorful people.

> **Right** I had a fascinating time on my trip to Mexico. It is a colorful country.

Shun the indefinite use of the pronoun *it*. In certain idiomatic phrases the indefinite use of *it* is acceptable. *(It is a fine day. It is a fact. It is necessary. It is likely. It is true.)* But when *it* is not part of an accepted idiom, avoid the indefinite use altogether.

> **Wrong** In the chapter on the second voyage, it reveals that Columbus sent five hundred Indian slaves as a gift to Queen Isabella.

> **Right** The chapter on the second voyage reveals that Co-lumbus sent five hundred Indian slaves as a gift to Queen Isabella.

Avoid the use of the impersonal *it* and the pronoun *it* in the same sentence.

> **Wrong** The car is in rough shape, and it will probably cost more to repair it than the price of a new one.

> **Right** The car is in rough shape, and the cost of repairing it will probably be more than the price of a new one.

Shun the indefinite use of the pronouns *you* and *they*. The indefi-nite use of these pronouns is acceptable in informal speech, but not in formal writing. In formal writing use *one* and *everyone*.

> **Informal** In the class I am taking, *you* are not permitted to take notes.

> **Formal** In the class I am taking, *one* (or *a student*) is not permitted to take notes.

Informal *They* greet tourists warmly in Holland.

Formal *Everyone* greets tourists warmly in Holland.

Verbs

A *verb* is a word or group of words that indicates action, condition (being), or process.

They *began* the boat race this morning; by six this evening they *will have sailed* halfway to the island.

He *was* a good dog. The house *seems* empty without him.

The rose *had become* an even deeper crimson.

Types of Verbs

Verbs may be classified according to four types:

1. A *transitive* verb requires a direct object to complete its meaning.

   Hilda *bathed* the *baby*. (The subject, *Hilda,* performs the action upon the direct object, *baby.*)

   Ulysses *plunged* the *stake* into the Cyclops' eye. (The verb *plunged* is transitive and the direct object is *stake*.)

2. An *intransitive* verb is complete within itself and does not require a direct object.

   Let us *pray*.
   We *felt* relieved.
   We *plunged* into the pool and *swam*. Then we *lay* in the sun.

Most verbs, like *plunge,* can be either transitive or intransitive. But *lie* is intransitive only. It is a troublesome verb because its past tense *lay* is frequently confused with the present tense of transitive *lay*.

	TRANSITIVE	INTRANSITIVE
PRESENT TENSE	lay (something down)	lie (on my bed)

| PAST TENSE | laid (something down) | lay (on my bed) |
| PAST PARTICIPLE | have laid (something down) | have lain (on my bed) |

3. A *linking verb* joins the subject to its complement, which is a predicate noun or adjective. The more common ones are:

appear	look
be	seem
become	smell
feel	taste
grow	turn

Most of these verbs are not exclusively linking verbs.

USED AS LINKING VERBS	USED AS OTHER VERBS
It *grew* colder.	He *grew* a beard. (transitive verb)
That *tasted* bad.	They *will taste* their soup. (transitive verb)
He *turned* pirate.	She stopped and *turned*. (intransitive verb)

4. An *auxiliary* verb helps the main verb of the sentence. It may be formed from *have, can, may, be, shall, will, might, must,* and *do* and appears before the main verb in a verb phrase.

We *can* go if we like.
She *might have been* told earlier.
I *am* finishing my letter.

Principal Parts

Verbs in English have three principal parts:

INFINITIVE OR BASIC FORM	to walk	to go
	to sleep	to bite
PAST TENSE USED IN THE SIMPLE PAST	walked	went
	slept	bit
PAST PARTICIPLE ("USED TO")	(has) walked	(has) gone
	(has) slept	(has) bitten

Complete Guide to Speech, Style and Grammar

Regular verbs form their principal parts by adding *-ed, -d,* or *-t* to the infinitive.

> wanted   placed   dealt

Irregular verbs change or retain the vowel of the infinitive and do not add *-ed, -d,* or *-t.*

> throw, threw, thrown
> choose, chose, chosen
>
> **Intransitive**   sit, sat, sat
>
> **Transitive**   set, set, set

Sometimes a verb may have more than one form:

> shine, shone (or shined), shone (or shined)
> dream, dreamed (or dreamt), dreamed (or dreamt)

Consult a recent dictionary if there is any question of a form's being irregular:

> see, saw (*not standard:* seen), have seen

Person and Number

Person and number present few problems in English verbs: the verb form usually changes only in the third person singular of the present tense, where an *s* is added (*I jump, he jumps; you cry, she cries*). A notable exception is the highly irregular verb *be,* but this is so frequently used it presents no practical difficulty.

Tense

The tense of a verb indicates the time of its action. There are six tenses in English:

1. The *present* tense uses three forms for positive statements.

SIMPLE
PRESENT: We *know.* You *say.* He *rides.*

PROGRESSIVE: I *am rushing.* You *are moving.* He *is standing* still.

EMPHATIC: I *do move.* He *does ride.*

In questions or in negative statements, the progressive or emphatic form is generally used.

PROGRESSIVE: *Are* you *coming?* She *is* not *coming.*
EMPHATIC: *Does* he *swim?* They *do* not *swim.*

2. The *past* tense indicates past time not continuing to the present. It uses three forms for positive statements.

SIMPLE PAST: I *took,* you *jumped,* she *sank*
PROGRESSIVE: He *was flying,* we *were laughing*
EMPHATIC: You *did believe,* they *did prove*

In questions or in negative statements, the progressive or emphatic form is generally used.

3. The *perfect* (or *present perfect*) tense indicates past time continuing to the present. It is formed by adding the past participle to *have* or *has.*

   I *have shown* her the ring.
   Have you *been* here long?
   He *has filled* the tub.

4. The *past perfect* tense indicates past time occurring before a definite time in the past. It is formed by adding the past participle to *had.*

   We *had been* in the new house for a week.
   You *had come* to visit us.
   Had she *set* the table yet?

Note: In the examples immediately above, any subsequent actions would still be in the past (She *set* the table when I arrived). But an action subsequent to those in the examples for the present perfect would naturally be in the present (He has filled the tub. He *is washing* now).

5. The *future* tense indicates future time continuing from the present. It has three forms.

We *will* not *leave*.
You *will be having* dinner.
Is he *going to tell* us?

The old distinction between *shall* (simple futurity) and *will* (future of determination) has virtually disappeared except in formal writing. It may also be used in the first person, to make clear an important difference in attitude.

I *shall* do it. (compliance)
I *will* do it. (desire)

6. The *future perfect* tense indicates future time occurring before a definite time in the future. It is formed by adding the past participle to the future tense of *have*.

He *shall have seen* them before you do.
Will they *have escaped* (before the house burns down)?

Note: The present tense may be used for future time (I *leave* for home tomorrow); past time, especially to add immediacy to a narrative (It *is* dark, this Christmas Eve, as Washington *approaches* Trenton); to make a statement that is presumably true at any time (Too many cooks *spoil* the broth); or to discuss a fictional past (When Huck *sneaks* ashore from the raft, we *see* intrepidity at its height).

Voice

A verb is in the *active voice* when its subject performs the action.

Tennyson published *In Memoriam* in 1850. (*Tennyson* is the subject and the verb *published* is in the active voice.)

A verb is in the *passive voice* when its subject is acted upon.

In Memoriam was published by Tennyson in 1850. *(In Memoriam* is the subject and the verb *published* is in the passive voice.)

Except for a reason of deliberate emphasis, choose the active voice in preference to the passive voice. It will make your writing more lively and vigorous. *Betty gave a party for all the children* is livelier than *A party was given by Betty for all the children*.

Mood

The *mood* of a verb refers to the manner in which a statement is expressed. There are three moods in English.

1. The *indicative* mood states a fact.

   I *spent* the holiday in New York.
   He *knew* you *had come*.

2. The *imperative* mood gives a command.

   Stop!
   Try and *make* me.

3. The *subjunctive* mood expresses a wish, a doubt, or a condition contrary to fact.

   I wish he *were* somewhere else.
   We wondered if we *were* going to get away with it.

   Note: The past subjunctive of the verb *be,* which is *were* in all three persons and both numbers, is the only subjunctive of any real importance in English. In informal writing and in speech, the indicative *was* is an acceptable substitute.

   Informal "I wish I *was* in Dixie."

   Formal If I *were* to tell you, . . .

   Formal Would that it *were* true.

   Other uses of the subjunctive are consciously formal (We request that this *be* omitted from the report; if this *proves* false, I shall resign), or preserved in automatic phrases (*come* what may, whatever it *cost*). The subjunctive mood has largely disappeared.

Finite and Nonfinite Verbs (Verbals)

A *finite* verb is capable of making a complete and independent assertion.

   She *finished* the book.
   You *have done* a good job.

A finite verb is limited to a specific person by a noun or a pronoun

Complete Guide to Speech, Style and Grammar

(the bear *roars;* he *climbs*). It is also limited in number, either singular or plural (she *laughs;* they *laugh*). And it is limited in time, by a tense form (we *sit;* we *sat*). A finite verb serves as a main verb in a sentence or clause.

> She *had eaten* before we *began*.

A *nonfinite* verb, commonly referred to as a *verbal,* is not thus limited. It cannot be used to make a sentence of the typical subject-verb pattern but is characteristically used in subordinate constructions. There are three classes of verbals:

1. The *infinitive* is one of the present forms of a verb, with *to* either present or understood.

	ACTIVE	PASSIVE
PRESENT	(to) push	(to) be pushed
PERFECT	(to) have pushed	(to) have been pushed

Most versatile of the verbals, the infinitive may be used as a noun:

> *To ride* is good sport. (subject)

> She wanted *to play* with the puppies. (object of a verb)

> They wanted nothing but *to be left* alone. (object of a preposition)

> His intention was *to have kissed* her. (subjective complement)

as an adjective:

> Ned Creeth is my choice *to represent* us. (modifies *choice*)
> He was courageous *to volunteer*. (modifies *courageous*)

as an adverb:

> I am sorry *to disappoint* you. (modifies *sorry*)
> *To find* work, he moved to the city. (modifies *moved*)

with an auxiliary as part of a finite verb:

> We must *find* a way. (*to* understood)

2. The *participle* is one of the present or past participle forms of a verb.

	ACTIVE	PASSIVE
PRESENT	trying	being tried
PAST	having tried	having been tried

It may be used as an adjective:

He shot the *leaping* deer.
The *broken* vase lay near the window.
Having paid our respects, we left.

as part of a finite verb:

We were *playing* leapfrog.

I have *had* enough for now.

in an absolute construction (a phrase grammatically independent of any other part of the sentence):

The city *having been taken,* Caesar moved on. (The entire phrase *The city having been taken* is the absolute construction.)

3. The *gerund* is one of the present participial forms of a verb, and is used as a noun.

Kissing is pleasant, but *being kissed* is a perfect joy. (subject, active and passive)

Many prefer *going* to the movies. (object of a verb)

Others waste their time in *bowling*. (object of a preposition)

Uncle Jack's favorite recreation is *sleeping*. (subjective complement)

Problems in Use

The following are some persistent problems in the use of verbs and verbals:

Complete Guide to Speech, Style and Grammar

- *SHALL (SHOULD)* and *WILL (WOULD)*
  In questions, *will* is properly used in all persons. However, *shall* is often used to convey a sense of propriety or obligation. *Won't* is the regular negative form.

  > *Shall* I write to thank her?
  > What *shall* I do to avoid it?
  > What *won't* you do?

  Do not overuse *shall*. It is neither more correct nor more elegant than *will*.
  Should and *would* suggest doubt or uncertainty.

  > That *should* be all right. (contrast: That *will* be all right.)

  In polite requests, *would* and *should* are used for the first person, *would* for the second.

  > I *would* (or *should*) be very grateful for your help.
  > *Would* you please pass the hominy grits?

- *CAN* and *MAY*
  Can is used to show ability; and *may* is used to show possibility.

  > You *can* do it if you try.
  > We *may* arrive in time.

  Can is used increasingly to express permission.

  > *Can* I come in?
  > You *can* choose the one you want.

  This use of *can* is still not considered formally correct. In writing, and even in speaking, it is preferable to use *may*.

  > *May* I come in?
  > You *may* choose the one you want.

- *LIE, SIT, RISE*
  Lie, *sit*, and *rise* are intransitive verbs. They should not be confused with their transitive counterparts *lay*, *set*, and *raise*. The best way to avoid difficulty with these troublesome pairs is simply to memorize their principal parts, and then to decide whether a construction calls for a transitive or intransitive verb.

	TRANSITIVE	INTRANSITIVE
PRESENT	lay, set, raise (something)	lie, sit, rise
PAST	laid, set, raised (something)	lay, sat, rose
PAST PARTICIPLE	(have) laid, set, raised (something)	(have) lain, sat, risen

Remember that a hen *sets* on her eggs, and the sun *sets* in the west.

- *GET*
  The past participle of the verb *get* is either *got* or *gotten*. The latter seems more common. (The only past participle of *forget* is *forgotten*.) Avoid *have got* and *have got to* (meaning *must*) where *have* and *have to* are sufficient.

    Wrong I have got some here. I haven't got any more. I have got to leave soon.

    Right I have some here. I haven't any more. I have to leave soon.

- *AIN'T*
  Ain't is a contraction of *am not, are not*, and occasionally *have not*. Despite its long history in English, it is a nonstandard form. Use the equally convenient contractions *I'm not, aren't*, and *haven't*. However, there is no completely satisfactory form for the first person singular negative interrogative: *am I not* is too formal for most speakers, and the clumsy *aren't I* is not everywhere accepted.

Misuse of Past Tense

One of the most common verb errors is to use the past tense instead of the past participle. Use the past participle whenever there is an auxiliary or helping verb.

    Wrong It wasn't until I left the house that I noticed I had *forgot* my books.

Complete Guide to Speech, Style and Grammar

> **Right** It wasn't until I left the house that I noticed I had *forgotten* my books. (The auxiliary verb *had* demands the past participle.)

Sequence of Tenses

Avoid unnecessary shifts from one tense to another in the same sentence. Make a verb in a subordinate clause (or an infinitive or a participle) agree in time with the verb in the main clause.

> **Wrong** Whenever he *said* yes, she *says* no. (The verb *said* in the subordinate clause does not agree in time with the verb *says* in the main clause.)

> **Right** Whenever he *says* yes, she *says* no. (Both verbs agree.) Whenever he *said* yes, she *said* no. (Both verbs agree.)

An exception to the above rule applies when one states a universal truth (a statement that is true regardless of time).

> Sally *said* that it *is* better to be wise than virtuous. (Disagreement between verbs is acceptable because a universal truth requiring the present tense is stated.)

When two past actions are stated in the same sentence, use the past perfect tense for the earlier action.

> **Wrong** Fred realized just in time that he already *drank* too much.

> **Right** Fred realized just in time that he *had* already *drunk* too much. (The action of the second verb occurred before that of the first verb.)

After *if,* use the auxiliary verb *had* instead of *would have*.

> **Wrong** If you would have used your head, you wouldn't be in this mess.

> **Right** If you had used your head, you wouldn't be in this mess.

The past infinitive is often used to express action not yet completed at the time of the main or preceding verb. This is wrong. The present infinitive is demanded in such constructions.

Wrong   We wanted *to have finished* the job by tonight.

Right   We wanted *to finish* the job by tonight. (The present infinitive *to finish* is demanded because its action has not yet taken place at the time of the main verb *wanted*.)

Agreement of Subject and Verb

A verb must always agree with its subject in person and number. It is often difficult to tell which is the true subject or whether a subject is considered singular or plural. The rules below govern the agreement of subject and verb.

The following pronouns, often taken to be plural, are singular and therefore require a singular verb: *each, everyone, everybody, either,* and *neither*.

Wrong   Each of the candidates are competent. Neither of us *are* ready.

Right   Each of the candidates *is* competent. Neither of us *is* ready.

The following nouns, plural in form, are considered singular in meaning and therefore require a singular verb: *news, economics, mathematics, politics, mumps,* and *measles. The United States* also takes a singular verb.

Wrong   The economics of the plan *are* hazardous.

Right   The economics of the plan *is* hazardous. Mathematics *is* difficult for some students. The United States *has* treated the American Indians abominably.

A collective noun generally takes a singular verb. However, when the individuals of the group are considered, the verb is plural.

Our team always *wins*.

The family *is* worried about my late hours. (Family regarded as a single unit—more usual.)

The family *have* gone about their chores. (Individuals of the family considered—less usual.)

Complete Guide to Speech, Style and Grammar

The words *there* and *here* are not subjects. In constructions introduced by *there* and *here*, look for the true subject to ascertain the number of the verb.

> **Wrong** *There's* several ways to skin a cat.

> **Right** There *are* several ways to skin a cat.

Fractions take a singular verb when bulk or a total number or amount is considered, a plural verb when individuals are considered. This rule applies also to words such as *all, any, none, some, more,* and *most.*

> Two-thirds of the student body *was* present.
> Two-thirds of the students *were* present.
> All the money *has* somehow vanished.
> All the members of the team *are* on the honor list.

When the word *number* is preceded by the definite article *the*, it usually takes a singular verb. When it is preceded by the indefinite article *a*, it takes a plural verb.

> The number on the team who can be counted on in a tight spot *is* small.

> A number of the team *have* proved their worth.

When subjects are contrasted, the verb agrees with the affirmative subject.

> **Wrong** She, not I, *am* responsible.

> **Right** She, not I, *is* responsible.

When the subject is a relative pronoun, look for the pronoun's antecedent to determine whether the verb is singular or plural. Relative pronouns are *who, which,* and *that.*

> **Wrong** Joe is one of the few students who *has* maintained an A average.

> **Right** Joe is one of the few students who *have* maintained an A average. (The antecedent of the relative pronoun *who* is *students*, hence it takes a plural verb.)

Words joined to a subject by *as well as, in addition to, with, together with, including,* and *rather than* do not affect the verb.

> **Wrong** The entire student body, as well as most of the members of the faculty, *have* denounced President Green's decision.

> **Right** The entire student body, as well as most of the members of the faculty, *has* denounced President Green's decision.

A compound subject joined by *and* generally takes a plural verb.

> **Wrong** Her arrival and departure *was* not even noticed.

> **Right** Her arrival and departure *were* not even noticed.

Do not use a plural verb when the subject is a compound that is regarded as a single entity.

> The long and short of the matter *is* that our front line is weak.

> Spaghetti and meatballs *is* my favorite.

> Bread and butter *is* all that we have for supper.

Singular subjects joined by *and* but preceded by *every* take a singular verb.

> **Wrong** Every man, woman, and child *are* accounted for.

> **Right** Every man, woman, and child *is* accounted for.

Singular subjects joined by *or, either . . . or, nor,* or *neither . . . nor,* take a singular verb.

> **Wrong** Neither Adams nor Williams *are* present.

> **Right** Neither Adams nor Williams *is* present.

When a verb has two or more subjects differing in person or number and connected by *or, either . . . or, nor,* or *neither . . . nor,* the verb agrees with the subject nearer it.

> **Wrong** Either he or you *is* wrong.

Right   Either he or you *are* wrong. (The verb agrees in person with the pronoun nearer it.)

Wrong   Either new players or a new play *are* needed.

Right   Either new players or a new play *is* needed. (The verb agrees in number with the noun nearer it.)

Irregular Verbs

To find the proper form of irregular verbs, consult a reliable dictionary. It is important to know how dictionaries enter the forms of irregular verbs. The main entry for all verbs is the infinitive (without the *to*) or present tense form. Following the verb's phonetic respelling comes, first, the past tense form; next, the past participial form; and finally, the present participial form. Acceptable variant forms are given. However, if any one form is the same as the one immediately preceding it, that form is not repeated. For verbs that are not irregular, the past tense and the past participle, when not given, are assumed to be formed in the usual way by adding *-d* or *-ed*.

Adjectives and Adverbs

Adjectives and adverbs are *modifiers*, words which change the meaning of other words to make them clearer, more exact, weaker, or stronger.

An *adjective* modifies a noun or pronoun. It may answer the questions How many? What kind? Which one?

	HOW MANY?	
three brothers	*one* dollar	*many* men
	WHAT KIND?	
early bird	*whole* truth	*beautiful* girl
	WHICH ONE?	
this visit	*whose* jug?	*her* book

Note that *this, whose,* and *her*—often used as pronouns—here function as *pronominal adjectives*. A pronominal adjective always accompanies a noun and cannot be a predicate adjective.

Also note that the indefinite article *a (an)* identifies something as one of its kind (*a* boy, *an* apple), or serves as a substitute for *each* or *every* (once *a* week). The definite article *the* identifies one or more persons or objects by separating them from all others of their kind. Both articles are therefore adjectives.

An *adverb* modifies a verb, adjective, or another adverb. It may answer the questions How? When? Where? How much?

HOW?

Come *quickly*. It moves *clockwise*.

WHEN?

They arrived *yesterday*.

WHERE?

They went *home*. *Here* it is.

HOW MUCH?

We are more active now, but *only partly* happy.

In addition, there are the conjunctive adverbs *(however, moreover, nevertheless, therefore),* and adverbs of assertion and concession *(yes, no, not, maybe, probably).*

Many adverbs may be distinguished from adjectives by their *-ly* ending *(happy, happily; hard, hardly; particular, particularly).* But some of the more common adverbs do not end in *-ly: now, quite, there, then, up, down, for.* The last four of these can also be adjectives; there is a long list of adjectives and adverbs with identical forms, including *better, early, fast, much, straight,* and *well.*

Some adverbs have two forms: *loud, loudly; slow, slowly; soft, softly; quick, quickly; wrong, wrongly.* Sometimes there is a clear difference of meaning between the two.

He tried *hard*   He *hardly* tried.

She came *late*.   *Lately* she has been coming at dinnertime.

With others, choice depends on sound or on level of usage. The *-ly* ending is more common in formal writing. It is almost invariably used when the adverb precedes the verb *(Tightly* he gripped the narrow ledge). The short form is used especially in commands (hold on *tight;* go *slow).* Do not drop the *-ly* from the adverbs *considerably, really, sincerely,* and the like. For any question of the standard form consult a dictionary.

Adjectives and adverbs in English do not change their forms to indicate person, number, or case. However, they do change their forms to indicate degrees of comparison. They are compared in three degrees, frequently by adding *-er* and *-est*.

	POSITIVE	COMPARATIVE	SUPERLATIVE
ADJECTIVE	long	longer	longest
ADVERB	far	farther	farthest

Some have irregular comparisons, but these rarely cause difficulty:

	POSITIVE	COMPARATIVE	SUPERLATIVE
ADJECTIVE	good	better	best
	bad	worse	worst
	many	more	most
	much		
ADVERB	well	better	best
	bad	worse	worst

Words of two syllables may have comparisons in *-er* and *-est*, or may use *more (less)* and *most (least);* the choice is determined by rhythm and emphasis. Words of three or more syllables are compared only with *more (less)* and *most (least)*.

	POSITIVE	COMPARATIVE	SUPERLATIVE
ADJECTIVE	lovely	lovelier; more (less) lovely	loveliest; most (least) lovely
	beautiful	more (less) beautiful	most (least) beautiful
ADVERB	beautifully	more (less) beautifully	most (least) beautifully

In informal speech, or for reasons of emphasis, the superlative is often used in place of the comparative. But the general rule in formal writing is to use the comparative in comparing two things, the superlative for three or more.

> **Informal** Put your *best* foot forward. May the *best* team win.

> **Formal** The *better* team won decisively. Rome is the *oldest* of European capitals.

Absolute adjectives cannot, strictly speaking, be compared; something is either *dead, possible, full, perfect, unique,* or it is not. But in informal usage absolute adjectives are often modified by comparisons, either for emphasis (*"deader* than a doornail") or because some of them have virtually lost their absolute meaning ("this box is *emptier* than that"). In formal usage, "more nearly empty" would be preferable.

Things compared should be of the same kind.

> **Wrong** Marlowe's plays are not so highly regarded as Shakespeare.

> **Right** Marlowe's plays are not so highly regarded as those of Shakespeare (or *as Shakespeare's*).

Other is used only when the things compared are of the same category.

> **Wrong** Helen is more intelligent than any *other* boy.

> **Right** Helen is more intelligent than any boy. She reads more widely than any *other* student.

Do not use *other* with superlative comparisons.

> **Wrong** Helen was the most intelligent of all the *other* students.

> **Right** Helen was the most intelligent of all the students.

An adjective may precede a noun (or pronoun), or follow one. Or an adjective may follow a linking verb.

> The *tired* nations sought a peace, one *secure* and *permanent*. (*Tired* precedes and modifies the noun *nations. Secure* and *permanent* follow and modify the pronoun *one;* this word order is not common but completely acceptable.)

> They hoped it would not prove *illusory*. (*Illusory* follows the linking verb *prove* and modifies the pronoun *it*.)

Notice in the example immediately above that an adjective, like a noun, may serve as subjective complement. This is not true of adverbs:

Wrong It seems *truly*.

Right It seems *true*.

Through frequent use, *I feel badly* is now sometimes acceptable in informal speech; but to be formally correct, say:

I feel *bad*.
I feel *ill*.
I feel *well*. (meaning: I do not feel ill.)
I feel *good*. (meaning: I feel positively happy, *or* healthy.)

Prepositions

A *preposition* connects a noun or pronoun with another word in the sentence and establishes the relationship between them.

Peter walked *to* the store. (connecting *walked* and *store*)
He returned *with* them. (connecting *returned* and *them*)

The following are some of the more common prepositions:

about	by	off
above	down	on
along	during	out
among	except	over
at	for	through
before	from	to
behind	in	under
below	like	up
beneath	near	with
beside	past	without
between	of	

The noun or pronoun introduced by the preposition is called *the object of the preposition* and must be in the objective case. This rule gives trouble only in the case of coordinated pronouns. Thus,

The waiter brought some *for her and me*. (NOT: *she and I*)

A preposition with its object is called a *prepositional phrase* and is used as an adjective or an adverb.

The boy *with the dog* is my brother. (adjective, modifying noun *boy*)

They are all playing *with the dog*. (adverb, modifying verb *are playing*)

He threw his hat *over the fence*. (adverb, modifying verb *threw*)

In informal conversation, prepositions are sometimes doubled, though this is not really necessary to the meaning of the sentence. Double prepositions are rarely used in writing.

Informal   We left *at about* nine o'clock.

Formal   We left *about* nine o'clock.

Never repeat the same preposition near the beginning and at the end of a sentence: She is the person *for* whom I took all that trouble *for*. This is a mark of carelessness. However, contrary to a frequent yet mistaken belief, a preposition may be used at the end of a sentence, whenever it sounds natural to the rhythm of the sentence.

Where does she come *from?*
Whom did she go *with?*

The first example below is obviously a much more natural (and effective) sentence than the second example, despite the two prepositions with which the first ends.

That's the kind of stupidity I won't put *up with*.
That's the kind of stupidity *up with which* I will not put.

One classic example ends with no fewer than five prepositions:

What did you put the book you were being read *to out of away for?*

This sentence, too clumsy for formal, written English, is perfectly clear (though not very elegant) as spoken language.

Problem Prepositions

As already stated, the major problem with most prepositions is their idiomatic use. The following prepositions often pose problems in general usage.

• *AMONG, BETWEEN*
Among is used when more than two persons or things are con-

sidered. *Between* is used when only two are considered. This rule, which may be relaxed in informal conversation, must be rigidly followed in written English.

Divide the money *among* Frank, John, and Bill.
We must choose *between* Frank and John.

An exception to this rule occurs when a mutual or reciprocal relationship is indicated. In this event, *between* is used for more than two.

A treaty was concluded *between* the three nations.

Frank, John, and Bill agreed *between* them that they would divide the prize.

* *AT, IN*
  At and *in* may often be used interchangeably. However, certain rules govern their usage when they indicate place or locality.
  In is used when the reference to the interior of a building is stressed; *at,* when the site itself is stressed.

  Please meet me *in* the reception room of the dean's office.
  Classes will be held *at* Judson Hall.

  In is used before the names of countries; *at* before the names of business firms, office buildings, schools, universities, etc.

  The International Conference will be held next year *in* Switzerland.

  I was educated *at* Princeton.

  In is used before the name of a city in local addresses; *at* before the street number.

  Bill lives *in* Newark *at* 562 Kensington Avenue.

* *BELOW, BENEATH, UNDER, UNDERNEATH*
  These prepositions are generally used interchangeably, and in most cases one will be as grammatically correct as the other. Choice is usually determined by courtesy. Thus, the use of *beneath* may imply inferiority or contempt where *below* would be more courteous. The example below implies inferiority:

Mary is in the class *beneath* me.

To substitute the word *below* does not make the construction more correct grammatically; however, it does make it more courteous and more in accord with accepted usage.

Mary is in the class *below* me.

- *BESIDE, BESIDES*
  Beside is used to mean *next to*. *Besides* (ordinarily an adverb) is used to mean *in addition to* or *moreover*.

  Please sit *beside* me.

  Besides a dog, I have three cats. (*Besides* modifies the verb *have*.)

- *IN, INTO*
  In refers to position. *Into* denotes motion from without to within.

  We ate a buffet supper *in* the living room.
  We marched *into* the dining room.

- *ON, ONTO, ON TO*
  On refers to position upon something; *onto* denotes motion toward the upper surface of something; the two-word form *on to* is used when *on* belongs to the verb.

  I rode *on* the horse.
  I got *onto* the horse.
  I hung *on to* the horse.

- *ITEMS IN A SERIES*
  Items in a series must always be parallel in form. This means that when a preposition is used to introduce a series, it should be either repeated before each ensuing item or dropped before each ensuing item.

  Wrong I shall send invitations to John, Bill, and to Mary.

  Right I shall send invitations to John, to Bill, and to Mary.

  Right I shall send invitations to John, Bill, and Mary.

Complete Guide to Speech, Style and Grammar

Conjunctions

A *conjunction* connects words, phrases, or clauses.

> black *and* blue (words)
> with a group *but* not part of it (phrases)
> He agreed, *though* he had reservations. (clauses)

Conjunctions may be classified according to four types:

* A *coordinating conjunction* connects equal words, phrases, or clauses. There are six coordinating conjunctions. These are *and, but, for, nor, or,* and *yet.*

  > We didn't walk, *nor* did we drive.
  > It rained, *yet* we enjoyed the farm.

  A coordinating conjunction may occasionally introduce a sentence closely related in thought to the preceding one.

  > We managed to win the first game. *But* we never had a chance for the championship.

* *Correlative conjunctions* are used in pairs to connect equal elements that are parallel in form. They replace a coordinating conjunction for greater emphasis.

  > We will go to Yellowstone Park *or* Yosemite. (coordinating conjunction)

  > We will go *either* to Yellowstone Park *or* Yosemite. (correlative conjunction)

  The most common correlative conjunctions are *both . . . and, neither . . . nor, either . . . or, whether . . . or,* and *not only . . . but (also).*

  > I didn't care *whether* we went *or* stayed home.
  > At the party we met *not only* the Jacksons *but* the Blairs.
  > *Not only* the husbands came *but also* the children.

* A *conjunctive adverb* connects clauses in addition to modifying a verb (or clause). The most common are:

accordingly	however	nevertheless
also	indeed	still

besides	likewise	then
furthermore	meanwhile	therefore
hence	moreover	thus

A group of words may also serve as a conjunctive adverb:

in fact	for that reason
in the first place	on the contrary
in the meantime	on the other hand

The conjunctive adverb always has a semicolon before it when it is used between independent clauses.

I hadn't set the clock; *hence,* I was late.

The search may have ended; *indeed,* it's likely.

We tried the engine; but *in the meantime,* the tire had gone flat.

- A *subordinating conjunction* introduces a dependent clause and subordinates it to an independent clause. It establishes the relation between the two clauses. This relation may be one of

CAUSE: *as, because, inasmuch as, since*

We went indoors, *as* it had grown quite dark.
Since he likes animals, they like him.

COMPARISON: *as . . . as, so . . . as, than*

Chaucer's language is not *so* difficult *as* you may think.
There was more smoke *than* (there was) fire.

CONCESSION: *although, though, while*

Although he works hard, he's not very efficient.
He doesn't write well, *though* he tries.

CONDITION: *if, provided that, unless*

She'll come *provided that* you do.
Unless you run, you won't catch her.

MANNER: *as, as if, as though*

Do *as* you would be done by
It seemed *as though* he would win.

PLACE: *where, wherever, whence, whither*

Where one is good, two are better.
"And *whence* they come and *whither* they shall go
The dew upon their feet shall manifest."

PURPOSE: *in order that, so that, that*

So *that* there will be enough for all, take no more than you need.

They died *that* we may live.

RESULT: *so that, so . . . that, such . . . that*

He studied hard, *so that* finally he was the recognized expert in the field.

Such was his optimism *that* we all were prepared for success.

TIME: *after, as, before, since, till, until, when, while*

Ruth arrived *as* they were leaving.
Until you spoke, I didn't know you were there.

Troublesome Conjunctions

The following are troublesome conjunctions:

- *AND, ALSO*
Also should not be used in place of *and* to connect items in a series.

    Wrong   I study English, French, Spanish, also Russian.

    Right   I study English, French, Spanish, and Russian.

- *AND, ETC.*
The abbreviation *etc.* means "and so forth." It is incorrect to use *and* to connect the last item in a series when the last item is followed by *etc.*

    Wrong   We need eggs, bacon, and bread, etc.

    Right   We need eggs, bacon, bread, *etc.*

- *AND WHICH, AND WHO*
  These should not be used unless preceded in the same sentence by *which* or *who*.

  Wrong I am looking for a course with four credits *and which* holds classes on Wednesday mornings.

  Right I am looking for a course *which* offers four credits *and which* holds classes on Wednesday mornings.

- *AND, BUT*
  And is used to show addition; *but,* to show contrast.

  Wrong Mary and I have been invited to a party, *and* I have to take care of my younger brother.

  Right Mary and I have been invited to a party, *but* I have to take care of my younger brother.

- *AS, AS IF, LIKE*
  As and *as if* are respectably used as conjunctions to introduce clauses of various kinds and to connect comparisons. *Like,* which is gaining respectability as a conjunction in informal usage, is treated only as a preposition in formal writing. Grammarians shudder when they see *like* usurping the role of *as* and *as if.*

  Informal You act *like* you're hurt.

  Formal You act *as if* you were hurt.

- *AS, BECAUSE, SINCE*
  Any one of these may be used to introduce clauses of cause or reason, that is, to connect the stated cause with a fact already given.

  I came *because* I was worried.
  As you won't go, I will stay.
  Since I can, I will.

  However, *because* is limited to introducing clauses of cause or reason. *As* and *since* are also used to introduce clauses involving time. To introduce duration of time, use *as*. To introduce sequence of time, use *since*.

I worked less and less *as* each day passed. (time duration)

I haven't done any work *since* last you were here. (time sequence)

- *BECAUSE, FOR*
  Because is used when the reason it introduces is based upon fact. *For* is used when the reason it introduces is based upon opinion or speculation.

  Come inside, *because* it is raining. (The reason given is an established fact.)

  We are going to have a storm, *for* there is a ring around the moon. (The reason given is based on speculation.)

- *IF, WHETHER*
  If introduces clauses of supposition or condition involving uncertainty or doubt.

  If I had known you were coming, I would have prepared a feast. (implies uncertainty)

  If may also stand for *even though* or *whenever*.

  If pigs could fly, I still would not go with you. (implies *even though*)

  If Mary ever arrives, we will go to the restaurant. (implies *whenever*)

  On the other hand, *whether* introduces clauses which involve an alternative. The alternative may be stated or understood. (*Whether* is the conjunction most likely to be followed by *or*.)

  It will not make any difference *whether* I know or not. (alternative stated)

  Please let me know *whether* I am right. (alternative implied)

- *WHEN, WHERE*
  When should not be used to introduce a definition unless the definition involves a time element; *where* should not be used unless the definition involves place or location.

Wrong   A foul is *when* (or *where*) the ball leaves the court.

Right   A foul is made *when* the ball leaves the court during the playing period. (time involved)

Right   A foul is made at the place *where* the ball crosses the foul line. (place involved)

- *WHEN, WHILE*
  When refers to a fixed period of time; *while* to duration of time.

  When you are willing to talk, I will listen. (fixed time: as soon as you are ready to talk)

  While you talk, I will listen. (time duration: during the time that you talk)

- *WHILE, ALTHOUGH, BUT, WHEREAS*
  While is often used colloquially to mean *although*, *but*, and *whereas*.

  Colloquial   I like Mary, *while* I like Jeanne better.

  Formal   I like Mary, *but* I like Jeanne better.

  Colloquial   Mary is fat, *while* Jeanne is slim.

  Formal   Mary is fat, *whereas* Jeanne is slim.

Interjections

An interjection is a word of exclamation which expresses emotion, but which has no grammatical relation to the rest of the sentence.

   Oh!   Hey!   Whoa!   Ouch!   Ha, ha!   Boo!

Many words that generally serve as other parts of speech may be used as interjections:

   Well!   Heavens!   Nuts!   Run!   Good!

Punctuation

Many of us look on marks of punctuation as annoying inventions of English teachers to make the hard job of writing even harder. Consequently, we ignore punctuation whenever we can, which is most of the time, and turn over the job of inserting the proper marks to instructors, copy editors, or to anyone else likely to get a mysterious pleasure from the process.

Actually, punctuation is almost as essential to clear writing as words themselves are. It is the function of words to identify meanings, and it is the function of punctuation to package the meanings in usable clumps, like phrases, clauses, and sentences. Imagine trying to read this page if all the letters were run together (for spacing is punctuation, too) with no capital letters, no breaks, and no clumping of word groups. Punctuation really *says* things, just as words do, but it says them more economically. A period, for example, says "Pause here. A complete thought has been expressed." And so with all the other marks.

Punctuation also serves another vital function, that of stylistic effectiveness. When you speak, you use physical means to achieve clarity and vigor. You raise and lower your voice; you emphasize a point with a gesture of your finger; you speak rapidly and then slowly to provide contrast; you say particular words with unusual stress. None of this is passed on to your reader, however, if you do not use punctuation marks. The reader of a well-punctuated page almost feels as if he or she were listening to you speak.

So do not underestimate the importance of punctuation. No writing is good if it is not clear, and no writing is clear if it is not well punctuated.

Terminal Marks

Marks of punctuation that have the power to end a sentence are called "terminal marks." A sentence may be brought to an end without necessarily being complete; that is, it does not have to possess a full subject and predicate. The terminal marks may be used with a phrase, or even a single word. The following are examples of how terminal marks may be used:

> **Questions and Answers**   Where to? Ash and 23rd Streets.
>
> **Exclamations**   What luck! Bah! Humbug!
>
> **Dramatic Effect**   He moved forward cautiously. One step, then another. A shot rang out.

We generally think that the period, question mark, and exclamation mark are the only terminal marks. This is not so. Two other marks have the power to end a sentence. The dash can interrupt or summarily end a sentence before it is completed; and the colon—essentially a mark of introduction—can terminate an introductory statement when what follows it begins with a capital letter.

> **Dash as a Terminal Mark** "I swear I never again will drive a—" The mad honking of automobiles cut him short.

> **Colon as a Terminal Mark** In conclusion, I make this promise: If elected, I shall serve you to the best of my ability.

These are only incidental uses of the dash and colon, however. The three chief terminal marks are still the period, question mark, and exclamation mark.

Period

The period (.) is the most common terminal mark of punctuation. The rules for use of the period are given below.

A period is used at the end of a declarative sentence.

> We have nothing to fear but fear itself.
> —*Franklin D. Roosevelt*

A period is used at the end of an imperative sentence.

> Go at once.
> She said, "Help me."

Do not use a period when an imperative sentence is so strong that it becomes an exclamation. Such a sentence is followed by an exclamation mark. Whether an imperative sentence is ended by a period or an exclamation mark depends entirely on the degree of emphasis desired.

> "Go at once!" he shouted.
> "Help!" she cried.

A period is used at the end of a sentence that is interrogative in form but to which an answer is not required.

> Children, will you stop that noise at once.

Complete Guide to Speech, Style and Grammar

Periods are used in courtesy titles and abbreviations of rank which appear before a name.

Mr. Jones	Lt. Jane Thomas
Ms. Brown	Mrs. Ralph Stone
Dr. Smith	Comdr. Edwards

A period is used to represent a decimal point.

17.4°   75.2% $1.75

A period is used after figures and letters to represent principal divisions of lists.

IV. Gross income
   A. Expenses
      1. Net income
         a. Net earnings per share

Do not use a period when the figures or letters are in parentheses.

(IV) Gross income
   (A) Expenses
      (1) Net income
         (a) Net earnings per share

A period is used with many abbreviations.

A.M.	P.M.	Mrs.	Ave.	etc.
Mon.	Jan.	treas.	i.e.	M.D.
F.D.R.	J.F.K.	H. L. Mencken		

Use periods for academic degrees when abbreviated.

B.A.   B.S.N.   Ph.D.

Do not use a period with abbreviations that are accepted as the shortened form of proper names.

TWA   FBI   NASA

But current practice is moving away from the period in some circumstances where periods were required in past years.

100 Maryland Ave. NE

Do not use a period with ZIP code abbreviations for states.

New York, NY 10115

Do not use a period after a person's nickname or after the shortened form of a person's name.

    Sue   Hank   Doug   Bob

Do not use a period after letters of the alphabet used in place of a person's name.

    Mrs. A told Mr. B

Do not use a period after the call letters of radio and TV stations or networks.

    WPIX   KLOB   ABC

Do not use a period after familiar shortened forms of words.

    tab   ad   el   lab

Do not use a period after Roman numerals except to represent principal divisions of lists.

Henry V	Ecclesiastes II
Act III	Pope John XXIII
Vol. II	

Do not use a period after ordinal endings of numbers.

    3rd   6th   21st   92nd

Do not use a period with mathematical equations, trigonometrical terms, or chemical symbols.

$$y \times 4 = y^2 \qquad \log \qquad \sin \qquad H_2O$$

Do not use a period with the abbreviated form of the words *manuscript* and *manuscripts*.

    MS   MSS

Do not use a period after the initials of the writer and the secretary in business letters (which appear in the bottom lefthand corner).

    JRS:BS   HTB:fn   rmm:ns   tdc/al

Complete Guide to Speech, Style and Grammar

Generally periods are not used in abbreviations which appear in tables and charts.

In some circumstances one abbreviation may need periods or not according to which meaning is desired.

MP   military police
M.P.   member of Parliament

The use of abbreviations should be avoided in most formal writing. When such use is accepted practice, follow the accepted style of the business or field in which you are working. When in doubt consult a reliable dictionary.

In Relation to Other Punctuation Marks The period is not used in addition to a question mark or an exclamation mark at the end of a sentence. It is always placed inside closing quotation marks.

The period is placed outside the closing parenthesis when the parenthesis encloses the last word of a sentence. The period is placed inside the closing parenthesis only when what is enclosed in parenthesis is a complete sentence and the first letter is capitalized.

> This is called the law of natural selection (Darwinism).

> This is called the law of natural selection. (This law cannot be too highly stressed in the study of biology.)

When a sentence ends with an abbreviation that requires a period of its own, no second period is added.

> For your first schoolday, you must remember to take paper, pencils, erasers, etc.

Question Mark

The question mark (?) follows an interrogative word, phrase, clause, or sentence. It has the power to end a sentence, yet it may also punctuate a quotation within a sentence without ending the sentence. This mark is always used to indicate a question.

A question mark should follow every direct question.

> Have you done your homework?
> "What time is it?" he asked.

Do not use a question mark after an indirect question.

> I was asked if I had finished my homework.
> He asked what time it was.

Do not use a question mark at the end of an interrogative sentence to which no answer is required.

> Will you please enter my name on your mailing list.

Do not use a question mark after a question that is actually an exclamation.

> How could you!   How dare you!

A declarative expression may be transformed into a question by the mere addition of a question mark.

> The train was late.   The train was late?
> Really.   Really?

A question mark is enclosed in parentheses after a fact that is doubtful.

> America was first visited by a white man in A.D. 1000 (?).
> The crowd numbered 650 (?) cheering students.

A question mark in parentheses should not be used in indicate irony.

> **Poor** This is a great (?) book.

> **Better** This is hardly a great book.

When more than one question is asked in a sentence, a question mark may or may not be used depending upon the degree of emphasis desired. For emphasis, each separate question begins with a capital letter and terminates with its own question mark. A single question mark is used at the end of a sentence when the questions within the sentence are related and form a unified thought.

> The teacher asked, "How large is Berlin? What is its population? and In what country is it located?"

> How am I expected to know the size, population, and location of a city when I don't have an atlas?

More than one question mark placed for special emphasis does not conform to accepted usage. A period or a comma is never used in addition to the question mark.

Wrong Did you really like that play?.

Right Did you really like that play?

Wrong "Will you come with us?," she asked.

Right "Will you come with us?" she asked.

The question mark should be placed inside quotation marks if it belongs to the quotation (as shown in the example immediately above). It should be placed outside quotation marks if it does not belong to the quotation.

Who first said, "Haste makes waste"?

Exclamation Mark

The exclamation mark (!) adds forceful emphasis to a declarative word, expression, or sentence. The exclamation mark is used after a strong command or exhortation.

"Get out!" she screamed.
"Don't shoot!" he pleaded.

The exclamation mark is used after an expression of strong emotion.

What a stroke of luck!
How the mighty are fallen!

An interjection is a word that expresses emotion. It may be strong enough on its own merit not to require an exclamation mark. The exclamation mark merely helps to strengthen it.

Oh, what a beautiful day!
Wow! What a blizzard.

The exclamation mark is placed either immediately after an interjection that begins a sentence, or at the end of the sentence introduced by an interjection.

Whew! That was a close call.
Oh, what a beautiful day!

Comma

The comma (,) is a comparatively weak but subtle mark of punctuation. It is used—and misused—more frequently than any other punctuation mark. This is because the comma has such varied functions. Chiefly, it introduces, separates, and encloses. In addition, it indicates omission. None of these functions is performed by the comma with the authority or finality of such marks as the colon, semicolon, or dash. All the comma indicates is a mild pause, hence its subtle, elusive nature. In the rules for comma usage that follow, the term "to separate" means that the comma separates a word, phrase, or clause from the rest of the sentence. A single comma is used to separate. The term "to enclose" means that an expression appearing within a sentence is enclosed in commas. Two commas are used to enclose: one comma is placed immediately preceding, and the other following, the expression. When an expression to be enclosed ends the sentence, a period is used instead of the second enclosing comma.

Quoted References

A comma is used to introduce a short quotation, maxim, or proverb.

> Helen said, "It's a lovely day."
> The saying is, "Time waits for no man."

Do not use a comma to introduce a formal quotation. A colon is used instead of the comma. Do not use a comma to introduce a quoted word or phrase that is the subject or object of a sentence.

> "Fourscore and seven years ago" is the most famous opening passage of any address ever made.

> The president spoke on "Our Relations with Latin America."

> Obey the "slow down" signs.

> Must you always ask "Why?"

> Can't you say "thank you" occasionally?

Do not use a comma preceding a quotation introduced by the conjunction *that*.

Wrong The travel poster suggested that, "California is the land of sunshine."

Right The travel poster suggested that "California is the land of sunshine."

A comma is used after a quotation to separate such expressions as *he said* and *she replied*. Commas are used to enclose such expressions when they break into or interrupt a quotation.

"It's a grand day," Bill said.

"The weather is perfect," she said, "for the Winter Carnival."

Do not use a comma in addition to a question mark or mark of exclamation following a quotation.

Wrong "Do you think we can leave early?," she asked.

Right "Do you think we can leave early?" she asked.

Series Separation

Commas are used to separate words, phrases, and clauses in a series. (In journalistic writing the comma is frequently omitted before the final conjunction in a series. This practice is not sanctioned in formal writing.)

Our American professors like their literature clear, cold, pure, and very dead.—*Sinclair Lewis*

All the things I really like to do are either immoral, illegal, or fattening.—*Alexander Woollcott*

Do not use commas when the conjunction is repeated before each item in a series.

Wrong It rained, and thundered, and hailed.

Right It rained and thundered and hailed.

Do not use a comma after the last item in a series.

Wrong We planted roses, violets, and nasturtiums, in our garden.

Right We planted roses, violets, and nasturtiums in our garden.

Commas are used to separate two or more coordinate adjectives modifying the same noun. Adjectives may be considered coordinate when they are in a series and the coordinating conjunction *and* can be readily substituted for the comma.

Caroline is a comely, tow-headed girl.
John is a short, stocky, powerful wrestler.

Do not use the comma to separate adjectives that appear as part of a compound noun, that is, if *and* cannot be readily substituted for the comma.

Wrong She is a comely, little girl.

Right She is a comely little girl.

Do not use the comma to separate one adjective that modifies another.

Wrong He has a deep, tan sunburn.

Right He has a deep tan sunburn.

Separation in Compound Sentences

A comma is used to separate the main (independent) clauses of a sentence joined by coordinating conjunctions like *and, but, or, nor, for,* and *yet.*

It's better to give than to lend, and it costs about the same. —*Philip Gibbs*

My folks didn't come over on the *Mayflower,* but they were there to meet the boat.—*Will Rogers*

We do not know what to do with this short life, yet we want another which will be eternal.—*Anatole France*

Arguments are extremely vulgar, for everybody in good society holds exactly the same opinions.—*Oscar Wilde*

Do not use a comma to separate main clauses when the clauses already contain commas within them. A semicolon is used instead of the comma.

Do not use a comma to separate main clauses when the second clause has the same subject as the first clause and the subject is not repeated.

> She was a brunette by birth but a blonde by habit.—*Arthur Baer*

> Poverty is very good in poems but very bad in the house; very good in maxims and sermons but very bad in practical life.—*Henry Ward Beecher*

Do not use a comma to separate main clauses when they are short and are closely connected in thought, provided that the omission of the comma will not lead to a misreading.

> **Wrong** Grace sang and she danced one number. (The omission of the comma in this sentence could be misread to mean that Grace sang and danced during one number only.)

> **Right** Grace sang, and she danced one number.

Introductory Phrases, Clauses

Use a comma to separate an introductory subordinate phrase or clause from a main clause. Such clauses often begin with subordinating conjunctions (*when, if, because, since, while, as, although, before, after,* etc.)

> Where all think alike, no one thinks very much.—*Walter Lippmann*

> When you get to the end of your rope, tie a knot and hang on.—*Franklin Delano Roosevelt*

Do not use a comma when a subordinate phrase or clause follows a main clause unless the subordinate clause expresses a nonlimiting idea.

> **Wrong** You must do this, because I said you must.

> **Right** You must do this because I said you must.

Right   Because I said you must do this, you must.

Right   You must do this, although I would much rather you did not.

A comma is used to separate an introductory phrase containing a participle or an infinitive used as an adjective or an adverb.

Drawing on my fine command of knowledge, I said nothing.—*Robert Benchley*

To keep your friends, treat them kindly; to kill them, treat them often.—*George D. Prentice*

Do not use a comma to separate a gerund or an infinitive phrase that is the subject of the sentence.

Wrong   Writing carelessly, causes bad grades.

Right   Writing carelessly causes bad grades.

To profit from good advice requires more wisdom than to give it.—*John Churton Collins*

Parenthetical Expressions, Appositives

Commas are used to enclose such parenthetical expressions as the following: *to tell the truth, in the main, generally speaking, you must admit, I should say, I know, I believe, we may understand, in short, for one thing, in the long run, for the most part,* and *in fact.*

Opera in English is, in the main, just about as sensible as baseball in Italian.—*H. L. Mencken*

The greatest of faults, I should say, is to be conscious of none. —*Thomas Carlyle*

Commas are used to enclose the parenthetical expressions *for example, for instance,* and *that is.*

Take, for example, the poets we have been reading.

Consider the books we have been reading, for instance.

This is not an adequate map, that is, not from an artist's point of view.

Commas are used to enclose nonlimiting (also called "nonrestrictive") phrases and clauses within a sentence. Though it may add information and help clarify meaning, a nonlimiting phrase or clause is not necessary to identify the word or words it modifies. It can be omitted from the sentence without changing the meaning. A limiting (also called "restrictive") phrase or clause, however, is necessary to identify the word or words it modifies. An integral part of the sentence, a limiting phrase or clause is *not* enclosed in commas.

> **Nonlimiting** *The Spirit of St. Louis,* which Lindbergh flew across the Atlantic, was a single-engine airplane.

> **Limiting** The airplane that Lindbergh flew across the Atlantic was *The Spirit of St. Louis.*

Commas are used to enclose a parenthetical aside that interrupts the free flow, or thought, of a sentence and that can be omitted without changing the meaning of the sentence. An aside—like other parenthetical expressions—may add information, but the essential thought of the sentence is complete without it.

> That, like it or not, is the way to learn to write; whether I have profited or not, that is the way.—*Robert Louis Stevenson*

> Age carries all things, even the mind, away.—*Virgil*

Commas are used to enclose words in apposition. An appositive is a noun or a pronoun (or any group of words used as a noun or a pronoun) that is set beside another noun or pronoun having the same meaning. An appositive adds information, but it is not absolutely essential to the meaning or clarity of the sentence.

> Helen, my sister, is coming to the prom.

> Roger Martin Du Gard, the author, was a close friend of André Gide.

Do not use commas to enclose limiting appositives. Because it actually identifies a particular person or thing, a limiting appositive is absolutely necessary to the meaning and clarity of the sentence. A limiting appositive is frequently part of a name.

My sister Helen is coming to the prom. (My sister Helen is coming—not my sister Barbara.)

The author Roger Martin Du Gard was a close friend of André Gide.

Expressions Not in Normal Order

Commas are used to enclose an expression that does not appear in its normal order in the sentence.

Not normal order   A cynic is a man who, when he smells flowers, looks around for a coffin.—*H. L. Mencken*

Normal order   A cynic is a man who looks around for a coffin when he smells flowers.

Omissions

A comma is used to take the place of one or more omitted words. Usually the comma takes the place of a verb or verb phrase.

To love and win is the best thing; to love and lose, the next best.—*William Makepeace Thackeray*

To eat is human; to digest, divine.—*Mark Twain*

Direct Address

A comma is used to separate a word or words in direct address, either at the beginning or the end of a sentence. When an expression in direct address appears within the sentence, commas are used to enclose it.

Sir, I wish to leave the room.
I move, Mr. Chairman, that the motion be put to a vote.

Contrasts

A comma is used to separate letters, words, phrases, or clauses that are contrasted. Such contrasts are generally introduced by the word *not*.

We live in deeds, not years; in thoughts, not breaths.—*Philip James Bailey*

Genius is born, not paid.—*Oscar Wilde*

Complete Guide to Speech, Style and Grammar

Direct Questions

A comma is used to separate a direct question from the rest of the sentence. The first word of the direct question may be capitalized or not, depending upon how much the writer wishes to emphasize the question. (The current trend, however, is away from capitalizing the question unless the emphasis desired is great enough to require a colon instead of the comma.)

> The question is, where do we go from here?
> Have you ever asked yourself the question, Why am I here?
> I wondered, what do I do next?

Interjections

A comma is used to separate mild interjections from the rest of the sentence. When the interjection appears within the sentence, commas are used to enclose it. (An interjection becomes an exclamation when it is followed by an exclamation mark.)

> Well, let me see now.
> Oh, why, oh, why did I ever do that?

Do not use a comma when such words as *well* and *why* are used as adverbs.

> Well done, team
> Why am I not good enough for you?

Do not use a comma immediately following the vocative *O* (that is, when *O* is used to emphasize the name of a person or persons being addressed).

> O ye Gods, grant us what is good, whether we pray for it or not, but keep evil from us, even though we pray for it. —*Plato*

However, you should use a comma after the interjection *O*.

> O, for a draught of vintage!—*John Keats*

Yes and No

A comma is used to separate the words *Yes* and *No* from the rest of the sentence.

Yes, it was a wonderful book.
No, you are not to leave.
I have already given my answer and that is, no.

Do not use a comma when the word *Yes* or *No* is a direct object.

Jane answered yes to the suggestion.

I said to tell him no.

Emphasis

A comma may be used to separate a word or words strictly for emphasis, or to add an element of surprise. This is a subtle use of the comma. The dash is used more frequently for emphasis and surprise.

I spent a year in that town, one Sunday.—*Warwick Deeping*

Ordinal Adverbs

Commas are used to separate ordinal adverbs (*first, second, third,* etc.) and ordinal adverb phrases such as *in the first place* and *in the second place*.

First, I wish to announce that the library will be open during the Christmas recess; second, that all borrowed books must be returned on or before the first day of classes.

In the first place, there isn't time; in the second, we don't have the facilities to do a proper job.

Numbers

Commas are used to separate the digits in numbers above 999. The comma is placed preceding every third digit, counting backward from the last digit. Note that in sums of money the digits denoting cents are not counted.

1,000	$99.00
1,999	$999,000
2,000	$1,000,000
12,605	$2,105,602,000.46

Do not use the comma in a number denoting a year.

The Trojan War began in 1194 B.C.

George Orwell's *1984* is a remarkable book.

Do not use the comma in page numbers, telephone numbers, and street numbers. The comma is also not generally used in serial numbers.

You will find the reference on page 1201.

Please phone me at 212-8915.

Do not use the comma in decimals.

.1329   .89641

A comma is used to separate a scene from an act in a play. (Either roman or arabic numerals may be used.)

Act III, scene ii   Act 3, scene 2

Do not use the comma in numbers denoting dimensions, weights, and measures.

6 ft. 3 in.   10 feet 11 inches
11 hr. 38 min.   11 hours 38 minutes

Commas are used to enclose the year when the year immediately follows the day of the month, but not the month from the year when no day is given or when the day precedes the month.

May 8, 1945, was the day Germany formally surrendered, ending World War II in Europe.

John moved to Los Angeles in December 1989.

The letter was sent 5 March 1992.

A comma is used to separate unrelated figures that appear next to each other.

In 1960, 68,837,000 presidential votes were cast—an increase of 6,800,000 from the presidential election of 1956.

Addresses

Commas are used to enclose the name of a state when it immediately follows the name of a city or town.

John moved from Denver, Colorado, to Los Angeles, California.

Do not use the comma in addresses to separate digits in street numbers, the street number from the street, or the state abbreviation from the ZIP code.

This is to notify you that I have moved my address from 1228 W. Jarvis Ave., Chicago, IL 60626 to 210 Old Hickory Blvd., Nashville, TN 37221.

Titles and Degrees

Commas are used to enclose an abbreviation or phrase that denotes a person's title or degree, when it follows the person's name.

George Bush, President of the United States, will address the United Nations.

Henry Nathan, M.D., and Lester Hawthorne, Ph.D., are the expert witnesses for the defense.

Initials

Commas are used to enclose a person's initials when the initials follow the person's name.

The authors are Johnson, L. M., and Scott, N. R.

Letters

A comma is used to separate the salutation of a friendly, informal letter from the body of the letter.

Dear Bill,   Dear Susan,   Dear Mother,

Do not use a comma after the salutation in a formal business letter. A colon is used instead.

Dear Mr. Marks: Dear Sir: Dear Editor:

A comma is used to separate the complimentary close of both informal and business letters from the writer's signature.

Affectionately,   Sincerely,   Yours truly,

Colon

The colon (:) is a formal mark of punctuation. It has two functions only: to introduce and to separate. As a mark of introduction, the colon introduces formal quotations, restatements or clarifying examples, and lists or enumerations. This construction gives more emphasis to these items than alternative sentence structures. As a mark of separation, the colon separates the salutation in a formal letter from the main body of the letter, titles from subtitles, the hours from minutes, etc.

A colon is used to call attention to a formal quotation.

> Franklin D. Roosevelt said: "We have nothing to fear but fear itself."

> The first line of Franz Kafka's *The Trial* reads: "Someone must have been telling lies about Joseph K., for without having done anything wrong he was arrested one fine morning."

Do not use a colon to introduce a maxim, a proverb, or a quotation of a single sentence in ordinary dialogue.

> The saying is, "A stitch in time saves nine."

> John said, "Let's go to the movies."

The colon may take the place of such expressions as *in effect, in other words,* and *namely* to introduce new statements, restatements, and clarifying examples.

> Readers are of two sorts: one who carefully goes through a book, and the other who as carefully lets the book go through him.—*Douglas Jerrold*

> Whatever you may be sure of, be sure of this: that you are dreadfully like other people.—*James Russell Lowell*

The colon is used to introduce formal lists and enumerations.

I have come to the following conclusions:
Please forward the items listed:
Mix the ingredients as follows:

But do not use a colon to introduce a list if the sentence does not have an introductory word or phrase to complete it.

>   **Wrong**   The crash injured: Bill, Tom, and David.

>   **Right**   The crash injured three students: Bill, Tom, and David.

>   **Right**   The crash injured Bill, Tom, and David.

>   **Wrong**   She ordered a breakfast of: eggs, bacon, toast, and coffee.

>   **Right**   She ordered a breakfast of eggs, bacon, toast, and coffee.

The colon is used in reference to time to separate hours from minutes.

>   10:15 A.M.   6:50 P.M.

The colon is used to separate a subtitle from a main title.

>   *Wheat: The Staff of Life*
>   *My Father: A Memoir of Mark Twain*

The colon is used to separate verse from chapter in the Bible.

>   The Song of Solomon 2:1
>   Ezekiel 10:6

In reference matter, the colon is used to separate the home office from the name of a publishing firm.

>   Deephaven, Minn.: Meadowbrook Books
>   New York: St. Martin's Press

The colon is used following the salutation in a formal business letter.

>   Dear Ms. Jones: Dear Sir: Gentlemen:

In Relation to Other Punctuation Marks

When the colon appears together with closing quotation marks, the colon always follows the quotation marks.

>   The teacher said, "Please answer the following questions":

The colon always follows a closing parenthesis.

> The librarian recommended the following books (all by Maugham):

The colon commonly used to be joined with the dash. This is no longer accepted usage.

> **Wrong**   We must follow these rules:—

> **Right**   We must follow these rules:

Semicolon

The semicolon, consisting of a period atop a comma (;), is strictly a mark of separation. Unlike a colon, it does not introduce; unlike a comma, it does not enclose; and, unlike a period, it does not terminate. Its sole function is to separate parts of sentences that cannot be separated by the comma. It marks a greater break or a longer pause than the comma, yet it does not carry the full authority of the period and other terminal marks to end a sentence.

A semicolon separates main (independent) clauses of a sentence when those clauses are not already joined by coordinating conjunctions like *and, but, or, neither, nor, for,* and *yet.*

> With educated people, I suppose, punctuation is a matter of rule; with me it is a matter of feeling. But I must say I have a great respect for the semicolon; it's a useful little chap.
> —*Abraham Lincoln*

A semicolon separates the main (independent) clauses of a sentence when the clauses are joined by coordinating conjunctions but when one or more already contain commas.

> Don't ever prophesy; for if you prophesy wrong, nobody will forget it; and if you prophesy right, nobody will remember it.—*Josh Billings*

> If you have charm, you don't need to have anything else; and if you don't have it, it doesn't matter what else you have.
> —*James M. Barrie*

A semicolon separates main (independent) clauses of a sentence that are joined by conjunctive adverbs like *thus, however, consequently, therefore, accordingly, besides,* and *moreover.*

> I do best in subjects that relate to science; consequently, I plan to major in science next year.

> He is taking six courses this semester; however, he has given up his part-time job and will have more time to study.

A semicolon separates items in a series when parts of the items are already separated by commas. The reason is that without the semicolon, the main parts would be indistinguishable.

> The winners were John, first; Bill, second; Tom, third.

> New York Central has railroad stations in Chicago, Illinois; Sante Fe, New Mexico; and Los Angeles, California.

In Relation to Other Punctuation Marks

A semicolon is always placed outside quotation marks.

> Play the "Appassionata Sonata"; play it with feeling this time.

A semicolon appearing next to words in parentheses is always placed after the closing parenthesis.

> The advanced math course intrigues me (with the possible exception of geometry); basketball practice, however, intrigues me more.

Dash

The dash (—) is roughly twice the length of a hyphen. On the typewriter or word processor it is indicated by two successive hyphens. The dash is extraordinarily versatile. It can perform any one of the four major functions of punctuation: introduction, separation, enclosure, and termination. In addition, the dash can indicate interruption and omission (of words, letters, numbers).

The dash is often used indiscriminately, especially by beginning writers, precisely because it is so versatile. It is, after all, a conspicuous, highly obtrusive mark of punctuation. Properly used, the dash is an ideal method of injecting an element of irony or surprise into a sentence; but to accomplish this; it must be used sparingly. Other marks of punctuation can usually take the place of the dash, and they should be substituted for it whenever one of the rules given below does not completely justify its use.

The dash is used without space between it and adjoining words. When a dash is used before a name indicating the source of the preceding material, space may precede the dash but none follows.

The dash indicates a sudden break or change of thought.

> Where was I on the night of last July 10? I was in my home— no, let me think, maybe I was at the theater.

> Are you—do you feel all right?

The dash is used to follow a direct quotation to indicate an interruption in discourse.

> "Really, now you ask me," said Alice, very much confused, "I don't think—"
> "Then you shouldn't talk," said the Hatter.—*Lewis Carroll*

Dashes may be used to set off a parenthetical thought to give it strong emphasis. Recourse to this use of the dash should be sparing.

> Yesterday, December 7, 1941—a date which will live in infamy—the United States of America was suddenly and deliberately attacked by naval and air forces of the Empire of Japan.—*Franklin D. Roosevelt*

Sometimes a parenthetical expression already contains punctuation within it and the expression cannot be enclosed in parentheses because it properly belongs to the sentence. Then dashes are used to set it off. This use of the dash frequently takes the place of commas that might otherwise be misread as series commas.

> His clothes—dirty, shabby, torn—belied his circumstances.

The dash may be used as a substitute for the expressions *that is, in other words,* and *namely.*

> He admits that there are two sides to every question—his own and the wrong side.—*Channing Pollock*

The dash may be used to set off a word or group of words to add an element of surprise, to show an unexpected turn of thought.

There are two things in life for which we are never fully prepared, and that is—twins.—*Josh Billings*

A pun is the lowest form of humor—when you don't think of
it first.—*Oscar Levant*

The dash is used before a summarizing expression such as *all
such, these,* and *all these.*

Barrymore, Gielgud, Evans—these were great Hamlets in
their time.

A long dash, called a 3-em dash, may be used to indicate a word,
or part of a word that has been omitted.

That fellow is a d—— fool.

In printed material an en dash—shorter than the usual em dash,
but longer than a hyphen—is used to indicate inclusion in dates, to
take the place of the words *to* or *through*. On the word processor or
typewriter, use the hyphen.

Vacation will be June–September.
He was here July 3–7.
I was in the Army 1963–1965.

Do not use the en dash or hyphen to indicate inclusion when the
words *from* or *between* precede the date.

Wrong   Vacation will be from June–September.

Right   Vacation will be from June to [*or* through] September.

An en dash is also used between other continuous numbers.

For a discussion of causes of the war, see pages 100–120.
The five children, ages six–twelve, watched with interest.

In Relation to Other Punctuation Marks

When the dash ends a sentence, all other terminal marks (period,
question mark, exclamation mark) are omitted.

Parentheses

When an expression cannot be sufficiently set off by commas or dashes, parentheses [( )] are used to enclose it. Generally, in order for a statement to be enclosed in parentheses, it must have no grammatical relationship to the rest of the sentence. Whatever is said in the parentheses should not be referred to again in the sentence. Statements within parentheses are completely independent of the rest of the sentence. Parentheses are used to set off a comment that may be only remotely connected to the meaning of the sentence itself.

> The astronomer reported (as the result of too much stargazing, I suppose) that the mean distance between the moon and the earth was 238 miles.

Parentheses are used to enclose references and directions.

> The book was hailed by at least one critic (see *The Saturday Review,* Nov. 30, 1963, page 43).

Parentheses may be used to enclose figures or letters marking the order of a series.

> (1). . . . .   (2). . . . .   (3). . . . .
> (a). . . . .   (b). . . . .   (c). . . . .

Do not let internal punctuation come between the parenthetical phrase and the word or phrase to which it is related.

> **Wrong** She brought a bottle, (the baby's) a book, and an empty box to the clubhouse.

> **Right** She brought a bottle (the baby's), a book, and an empty box to the clubhouse.

Brackets

Brackets ([ ]), like parentheses, enclose statements that are independent of the rest of the sentence. Unlike parentheses, brackets enclose parenthetical material inserted by someone other than the author of the sentence. Brackets are generally used by editors to supply missing material to make an author's meaning clearer or to draw attention to an author's error of fact. Brackets are used to enclose an explanatory comment in quoted material.

> She [Gertrude Stein] used to counsel Hemingway at great length.

Brackets are used to enclose a correction of a quoted statement of fact.

> Douglas Fairbanks, Junior [Senior] was married to Mary Pickford.

Brackets are used to enclose the word *sic,* which is Latin for "thus," to call attention to the fact that some remarkable or inaccurate expression, misspelling, or error is being quoted literally.

> In his speech he suggested that Li'l Abner was the most literate [sic] cartoon in America.

Brackets may be used to take the place of parentheses within parentheses.

> An interesting comment on the Witches Sabbath is contained in the author's previous book (see *Medieval Europe* [2d ed.], pp. 204–229).

Quotation Marks

A chief function of quotation marks (" ") is to identify words spoken in direct discourse. Another chief function is to identify words said or written by one person and quoted or reproduced by another.

Modern journalistic practice is to use quotation marks as an actual substitute for italics. Newspapers and magazines often use quotation marks, for example, to set off the titles of books and plays—a practice not countenanced in formal writing. Formal writing limits quotation marks to subdivisions: the titles of chapters of books, the titles of stories and articles appearing in books or magazines, and the titles of episodes from a radio or television series. Quotation marks are used at the beginning and end of every direct quotation except when the direct quotation is continued beyond the first paragraph. A direct quotation consists of the exact words of a speaker and the exact words used in reproducing a quoted passage.

> "Speak for yourself, John," suggested Priscilla.

> "Even when laws have been written down," said Aristotle, "they ought not always to remain unaltered."

Quotation marks are not used with an indirect quotation.

> Aristotle suggested that even when laws are written down,
> they ought not always to remain unaltered.

When a quotation consists of more than one paragraph, place the quotation marks at the beginning of each new paragraph and at the end of the last paragraph only.

A single quotation mark is used to enclose a quotation within a quotation. Double quotation marks are used to enclose an additional quotation within the second.

> He said, "Mary said that John told her the answer to ques-
> tion 3 was 'John Phillips Sousa, when he wrote "The Stars
> and Stripes Forever."'"

Quotation marks may be used to set off slang terms in formal writing, not generally, however, in informal writing, and almost never in dialogue.

> He has the job "sewed up."

In References to Some Titles and Headings

Quotation marks are used to set off quoted references to chapter headings of a book, titles of articles, stories, poems, etc., appearing in magazines and other periodicals. Quotation marks are also used on quoted titles of episodes from radio and television series. Such larger works, together with books and plays, are printed in italics if available and underlined if not.

> Chapter II: "My Early Years"

> Have you read "Backstairs at the White House" in last
> month's *Digest?*

> *Star Trek*'s "The Cage"

Quotation marks are used to set off the title of a book series.

> "Great Art of Western Civilization" series

Quotation marks are used to set off quoted references to the title of a lecture, sermon, or speech unless it has been established as virtually public domain.

Dr. Jones will speak on "The Meaning of Christmas."
the Sermon on the Mount
the Gettysburg Address

Quotation marks are used to set off quoted reference to the titles of songs and short musical works.

"Say It with Music"
"Slaughter on Tenth Avenue"

Quotation marks are used to set off quoted reference to the titles of paintings and sculpture.

"Nude Descending a Staircase" by Duchamp
"Bird in Flight" by Brancusi

In Relation to Other Punctuation Marks

The period and comma are always placed inside the quotation marks.

Henry Ford said, "History is the bunk."

Although Anne said, "That was a fine play," she did not mean it.

A colon or semicolon after a quotation always appears outside the quotation marks.

Mary said, "Of course not"; and she meant it.

All other marks of punctuation are placed inside the quotation marks if they refer specifically to the quotation. They are placed outside if they refer, not to the quotation, but to the sentence as a whole.

"Has it occurred to you that your parents have been waiting all day?" he asked.

Did you remember to say "thank you"?

She exclaimed, "My gosh, I forgot!"

Quotation marks may be omitted when a single word is used.

What can we do if they all say yes?

Complete Guide to Speech, Style and Grammar

Apostrophe

The apostrophe mark (') is essentially a spelling device used to indicate the possessive case of nouns. As a mark of punctuation, it is used to denote the omission of one or more letters or figures.

o'clock	the Spirit of '76
shouldn't	the class of '63
don't	

Do not use the apostrophe in words that are accepted shortened forms. Generally, such words would otherwise have an apostrophe preceding their first letter.

phone	cello	Frisco
plane	possum	copter

Points of Ellipsis

The points of ellipsis consist of three consecutive periods (. . .). They indicate an omission, a lapse of time, or a particularly long pause. When the points of ellipsis fall at the end of a sentence, a fourth—the terminal period—is added next to the final word.

The points of ellipsis indicate the deliberate omission of one or more words from a quoted passage.

> The playbill quoted Wolcott Gibbs as saying "I couldn't leave the theater . . ." when what he really said was "I couldn't leave the theater soon enough."

A full line of points of ellipsis indicates the omission of one or more paragraphs from a quoted passage. It may also indicate the omission of one or more lines of poetry.

The points of ellipsis indicate passage of time.

> Three . . . two . . . one . . . zero.

The points of ellipsis may be used to indicate that a statement is deliberately left unfinished.

> Even before the act was half over, I thought, "Well. . . ."

In advertising, the points of ellipsis may be used between short groups of words for emphasis; but the practice is not acceptable in formal writing.

Don't hesitate . . . send for your copy today.

Multiple points of ellipsis are sometimes used in textbooks, examinations, and commercial coupons to indicate words to be filled in.

Four kinds of citrus fruits are . . . , . . . , . . . , ...

Enclosed find $ . . . for . . . copies at . . . each.

Name . . . .

Address . . . .

City . . . . State . . . . . . Zip . . . .

In Relation to Other Punctuation Marks

The points of ellipsis are always placed inside quotation marks, whether they fall at the beginning or end of the sentence. Current journalistic practice is to omit points of ellipsis when they fall at the beginning or end of quoted material, but in formal writing, the omission should be indicated.

Jean said, ". . . and, furthermore, I wouldn't have gone even if. . . ."

Hyphen

The hyphen (-) both connects and separates words. As a connector, it joins compound words. As a word separator, it marks the division of an uncompleted word at the end of a line when there is no room for all of it, so that part of the word must be carried over to the next line. Such division of words is known as *syllabication* because such division should only occur between syllables. Do not use a hyphen to separate parts of a monosyllabic word such as church. Other, minor uses of the hyphen include the following:

The hyphen is used to break up telephone numbers, Social Security numbers, account numbers, etc.

555-1212
032-16-1379
Acct. No. 3060-6030-3663
Library of Congress Catalogue Card Number 64-20010

When the en dash is not available, the hyphen is used to indicate inclusion of continuous numbers in street addresses, dates, pages, etc.

> 14-18 Sunset Blvd.
> checks numbered 134-139
> pages 400-414

Asterisk and Superior Figure

The asterisk (*), once the universal mark of omission, is now little more than a reference mark. Even in this capacity it is rapidly being superseded by the superior figure. The asterisk may be used as a footnote reference when only a few such references are planned.

> Allergy diseases are often caused by psychogenic factors.*

> *William Nesbitt, *Psychosomatic Medicine* (Philadelphia: Saunders, 1959), pp. 26–49.

The superior figure is used when many footnote references are planned and when endnotes are to be used instead of footnotes.

> "It is proper for an escort to precede a lady through a revolving door."[4]

> [4]Sophie Hadida, *Manners for Millions* (New York: Perma-books, 1934), p. 38.

Slash (Virgule)

The slash/diagonal/virgule is used to indicate that any of the terms so joined may be used in the sentence without altering the meaning. Such use, however, is rarely acceptable in formal writing. When running together lines of quoted poetry, use the slash or solidus, as it is less commonly known, to indicate the correct ending of lines.

> A thing of beauty is a joy forever;/Its loveliness increases; it will never/Pass into nothingness; but still will keep/A bower quiet for us, and a sleep/Full of sweet dreams, and health, and quiet breathing./—*John Keats*

Use the slash, in addresses, to separate the letters *c* and *o* to form the symbol meaning *in care of*.

> *c/o* Richard Watts Smith

The slash is sometimes used in informal notes and memoranda in the contractions of dates.

>January 8, 1964   1/8/64

The slash is occasionally used in business reports and in technical writing to indicate the omission of such words as *per* and *as*. Note that when the slash is used in abbreviations, the period that ordinarily follows the abbreviation is omitted.

>barrels per day   barrels/day   bbls/day

Caret

The word *caret* is Latin and literally means "it is missing." The caret (‸) is used to indicate where letters or words are to be inserted in a written line, or between lines. Use the caret freely on rough drafts, sparingly—if at all—on the finished composition. A single page with more than one insertion should be rewritten or retyped. On the word processor, all corrections should be entered and the document reprinted.

The keyboards of standard typewriters do not carry the caret, and the current practice is to use the slash or diagonal as follows:

>find
>Look before, or you'll / yourself behind.—*Poor Richard's Almanac*

The caret itself has to be written in by hand. Write the caret as an inverted *v*. Since it is such a conspicuous mark, the caret should be made small and in light, not heavy lines.

>We visited the capitol in Boston, Massachusetts.

>upon
>All experience is an arch, to build.—*Henry Brooks Adams*

Ditto Marks

Ditto Marks (″) are used where considerable repetition occurs, to take the place of words and groups of words. Ditto itself is derived from the Latin *dicere* (to say) and means "the aforementioned thing." The marks are restricted chiefly to lists and tabulations.

The ditto is another mark that does not appear on standard typewriter keyboards. Quotation marks are the acceptable substitute.

Capitalization

First Words

Capitalize the first words of sentences, lines of poetry, and items in an outline.

> The book is on the shelf.
> The question is, Shall the bill pass?
> He asked, "And where are you going?"

> Sad soul, take comfort, nor forget
>   That sunrise never failed us yet.
>   —Celia Laighton Thaxter

> The rose upon my balcony
>   the morning air perfuming,
> Was leafless all the winter time
>   and pining for the spring.
>   —William Makepeace Thackeray

> I. Select the subject of your paper.
>   A. Decide on a general topic.
>   1. Survey available resources.
>   2. Note the various aspects of the subject.
>   B. Limit your topic to a narrow aspect.

Proper Names

Proper names are capitalized.

Rome	John Macadam	Italy
Brussels	Macadam family	Anglo-Saxon

Derivatives of Proper Names

Derivatives of proper names used with a proper meaning are capitalized.

Roman (of Rome)	Johannean	Italian

Derivatives of proper names used with acquired independent common meaning, or no longer identified with such names, are lower-cased. Consult a dictionary when in doubt.

roman typeface	macadam (crushed rock)	italicize
brussels sprouts	watt (electric unit)	anglicize
venetian blinds	plaster of paris	pasteurize

Common Nouns and Adjectives in Proper Names

A common noun or adjective forming an essential part of a proper name is capitalized; the common noun used alone as a substitute for the name of a place or thing is not capitalized.

Massachusetts Avenue; the avenue	Cape of Good Hope; the cape
Modoc National Forest; the national forest	Jersey City; *also* Washington City; *but* city of Washington;
Panama Canal; the canal	the city
Johnson House (hotel); Johnson house (residence)	Cook County; the county
Crow Reservation; the reservation	Lower California; *but* lower Mississippi

If a common noun or adjective forming an essential part of a name becomes separated from the rest of the name by an intervening common noun or adjective, the entire expression is no longer a proper noun and is therefore not capitalized.

> Union Station; union passenger station
> Eastern States; eastern farming states

A common noun used alone as a well-known short form of a specific proper name is capitalized.

> The Capitol (at Washington); *but* state capitol (building)
> the Channel (English Channel)

The plural form of a common noun capitalized as part of a proper name is also capitalized.

Seventh and I Streets	State and Treasury Departments
Lakes Erie and Ontario	Presidents Washington and Adams
Potomac and James Rivers	

Complete Guide to Speech, Style and Grammar

A common noun used with a date, number, or letter to denote time or sequence or to provide reference or record designations does not form a proper name and is therefore not capitalized.

apartment 2	page 2	section 3
appendix C	paragraph 4	spring 1926
article 1	part I	station 27
collection 6	phase 3	table 4
column 2	plate IV	title IV
exhibit D	region 3	treaty of 1919
figure 7	room A722	ward 2
mile 7.5	rule 8	

Definite Article in Proper Place Names

To achieve greater distinction or to adhere to the authorized form, the word *the* (or its equivalent in a foreign language) used as a part of an official name or title is capitalized. When such name or title is used adjectively, *the* is not capitalized.

> *British Consul* v. *The Mermaid* (title of legal case)

> The Dalles (Ore.); The Weirs (N.H.); *but* the Dalles region; the Weirs streets

> The Hague; *but* the Hague Court; the Second Hague Conference

> El Salvador; Las Cruces; L'Esterel

> The Netherlands; *but* the Congo, the Sudan

Particles in Names of Persons

In foreign names such particles as *d', da, de, della, den, du, van,* and *von* are capitalized unless preceded by a forename or title. Individual usage, if ascertainable, should be followed.

> Da Ponte; Cardinal da Ponte
> Den Uyl; Johannes den Uyl; Prime Minister den Uyl
> Du Pont; E. I. du Pont de Nemours & Co.
> Van Rensselaer; Stephen van Rensselaer
> Von Braun; Wernher von Braun
> *but* d'Orbigny; Alcide d'Orbigny; de la Madrid; Miguel de la Madrid

In anglicized names such particles are usually capitalized, even if preceded by a forename or title, but individual usage, if ascertainable, should be followed.

Justice Van Devanter; Reginald De Koven
Thomas De Quincey; William De Morgan
Henry van Dyke (his usage)
Samuel F. Du Pont (his usage); Irénée du Pont

If copy is not clear as to the form of such a name (for example, *La Forge* or *Laforge*) the two-word form should be used.

De Kalb County (Ala., Ga., Ill., Ind.); *but* DeKalb County (Tenn.)

Names of Organized Bodies

The full names of organizations and their shortened names are capitalized; other substitutes usually are not capitalized.

U.S. Congress, 98th Congress, the Congress; the Senate; the House; Committee of the Whole
Department of Agriculture, the department
Bureau of the Census, the Census Bureau, the bureau
Geological Survey, the survey
Department of Defense, Armed Forces; all-volunteer forces, armed services
U.S. Army, the Army, the Infantry, 81st Regiment, the Army Band, Army officer, Regular Army officer, Reserve officer; *but* army shoe, Grant's army, Robinson's brigade, the brigade, the corps, the regiment, infantryman
U.S. Navy, the Navy, the Marine Corps, Navy officer; *but* naval shipyard, naval officer, naval station
U.S. Air Force, the Air Force
U.S. Coast Guard, the Coast Guard
French Ministry of Foreign Affairs; the Ministry; French Army; British Navy
United Nations: the U.N. Council, the U.N. Assembly, the U.N. Secretariat
Montgomery County Board of Health *or* the Board of Health, Montgomery County; the board of health, the board

Complete Guide to Speech, Style and Grammar

The names of members and adherents of organized bodies are capitalized to distinguish them from the same words used merely in a descriptive sense.

a Representative (U.S. Congress)	an Odd Fellow
a Republican	a Communist
an Elk	a Boy Scout
a Shriner	a Knight (K.C., K.P., etc.)

Names of Countries and Administrative Divisions

The official designations of countries, national domains, and their principal administrative divisions are capitalized only if used as part of proper names, as proper names, or as proper adjectives.

United States
New York
Lorain County
Northwest Territories, territory of Guam
Dominion of Canada
Ontario Province
Crown Colony of Hong Kong
Grafton Township

The designations *commonwealth, confederation (federal), government, nation (national), powers, republic,* etc., are capitalized only if used as part of proper names, as proper names, or as proper adjectives.

British Commonwealth
Commonwealth of Virginia
Swiss Confederation
Cherokee Nation
Republic of South Africa

Names of Regions, Localities, and Geographic Features

A descriptive term used to denote a definite region, locality, or geographic feature is a proper name and is capitalized; also for temporary distinction a coined name of a region is capitalized.

the North Atlantic States; the Gulf States; the Central States; the Pacific Coast States; the Lake States; East

North Central States; Far Western States
the West; the Midwest; the Middle West; Far West; East
    Coast
the Eastern Shore (Chesapeake Bay)
the Badlands (S.D. and Neb.)
the Continental Divide (Rocky Mountains)
Deep South; Midsouth
the Occident; the Orient
the Far East
the East
Middle East, Middle Eastern, Mideast, Mideastern (Asia)
Near East (Balkans, etc.)
the Promised Land
the Continent (continental Europe)
the Western Hemisphere
the North Pole; the North and South Poles
the Temperate Zone; the Torrid Zone
the East Side, Lower East Side (sections of a city)
lower 48 (States); the Northeast corridor

A descriptive term used to denote mere direction or position is not
a proper name and is therefore not capitalized.

north; south; east; west	central Europe; south
east Pennsylvania;	Germany;
northern Virginia	southern France
west Florida; *but* West	North Korea,
Florida (1763–1819)	South Korea
north-central region	(political entities)

Names of Calendar Divisions

The names of days and months are capitalized, but seasons are not.

January; February; March; etc.
Monday; Tuesday; Wednesday; etc.
spring; summer; autumn (fall); winter

Names of Historic Events, etc.

The names of holidays, ecclesiastic feast and fast days, and historic events are capitalized.

Battle of Bunker Hill	Reformation
Christian Era; Middle	Renaissance
Ages; *but* 20th century	Veterans Day
Feast of the Passover;	War of 1812;
the Passover	World War II;
Fourth of July;	*but* war of 1914;
the Fourth	Korean war

Trade Names

Trade names, variety names, and names of market grades and brands are capitalized. Common nouns following such names are not capitalized.

Foamite	Choice lamb
(trade name)	(market grade)
Plexiglas	Yellow Stained cotton
(trade name)	(market grade)
Snow Crop	Red Radiance rose
(trade name)	(variety)

Scientific Names

The name of a phylum, class, order, family, or genus is capitalized; the name of a species is not capitalized, even though derived from a proper name. (Note italics on genus and species.)

Arthropoda (phylum), Crustacea (class), Hypoparia (order), Agnostidae (family), *Agnostus* (genus)

Agnostus canadensis; Aconitum wilsoni; Epigaea repens; Homo sapiens (genus and species)

In scientific description coined terms derived from proper names are not capitalized.

aviculoid   crustacean   menodontine

A plural formed by adding *s* to a Latin generic name is capitalized.

Rhynchonellas   Spirifers

In soil science the 24 soil classifications are capitalized.

Alpine Meadow   Bog   Brown

Written Communication

Capitalize the names of the celestial bodies Sun and Moon, as well as the planets Earth, Mercury, Venus, Mars, Jupiter, Saturn, Uranus, Neptune, and Pluto. Lowercase the word *moon* in such expressions as "the moons of Jupiter."

Fanciful Appellations

A fanciful appellation used with or for a proper name is capitalized.

Big Four	Hub (Boston)	Prohibition
Dust Bowl	Keystone State	Great Depression
Great Society	Space Age	Third World
Holocaust	New Frontier	

Personification

A vivid personification is capitalized.

> The Chair recognized the gentleman from New York.
> For Nature wields her scepter mercilessly.
>> All are architects of Fate,
>>> Working in these walls of Time.

Religious Terms

Words denoting the Deity, names for the Bible and other sacred writings, names of confessions of faith and of religious bodies and their adherents, and words specifically denoting Satan are all capitalized.

> Heavenly Father; the Almighty; Lord
> Mass, Communion
> Son of Man; Jesus' sonship; the Messiah; *but* a messiah, messianic, christology
> Bible, Holy Scriptures, Scriptures, Koran; *but* biblical, scriptural
> New Testament; Ten Commandments
> Apostles' Creed; Augsburg Confession; Thirty-nine Articles
> Episcopal Church; an Episcopalian; Catholicism; a Protestant
> Christian; *also* Christendom; Christianity; Christianize
> Black Friars; King's Daughters; Ursuline Sisters

Satan; His Satanic Majesty; Father of Lies; the Devil; *but* a devil

Titles of Persons

Civil, religious, military, and professional titles, as well as those of nobility, immediately preceding a name are capitalized.

President Reagan	Nurse Chapel	*but* baseball
King George	Professor Leverett	player Jones
Ambassador Gibson	Examiner Jones (law)	maintenance man
Lieutenant Fowler	the Rev. Ray Black	Smith
Chairman Smith	Vice-Presidential	Sue Fowler, a
Dr. Bellinger	candidate White	police lieutenant

Only the titles of the President of the United States, Vice President of the United States and Secretary General of the United Nations should be capitalized when they stand alone or follow a name in text.

the President	George Bush, President	Queen Elizabeth II
President Bush	of the United States	the queen

In formal lists of delegates and representatives of governments, all titles and descriptive designations immediately following the names should be capitalized if any one is capitalized.

Titles of Publications, Papers, Documents, Acts, Laws, etc.

In the full or short English titles of periodicals, series of publications, annual reports, historic documents, and works of art, the first word and all important words are capitalized.

Atlantic Charter
Balfour Declaration
Chicago's American
Reader's Digest
New York Times Magazine
Newsweek magazine
Bulletin 420, House Resolution 45, Presidential Proclamation No. 24, Executive Order No. 24, Royal Decree No. 24, Calendar No. 80, Senate bill 416, House bill 61

Declaration of Independence
Constitution (United States or with name of country)
Kellogg Pact, Treaty of Versailles, treaty of peace, the treaty
    (descriptive designations); treaty of 1919
United States v. *Four Hundred Twenty-two Casks of Wine*
    (law)
The Blue Boy, Excalibur, Whistler's Mother (paintings)

All principal words are capitalized in titles of addresses, articles, books, captions, chapter and part headings, editorials, essays, headings, headlines, motion pictures and plays (including television and radio programs), papers, short poems, reports, songs, subheadings, subjects, and themes.

In the short or popular titles of acts (federal, state, or foreign) the first word and all important words are capitalized.

Revenue Act; Walsh-Healey Act; Freedom of Information Act; Classification Act; *but* the act; Harrison narcotic law; Harrison narcotic bill; interstate commerce law; sunset law

The first word of a fragmentary quotation is not capitalized.

He objected "to the phraseology, not to the ideas."

The first word following a colon, an exclamation point, or a question mark is not capitalized if the matter following is merely a supplementary remark making the meaning clearer.

Revolutions are not made: they come.

Intelligence is not replaced by mechanism: even the televox must be guided by its master's voice.

The first word following *Whereas* in resolutions, contracts, etc., is not capitalized; the first word following an enacting or resolving clause is capitalized.

Whereas the Constitution provides . . . ; and
Whereas Congress has passed a law . . . ;
Whereas the Senate provided for the . . . : Now, therefore, be it *Resolved,* That . . . ; and be it further

Spelling and Vocabulary

Spelling is not the horrendous problem that many students think it is. By the time they have reached senior high school, and certainly by the time they finish college, most people have learned most of the words they will ever use, and they spell most of them correctly. The problem is caused by those few words which are misspelled over and over again. Another, but quite separate, problem is the rapid rate at which new words are added to our vocabulary, notably those emerging from enlarging technology and from areas of professional specialization.

For the average person afflicted with habits of bad spelling, corrective measures are not difficult to determine or apply. If you fall in this category, you probably spell most words quite correctly, and only fall down, with depressing recurrence, on certain kinds of words. To improve, you need not relearn how to spell, but only ferret out and concentrate on those specific areas where you have trouble. You will probably find that your problems are confined to certain special areas. Perhaps you are confused by words with *-able* or *-ible* endings, or by the question of whether to double final consonants or not. Once you have a list of such troublesome words—and the real job is running them down—you can take effective curative measures. Brief periods devoted to memorizing the correct spellings will quickly produce results, particularly if the memorizing period is just before you go to bed or at a time you have found to be your most effective learning period. Regularity is the critical factor as good intentions without practice have never improved anyone's spelling.

One way to locate your recurrent spelling problems is to use a computer if you have access to one with spell-checking capabilities. Run the program to locate misspelled words, making note each time of those words you misspelled. Review lists compiled during several spelling checks to identify your problem area or areas.

Never rely on the computer to correct or call your attention to all the errors. It will recognize correctly spelled words without noting that a word is the wrong word in the sentence. For example, *"And time you wish"* should read *"Any time you wish."* Sometimes the problem is with the computer operator, who, having chosen not to add a name or unusual word to the computer's memory, fails to adequately check the spelling each time the same word is presented. In addition, most computers are not able to check for errors in capitalization or punctuation.

Building a Vocabulary

We tend to avoid words we do not know how to spell, and in so doing we forget them by nonuse. With the spelling handicap reduced, we can explore the various ways of acquiring a large and useful vocabulary.

In school the teacher advises, "Look up in the dictionary every word you don't know and write it, with its definition, in a notebook. Then examine the meaning of its root, or roots, suffix or prefix. Pronounce the word to yourself, and finally use it in speaking and writing." This remains the surest technique, but it is slow and demands more conscientious application than most people are prepared to bring to it.

The best way to build a vocabulary is to broaden one's intellectual horizons. An interest and a delight in words and the ideas they convey will bring about attentive listening and wide and thorough reading. It can give impetus to frequent use of the dictionary, memorization of selected vocabulary lists, and the study of the origin and development of words (etymology).

We all possess three basic vocabularies—speaking, writing, and reading vocabularies. Of the three, the reading vocabulary contains by far the largest number of words. As we read extensively, all three vocabularies will expand, but at surprisingly different rates. The reading vocabulary increases the fastest. Only relatively few words will seep down into the speaking and writing vocabularies. We recognize any number of words when we see them in print, but they are neither on the tips of our tongues nor on the points of our pens for use when they are applicable.

The main problem is to make the newly learned words accessible when we are speaking—but more especially when we are writing. The words we have learned must become familiar friends; not only should they be recognizable when we see and hear them again, but they should be instantly available.

A much surer way than the list method for making a new word your very own is to use the word in a sentence of your own construction. Do not attempt to do this with every new word you encounter. Be selective. Take the words that appeal to and interest you—words that you think you may want to use again in the future. When a word does appeal to you, go to the dictionary for help in defining it precisely. When you have the definition (or, rather, definitions, for most words have a number of meanings), do not simply accept the dictionary example of how it is used. Compose your own illustrative sentence to fix the newfound word in your mind. Let the sentence express something that is essentially *you*—some interest of yours.

A few words of caution: Do not be too quick to flaunt the new words in public. Do not insist on forcing them into your very next composition or report. You may have a fair idea of the meaning of a word; you may have a good sentence in mind. At the same time, you may not be using the word in precisely its right context. A good idea is to wait a bit before exposing the word to public hearing or view. For example, if the word has to do with biology, try the sentence out on a friend who is at home in this field, and ask him or her whether you are using it correctly. This is the most creative way of fixing new words in your mind. It works; the new words will be ready for recall and use when the occasion arises.

Frequently Misspelled Words

Words below shown with an asterisk also have an alternate correct spelling. See any good dictionary for the alternate spelling.

A

abominable	accidental	accusing
abridgment	accidentally	accustom
absence	acclaim	achievement
abundance	accommodate	achieving
abundant	accompanied	acknowledgment*
academic	accompanies	acquaintance
academically	accompaniment	acquire
academy	accompanying	across
accelerating	accomplish	actuality
accentuation	accountant	actually
acceptable	accuracy	acutely
acceptance	accurate	adequately
accepting	accurately	adhering
accessible	accuser	admirable
accessory*	accuses	admissible*

admission
admittance
adolescence
adolescent
advancement
advantageous
adversaries
advertisement*
advertiser*
advertising*
advice
advise
aerial
aesthetic
affect
affiliate
afraid
against
ageless
aging
aggravate
aggressive
alibis
allegedly
allergies
alleviate
allotment
allotted
allowed
allows
all right*
all together
already
altar
alter
alternate
alternative
altogether
amateur

amenable
amiable
amicably
among
amount
amplified
amusing
analogies
analysis
analyze
anarchy
anecdote
angrily
annihilate
announcing
annually
anonymous
another
anticipated
antique
anxieties
apiece
apologetically
apologized
apology
apostrophe
appall*
apparatus
apparent
appearance
applies
applying
appraise
appreciate
appreciation
apprehend
approaches
appropriate
approval

approximate
apropos
aptly
aquarium
arbitrary
arduous
area
aren't
arguing
argument
arise
arising
armies
arouse
arousing
arrangement
arrears
arriving
artfully
article
artificial
ascent
ascetic
asinine
asphalt
asphyxiation
aspiration
assassin
assemblies
assertiveness
assiduous
assignment
assimilate
assistance
associating
assortment
assuming
asthma
astonish

astronaut
astute
asylum
atheist
athlete
athletic
atrocious
atrocity
attachment
attack
attempts
attendance
attendant
attended
attirement
attitude
attractive
attribute
audacious
audacity
audience
augment
auspicious
authenticity
author
authoritarian
authoritative
authority
authorization
authorize
autumn
available
awareness
awesome
awfully

B

babbling
balancing

ballerina
balminess
baloney*
bankruptcy
bare
barely
bargain
barrenness
barrier
barroom
bashfulness
basically
basis
battling
bawdiness
bazaar
bearable
beauteous
beautified
beautiful
beautifying
beauty
become
becoming
before
began
beggar
beginner
beginning
begrudging
beguile
behaving
behavior
belatedly
belief
believe
belittling
belligerence
beneath

benefactor
beneficent
beneficial
benefited*
benevolence
benign
biannual
bicycle
bicycling
bigamy
bigger
biggest
binoculars
biscuit
biting
bitten
blameless
bluing
blurred
blurry
boastfully
bohemian
boisterous
booby trap
boring
born
borne
bossiness
botanical
bottling
boulevard
bouncing
boundary
bounties
braggadocio
breath
breathe
breezier
brief

brilliance
brilliant
brimming
Britain
Britannica
brochure
bronchial
brutally
budget
bulging
bulletin
bumptious
buoy
buoyant
buried
bursar
bury
bushiness
business
busy

C

cabaret
cafeteria
caffeine
calamity
calculation
calendar
callous
callus
calves
camaraderie
canceled*
candescence
canniness
canning
canoeing
capably
capacity

capitalism
capital
capitol
capricious
captaincy
captivity
careen
career
careless
cargoes
caribou
caricature
caring
carnally
carousel*
carousing
carpentry
carpeted
carried
carrier
carries
carrying
cascade
casserole
casually
cataclysmal
cataloged*
catalyst
catastrophe
category
caught
causally
causing
caustic
cautious
ceaseless
celibacy
celluloid
cemetery

centrifugal
centuries
ceramics
cerebellum
certainly
certificate
certified
cessation
chafe
chagrined
chalice
challenge
chancing
changeable
changing
chaotic
characteristic
characterized
charging
charlatan
chastise
chatty
chauffeur
chauvinism
cheerier
chief
children
chilliness
chiseling*
chivalry
choice
choose
choosing
chose
choreography*
Christianity
chronically
chronicle
cigarette

cinema
cipher
circling
circuit
circulating
circumstantial
cite
citizen
claimant
clairvoyance*
clamorous
clarify
classification
claustrophobia
cleanly
cleanness
cleanse
clemency
climactic
climatic
closely
clothes
cloudiest
coarse
cocoa
coerce
cognizance*
cohort
coincidence
collaborate
collectively
collegiate
collision
colloquial
colossal
combining
comfortable
coming
commentary

commercial
commiserate
commission
commitment
committee
commodities
commotion
communicate
companies
comparative
comparing
compassion
compatible
compel
compelled
competition
competitive
competitor
complacence
complement
completely
compliment
comprehendible
comprehensible
compromising
concede
conceit
conceive
conceivable
concentrate
concern
concession
condemn
condescend
conditionally
conferred
confidentially
confuse
confusion

congenial
conniving
connotation
connote
conquer
conscience
conscientious
conscious
consciousness
consequence
consequently
conservatively
considerably
considerately
consistency
consistent
conspicuous
constancy
consul
contagious
contemporary
contemptible
contemptuous
continuing
continuously
contrarily
contritely
contrivance
controlled
controlling
controversial
controversy
convalesce
convenience
convenient
conveyance
convincingly
coolly
cooperate

cooperative
coordinate
coordination
corporal
correlate
correspondent
corroborate
corruption
council
counsel
counselor*
countenance
countries
courtesy
cowardice
cozier
crazily
create
credibility
crescendo
crescent
crevice
criminally
cringing
criticism
criticize
crucially
crudely
cruelly
cruelty
crystal
cultivating
cultural
cunning
curing
curiosity
curious
curriculum
cycle

cynicism

D

dahlia
dallying
dauntless
dazedly
debatable*
deceased
deceitfully
deceive
decent
decided
decision
dedicating
deductible
defenseless
deferred
deficiency
define
definitely
definition
degeneracy
deliberating
delicately
delightfully
delinquency
demoralize
denied
denominational
denouncement
department
dependent*
deplorable
depreciate
depressant
depression
derangement
derisive

descend
describe
description
desert
deservedly
desirability
desire
desolately
despair
desperate
desperation
despising
despondency
desert
dessert
destitution
destruction
detach
deteriorate
determining
detriment
deuce
devastating
development*
deviation
device
devise
dexterity
diabolic
diagonally
dialogue
dictionary
difference
different
difficult
dilapidated
dilemma
diligence
diminutive

diner
dinghy
dining
dinner
dinosaur
diphthong
dipsomania
direness
disagreeable
disappear
disappoint
disapproval
disarray
disastrous
disbelief
discernible*
disciple
discipline
disconsolately
discourteous
discreditable
discrimination
discussion
disease
disguise
disgusted
dishevelment
disillusioned
disintegrate
dismally
dismissal
disparaging
disparity
dispersal
dispirited
dispossess
disprove
disqualified
disreputable

dissatisfied
dissension
dissoluteness
dissolve
dissuading
distraught
distressingly
disuse
diversely
divide
divine
divisible
docilely
doesn't
dolorous
dominant
dormitories
double
doubtfulness
drastically
dropped
drudgery
dually
during
duteous
dye
dyed
dyeing
dying

E

eager
easel
easily
eccentric
echelon
ecstasy*
eczema
edified

educating
eerily
effect
efficiency
efficient
effortlessly
egotistical
eighth
eightieth
either
elaborate
elapse
elegy
element
elementary
eligible
eliminate
emaciate
embarrass
embarrassment
embellish
embitter
emergencies
emerging
eminence
emperor
emphasize
employment
emptiness
emulate
enabling
enamel
enamored
encourage
encyclopedia
endeavor
energies
engaging
enjoy

enormous
enough
enrapture
enroute
ensconce
ensuing
enterprise
entertain
entertainment
enthusiastic
enthusiastically
enticement
entirely
entrance
enumerate
enunciate
envelop
envelope
enviable
environment
epitome
equable
equally
equipment
equipped
erratic
erroneous
escapade
escape
especially
essence
et cetera*
ethical
etiquette
eulogy
evacuate
evaporate
eventful
everything

evidently
exaggerate
exceed
excellence
excellent
except
excessive
excising
excitable
excruciating
excusing
exercise
existence
existent
expelled
expense
experience
experiment
explanation
expulsion
extensively
extenuate
extremely

F

fabricator
facetious
facility
facing
facsimile
factually
fallacy
falsely
falsified
familiar
families
fanatical
fancied
fantasies

fantasy
farewell
fascinate
fashions
fastidious
fatally
fatigue
favorable
favorite
feasible
ferocity
fertility
fetish
fiancé
fiancée
fickleness
fictitious
fidelity
field
fierce
fifteenth
figuring
finally
financially
financier
finesse
fitfully
flamboyant
flammable
flatterer
flexible
flimsiness
flippancy
flourish
fluidity
fluorescent
forbearance
forbidding
foreigners

forfeit
forgotten
formally
formerly
formidable
fortieth
fortitude
fortunately
forty
forward
fourth
freer
frequency
friendliness
frightfully
frivolous
fulfill
fundamentally
furrier
further

G

gaiety
galvanizing
gamble
gambol
garish
garnishee
garrulous
gaseous
gauche
gauging
gazette
generally
generating
generic
geniality
genius
gentlest

gesticulating
ghastliest
gladden
glamorous
glamour*
glorified
gluttony
government
governor
gradually
grammar
grammatically
grandeur
grandiloquence
grandiose
graphically
gratefully
gratification
gratuitous
greasing
grieving
grimacing
group
grudgingly
gruesome
guaranteed
guidance
guiding
guileless
guillotine
gullible
gutturally
gypped

H

habitable
hackneyed
hallucination
halving

hamster
handicapped
handled
handsomely
happen
happened
happiness
harangue
harassment
harmfully
harmonizing
hear
height
heinous
hemorrhage
hereditary
heresy
heretofore
heroes
heroic
heroine
hesitancy
heterogeneity
heuristic
hibernate
hierarchy
hilarity
hindrance
hirable
hoarsely
holocaust
homage
homely
homilies
homogeneous
hopeful
hopeless
hoping
horizontally

horrendous
horrified
hospitality
hospitalization
huge
human
humane
humanistic
humidified
humiliating
humorist
humorous
hundred
hundredth
hunger
hungrily
hungry
hydrophobia
hygiene
hygienic
hyphenation
hypnotizing
hypocrisy
hypocrite
hypothesis
hysterical

I

icicle
ideally
ideologies
idiocy
idiomatic
idiosyncrasy
ignoramus
ignorance
ignorant
illegible
illiteracy

illuminate
illusory
imagery
imaginary
imagination
imagine
imbibing
imitating
immaculate
immanent
immediately
immense
immigrant
imminent
immobilized
impartially
impasse
impeccable
impeding
imperceptible
impersonally
impinging
implausible
imploring
impoliteness
importance
impresario
impressionistic
improbability
improvement
inadequacy
inappeasable
inattentively
incalculable
incessantly
incidentally
incomparable
incomprehensible
inconceivable

inconsequential
inconstancy
incorrigible
increase
indefinite
independence
independent
indeterminate
indexes*
indispensable
individually
industries
inebriation
inefficiency
inevitable
inexcusable
inferred
infinitely
inflame
inflammation
inflammatory
influence
influential
informally
infringement
infuriating
ingenious
ingenuity
ingenuous
ingratiate
ingredient
inimitable
initiative
injurious
innervate
inoculate
inquiries
inscrutable
inseparable

insincere
insouciance
installment
instinctive
insuperable
insusceptible
intangible
intellect
intelligence
intelligent
interceding
interchanging
interest
interference
interim
interlining
intermediary
intermittent
internally
interpretation
interrogator
interrupt
intervening
intimately
intricately
intrigue
intuition
involve
invulnerability
irascible
ironical
irrationality
irrefutable
irrelevant
irreproachable
irresistible
irreverence
irreversible
irritable

irritating
irruptive
issuing
itinerary
its
it's

J

jauntily
jealousy
jeopardy
jettison
jocundity
jolliness
jovially
judgment*
judicially
juiciness
juvenile

K

kaleidoscope
keenness
khaki
kidnaped*
kindlier
kinescope
knowledge

L

laboratory
laborer
laboriously
labyrinth
laconic
laid
lamentable
languorous
largess*
laryngitis

lascivious
lassitude
lately
later
laureate
lazier
lead, led (v).
lead (n.)
leafy
learnedly
legacy
legality
legibility
leisurely
lengthening
leniency
lenses
lesion
lethally
lethargy
letup
levying
libelous*
liberally
libidinous
license*
licentious
liege
likelihood
likely
likeness
limousine
linage
lineage
listener
literally
literary
literate
literature

litigation
liveliest
livelihood
liveliness
lives
lodging
loneliness
lonely
longitudinal
looniness
loose
lose
losing
loss
lugubrious
luminosity
lustfulness
luxury
lyricism

M

macabre*
macaroni
mademoiselle
magazine
magnanimity
magnificence
magnificent
maintenance
malefactor
malleable
manageability
management
maneuver
manful
manginess
maniacal
manifesto
manner

manning
manually
manufacturers
marauder
marionette
marriage
marveled
masquerade
massacre
massacring
material
maternally
mathematics
matriculating
matter
maturely
maturing
mausoleum
maybe
meant
measurement
mechanics
medallion
medical
medicine
medieval*
mediocrity
melancholia
melancholy
melee
meltable
memorability
memorizing
menacingly
mentally
merchandise
mere
merely
methods

microscopic
middling
mien
mightily
mileage
milieu
millennium
millionth
mimicker
mincingly
miniature
minority
minuscule
minutes
miraculous
mirrored
misalliance
misanthrope
miscalculation
miscellaneous
mischief
mischievous
misconstruing
mismanagement
misshapen
misspell
mistakable
moderately
moisturize
mollification
momentarily
monetary
monitor
monopolies
monosyllable
monotonous
monstrosity
moodily
moral

morale
morally
morbidity
morosely
mortally
mortifying
mosaic
mosquitoes
motif
mottoes*
mousiness
movable*
mucilage
multiplicity
multitudinous
mundanely
munificent
musically
musing
mutuality
mysterious

N

naïve*
naïveté*
namely
narcissus
narrative
natively
naturalistic
naturally
naughtily
nauseate
nearly
necessary
needlessly
nefarious
negativism
negligence

negligible
Negroes
neighbor
neither
neurotic
nevertheless
nicety
niggardly
nihilism
nimbly
nineteen
ninetieth
ninety
ninth
noble
noisily
nominally
noncombustible
normally
nostalgia
noticeable
noticing
notifying
notoriety
nourishment
nudity
nuisance
nullify
numerous
nuptial

O

obedience
objectively
obliging
obliquely
obliterate
obsequious
observance

obsess
obsolescent
obstacle
obstinately
obtuseness
occasion
occupancy
occupying
occur
occurred
occurrence
occurring
o'clock
oculist
oddly
odoriferous
odyssey
Oedipus
off
offense
offensively
officially
officiating
officious
omission
omit
omitted
oncoming
opaque
operate
opinion
opponent
opportunely
opportunity
oppose
opposite
oppression
optimism
optionally

oracular
orating
orderliness
ordinarily
ordinary
organization
original
ornamental
ornateness
orthodoxy
oscillate
ostentatious
ostracism
outrageous
outweigh
overdevelopment
overrun

P

pacified
pageant
paid
painstaking
palatable
palladium
palpitating
pamphlets
pancreas
panicky
pantomime
papier-mâché*
parable
parading
paradoxically
parallel
paralleled
paralyzed
parental
parentheses

parenthesis
parliament
paroxysm
parsimonious
partaking
partiality
participating
participial
participle
particular
passable
passed
passionately
passivity
past
pasteurize
pastime
pastoral
pastorale
pastries
pathetically
pathologist
patriarch
patriotically
patrolling
patronize
paunchy
pausing
peace
pealing
peculiar
pecuniary
pedagogue
padagogy
pedantic
pedestrian
peeve
peignoir
penetrate

penicillin
penitent
penniless
penology
penury
perambulating
perceive
perceptible
percipience
peremptorily
perfidious
performance
perfunctory
perilous
periodic
permanent
permit
perpetually
persevering
persistent
personal
personally
personnel
perspicacity
persuade
pertain
perversely
pessimism
pestilence
petticoat
petulancy
pharmaceutical
phase
phenomenon
philosophy
phlegmatic
phobia
phonetically
phosphoric

photogenic
phraseology
phrasing
physical
physician
physique
pianos
picayune
piccolo
picnicked*
pictorially
piece
piecing
piling
pinnacle
piquancy
pirouette
piteous
pitifulness
placating
placidity
plagiary
plaintively
planetarium
planned
platitude
plausible
playwright
pleasant
pleasurable
plebeian
plenteous
pliability
poetically
poignant
politely
political
politician
polyethylene

pontifical
popularize
populous
pornographic
porosity
portable
portfolios
positively
possession
possibility
possible
postponement
potentiality
practicability
practical
practically
practice
precautionary
precede
precipice
precipitous
precisely
precursor
predecessor
predictable
predominant
preexistence
preferred
prejudice
prematurely
prepare
preposterous
presence
preservable
prestige
presumedly
pretension
prettily
prevalent

primitive
principal
principle
prisoners
privilege
probably
procedure
proceed
producible
profession
professor
proficient
prognosticating
progressively
prominent
promissory
pronounce
pronunciation
pronouncing
propaganda
propagate
prophecy*
prophesy*
psychoanalysis
psychology
psychopathic
psychosomatic
ptomaine
puerile
pugnacity
punctilious
purposeless
pursue

Q

quadruplicate
quantity
quarreled*
queasiness

querulous
questionnaire
queue
quiescent
quintessence
quipster
quixotic
quotable
quotient

R

rabies
raconteur
radiating
raising
ramification
rapidity
rarely
rarity
rationalize
readily
readmitted
reality
realize
really
reasonable
rebel
receive
receiving
receptacle
recipient
recognize
recollect
recommend
reconciling
recoup
recoverable
recreation
rectangular

rectified
recurrence
redoubling
reexamining
referring
refrigerate
regard
registrant
regretful
regulating
rehearsal
reimbursement
reissuing
reiterate
rejuvenate
relative
relevant
reliability
relieve
religion
remarkable
remember
reminisce
remotely
renaissance
repeatedly
repelled
repentance
repetition
replacement
reprehensible
represent
reprieve
reproachfully
reproducible
repudiating
repulsion
reputable
requisite

rescind
resembling
resignedly
resources
respectful
response
responsible
restaurant
resurrect
resuscitate
retaliating
retrieve
revealed
revenging
reverence
revering
reversible
revising
revocable
revolutionize
rhapsodies
rhinoceros
rhyming
rhythm
ricochet
ridicule
ridiculous
rigidity
risqué
ritualistic
rogue
rollicking
romantically
roommate
rottenness
rudely

S

sabbatical

sacrifice
sadistically
safety
salacious
salutary
sanatorium*
sanitarium*
sapphire
sarsaparilla
satellite
satiety
satisfied
satisfy
saturating
sauerkraut
saxophone
scandalous
scared
scarred
scene
schedule
schemer
scintillating
scissors
sclerosis
scoundrelly
scrupulous
scurrilous
scurrying
secretive
secureness
sedentary
seducible*
seemingly
seize
self-abasement
self-conscious
selves
semantics

senatorial
sensitivity
sensuality
sentence
sentience*
sentimentality
separable
separate
separation
sergeant*
serviceable
seventieth
sexually
Shakespearean*
shamefacedly
shellacked*
shepherd
shining
short circuit
short-lived
shredded
shrinkage
shrubbery
shyly
sibilance
sickliness
sidesplitting
sideways
siege
significance
silhouette
similar
simile
sincerely
situating
skied
skyscraper
slatternly
sleepily

sleigh
sleight of hand
sliest
slipperiness
slurred
smoky*
smuggest
snobbery
snowcapped
sobriety
sociability
socialistic
sociology
solemnity
solicitude
solidity
solitaire
solvable
somnambulist
soothe
sophomore
soporific
sorcery
sorely
sorrier
source
souvenir
spaghetti
sparing
sparsely
speaking
spectrum
speech
speedometer
spirituality
spitefulness
sponsor
spontaneity
spurious

squalid
squarely
squaring
stabilization
starry
startling
stationary
stationery
statuary
stealthily
stealthy
stepped
stiffen
stimulating
stodginess
stoically
stolidity
straight
strangely
strategy
strength
stretch
stretchable
stubborn
studying
stultify
stupefaction
stylistic
suavely
subjectivity
sublimity
submissiveness
submitted
subsidiary
subsistence
substantial
substituting
subterranean
subtle

succeed
succession
sufficient
suggestible
suitable
summary
summed
superannuate
superficially
superintendent
superlatively
supersede*
superstitious
suppress
supremacy
surcease
surfeited
surreptitious
surrounding
surveillance
susceptible
suspense
suspicious
sustenance
swimming
syllabication
syllable
symbol
sympathetic
symphonic
synonymous
synthesis
systematically

T

tableau
tabooed*
taciturn
tactically

talkativeness
tangible
tassel
tasteless
taught
taut
tawdriness
technique
tedious
telepathy
temperament
temporarily
tenacious
tendency
tentatively
tenuous
terminology
terrifically
terrifying
testicle
thankfully
thatched
themselves
theories
theory
therapeutic
therefore
thesaurus
theses
thesis
thief
thieve
thinkable
thirstily
thirties
thorough
thought
thriving
through

ticklish
timidity
timing
tiresomely
titillate
to
tobaccos
together
tolerable
tomato
tomatoes
tomorrow
too
topography
tormentor
torpedoes
torrential
totally
tousled*
tragedy
tragically
tranquillity*
transcendental
transferred
translucence
transmitter
transparent
treachery
tremendous
trichinosis
tricycle
trivially
tropical
truculence
tubular
tumultuous
tuneful
turmeric*
turquoise

tying
typewriter
tyranny

U

ugliness
ukulele*
ultimately
umbrella
unaccountable
unanimous
unconcernedly
unctuous
undeniable
undoubtedly
unfortunately
uniformity
uniquely
unlikely
unnecessary
unoccupied
unprincipled
unruliness
unusually
urbanely
useful
useless
using
utterly

V

vacating
vacillate
vacuum
validity
valuable
vanquish
vaporous
variegated
varies

various
velocity
venerable
vengeance
ventriloquist
veracity
veritable
vernacular
versatility
vicarious
vicissitude
villain
vinegar
virtually
virulence
visibility
visitor
visualize
vitally
vivacity
vocalist
vociferous
voicing
voluminous
voluntarily
voluptuous
voracity
voucher
vulnerable

W

wakefully
wantonness
wariness
warrant
watery
weakened
wearisome
weather

weighty	willness	won't
weird	willfully*	workable
weren't	winery	worrying
wheeze	wintry	wrathfully
where	wireless	wrench
whether	wishful	wretchedness
whistling	witticism	writhe
whole	woeful	writhing
wholly	wonderfully	writing
whose	wondrous	wryly
wieldy	wont	

Misuse of the Word

Faulty Diction

Aggravate, *to increase,* does not mean *to irritate.*

Ain't, a contraction of *am not,* should be avoided.

Alternative, *one of two things,* may not correctly be applied to more than two.

Among should be applied to more than two persons or things; *between* to two.

Any (every, no, some) place should not be used adverbially for *anywhere (everywhere, nowhere, somewhere).*

And which should be used only when preceded by *which.*

As should not take the place of *that* or *whether,* and preferably not of *because.*

As . . . as are correlatives to be used with positive; with negative use *so . . . as.*

As good as and **better than** are idioms. If they are used in the same sentence, neither *as* nor *than* may be omitted. The following sentence is, therefore, incorrect: *Brazil is as good as, if not better, than Argentina in climate.* Correctly, it would read as follows: *Brazil is as good as, if not better than, Argentina in climate.*

As yet is redundant. Omit *as.*

Awful means *profoundly impressive.* It should not be used loosely to mean *very bad.*

Badly should not be used for *very much.*

Balance should not be used for *remainder* except in connection with a financial statement.

Complete Guide to Speech, Style and Grammar

Barefoot is preferred to *barefooted*.

Because should not be used instead of *that* if preceded by *the reason why . . . is*. Nor should it be used instead of *the fact that*.

Blame it on him should not be used for *place the blame for it on him* or *blame him for it*.

Bring up or **rear** is preferable to *raise* in speaking of children.

Bursted, bust and **busted** should not be used for *burst*.

But should not be used with a negative in expressions like *isn't but*.

But what is less desirable than *but that*.

Cannot but should not be confused with *can but*.

Certainly should not be overused.

Claim is a strong word. It should not be used for *maintain*.

Common, meaning *shared similarly,* should not be confused with *mutual,* meaning *reciprocal*. The expression *a friend in common* is naturally preferable to *a common friend*.

Comparison. Two standards should not be combined in one sentence. *Largest (tallest, best)* should be followed by a singular; if preceded by *one of,* by a plural. It is, therefore, incorrect to say, *The* Paul Revere *is New England's fastest, and one of America's best, planes.*

Considerable is overused. It may not be used as a noun.

Contact, used as a verb in business, should be avoided.

Convince must be followed by a phrase or clause beginning with *of* or *that,* but persuade is followed by an infinitive.

Could of is illiterate for *could have*.

Cute is used colloquially to mean *clever*. The word should be avoided.

Criticize, in literature, means *to judge*.

Date may not be used as a verb to mean *make an appointment,* or as a noun to mean *the one with whom an appointment has been made;* it is colloquial for *appointment*.

Different from is the preferred idiom.

Don't, a contraction of *do not,* may not be used in the third person singular.

Drownded is illiterate.

Each other should be used only with two persons or things; *one another* with more than two.

Either and **neither** should be used only with two persons or things.

The elements of the correlatives *either . . . or* and *neither . . . nor* may not be interchanged.

Enthuse, a colloquialism, may not be used in formal writing.

Etc. is an overused and almost meaningless abbreviation. It should not be used, especially with *and*.

Every bit is colloquial.

Except, which is not a conjunction, should not be used for *unless*.

Expect should not be used for *think* or *suppose*.

Extra means *beyond that which is usual,* not *extraordinarily*.

Feel bad (not *badly*) is correct but confusing; *feel ill* is preferable. *Feel good* refers to a moral, not a physical, state.

Fellow is colloquial when it means *person* or *fiancé*.

Fewer is used with number; *less* with degree or quantity.

Fine means *finished, refined,* or *perfect*. It should not be used loosely.

Fix (up) is colloquial for *to arrange* or *to repair*.

Former may be used with only two persons or things; likewise *latter*.

Get to go is provincial for *to be able to go*.

Goings on is a vulgar expression.

Good may not be used as an adverb to mean *well*.

Got is an abused word: it is colloquial for *possess,* as is *have got* for *must*.

Gotten, except in a few crystallized expressions, has now been supplanted by *got*.

Grand means *magnificent* or *impressive*. It should be used with care.

Guess, when used to mean *believe or suppose,* although possessing a long history in that sense, should be used infrequently if at all.

Had ought is illiterate.

Hardly should not be used with a negative in expressions like *couldn't hardly*.

Have got is both colloquial and redundant. Omit *got*.

Heap(s) is colloquial when meaning *much* or *many*.

Hear to it is vulgar.

Honorable should be preceded by *the* and followed by the first name, *Ms.,* or *Mr.*

If is less desirable than *whether* after *ask, doubt,* and similar words.

Complete Guide to Speech, Style and Grammar

Inside of for *within* is colloquial; in other cases, *of* should be omitted.

Kind and **sort** are singular: *this kind* or *these sorts*.

Kind of and **sort of** are colloquial when meaning *rather*. These phrases in sentences like *You plan to create a kind of game preserve?* should not be followed by the indefinite article, for the noun is used generically.

Lady is correctly applied to one of culture or social distinction; *woman* is, however, entirely correct and is preferred in compounds like *saleswoman*.

Learn means *to gain knowledge; teach* means *to give instruction*. These words must not be confused.

Let's, a contraction of *let us,* should not be followed by *we, don't,* or any other illogical words.

Like, never a conjunction, may not be followed by a clause, thus taking the place of *as* or *as if*.

Line is slang for *kind,* as in *line of work*.

Literally means *true to the fact*. It should not be used untruly for intensification.

Locate means *to place;* it is colloquial when it means *to take up residence*.

Lose out is redundant; omit *out*.

Lovely means *delicate* or *exquisite*. It should not be overused colloquially to mean *very pleasing*.

Mad means *insane* or *enraged,* not *angry*.

Mean, as an adjective, is a synonym for *humble* or *ignoble;* it is colloquial for *ill-tempered* or *selfish*.

Mighty means *powerful* or *wonderful*. *Mighty tired* is, therefore, incorrect.

Miss, Ms., Mr., Dr., Professor, and similar titles must be followed by the name.

More than means *in a greater number* or *amount;* it should not be confused with *over*, which indicates place.

Mrs. should never be followed by the title or profession of the husband of a married woman: *Mrs. Judge Watson, Mrs. Lawyer Williams, Mrs. Major Wilkinson, Mrs. Director of Public Works Warren*.

Nice means *discriminating, pleasing,* or *scrupulous*. A more precise word is preferred.

No good is colloquial when used to modify a noun.

Notorious means *discreditably known; noted* as an adjective means *celebrated*.

No use, except in informal speech, should be preceded by *of*.

Nowhere near is colloquial for *not nearly*.

Of is redundant when preceded by *outside (the house)* or *off*; it is illiterate when used for *have*, as in *could of*.

On account of is not a conjunction and may not be followed by a clause.

One repeated is stiff: *One may earn one's living if one tries*. But using the singular male pronoun generically is no longer acceptable. Rework the sentence. Often using the plural is best when not speaking of a specific person.

Only should be placed properly in a sentence. Note the difference in meaning: *Only America won the war. America only won the war. America won the only war. America won the war only*.

Out loud, a colloquialism, should be replaced by *aloud*.

Outside of, meaning *besides* or *except for*, is objectionable.

Over with is redundant; omit *with*.

Overly is unknown to good usage.

Party means one person on one of two sides of a cause or one entire group. It does not mean *any person*.

Per, coming from the Latin, should be used only with Latin like annum, capita, cent, not with *acre, dozen*, and similar words.

Percent should be used only after numbers; otherwise *percentage* should be used.

Perfectly is an abused and often unnecessary adjective, as in *perfectly darling* or *perfectly beautiful*

Piano, voice, violin, vocal, and **instrumental** should not be used alone when speaking of instruction: *lessons* or *instruction* should follow.

Plan on is redundant; omit *on*.

Proven, except in the law, is archaic; *proved* is the modern past participle.

Quite means *completely;* when used to mean *to a great extent*, it is colloquial. It should not be used as by the English, excessively and often absurdly, as a meaningless ejaculation.

Quite a (bit, few, little, number) is colloquial.

Complete Guide to Speech, Style and Grammar

Rarely ever and **seldom ever** should be avoided as confusions of *hardly ever* or *rarely (seldom) if ever*.

Real is an adjective or a noun; *really* is an adverb. *I was real happy* is, therefore, incorrect.

Render means *to give, to yield, to extract,* or *to inflict.* One may *render lard,* but one should not *render a vocal selection.*

Reverend should be preceded by *the* and followed by the first name or *Mr. or Ms.*

Right, meaning *precisely (right here and now)* or *to a large degree (right nice girl)* is colloquial. *Right smart* is dialectal.

Right along (away, off) is colloquial.

Run, when meaning *to conduct* or *to manage,* is colloquial.

Said, when meaning *previously mentioned,* should be avoided except in the law. *Aforesaid* is permissible.

Same, except in the law, should not be used as a pronoun.

Says is the third person singular of *say;* it may not be used with *I. Says* should not be used when the past tense, *said,* is required.

See where is a misuse of *see that.*

Show is colloquial for *drama* or *concert.*

Show up is colloquial for *appear.*

So should not be used as a mere intensive in an incomplete construction: *I am so angry. Because* is preferable to the colloquial *so* in joining coordinate clauses: *He came; so we held a reception* should be rephrased: *Because he came, we held a reception. So* should not be used instead of *so that.* The correlative *as . . . as* is used positively; *so . . . as* is used negatively.

Some is colloquial for *somewhat.*

Stop means *to arrest progress.* A person *stays* at a hotel.

Such should not be used as a mere intensive in an incomplete construction: *I have heard such good things about you* is incomplete. A clause of result following *such* should be introduced by *that,* not as: *There was such a noise that I could not hear.* A relative clause following *such* should be introduced by *as: He will follow such directions as the governor may give.*

Superlatives should not be used for intensification in an incomplete construction, as in *I had the best time.*

Sure is slang when it means *certainly. Surely* should be used.

Suspicion may never be used as a verb.

Take or **take it** should not be used to introduce an example.

The should not take the place of *a: Bittersweet candy is fifty cents the pound* is incorrect because a specific pound is not intended.

That is used colloquially to mean *to such a degree: I am not that tired that I must rest. So* should be used.

There as an expletive should be avoided.

This here *(these here, that there, those there)* is a vulgarism.

These should not be used loosely without any feeling of the demonstrative: *He is one of these modern cowboys who broadcast.*

Those should be followed by a relative clause: *He is one of those militarists* should be completed by adding a clause like *who would involve us in war;* or *He is a militarist.*

Through should not be used before a gerund: *I am through working* should be changed to *I have finished my work.*

Try and should be replaced by *try to.*

Ugly means *hideous* or *offensive morally.* It is used colloquially to mean *unpleasant.*

Up is redundant when preceded by a verb. It may not be used as a verb to mean *to increase,* as in *He upped the price ten dollars.*

Used to could is illiterate.

Verse, when used with the indefinite article, means *a line of poetry.* It should not be confused with *stanza,* a group of verses.

Very much is preferred to *very* when followed by a past participle not yet recognized as an adjective.

Way must be preceded by a preposition if used adverbially: *He works in that way.*

Who is this? when spoken over the telephone is both illogical and impolite.

Which as a relative pronoun should be used if the antecedent is inanimate or an animal; *who* if the antecedent is a person.

Without may not be used as a conjunction.

Words Commonly Confused

accept: to receive	**affect:** to influence
except: to exclude	**effect:** to execute
access: approach	**aisle:** passage
excess: superfluity	**isle:** island

Complete Guide to Speech, Style and Grammar

alley: lane
ally: associate

all ready: entirely prepared
already: at this time

all together: grouped
altogether: completely

allude: indirectly refer to
elude: evade

allusion: indirect reference
illusion: deceptive appearance

altar: table
alter: vary

anachorism: violation of
    geography
anachronism: violation of time

angel: spiritual being
angle: corner

assure: to reassure (requires
    indirect object)
insure: to obtain or supply
    insurance
ensure: to make certain

barbarous: almost savage
barbaric: showy, lacking
    restraint

berth: sleeping compartment
birth: beginning

beside: by the side of
besides: in addition to

boarder: one who takes meals
border: margin

Calvary: site of Christ's
    crucifixion
cavalry: horsemen

canvas: cloth
canvass: to solicit

capital: principal
capitol: statehouse

censor: examine
censure: condemn

centrifugal: proceeding from
    center
centripetal: proceeding toward
    center

chord: combination of tones
cord: small rope

cite: summon, quote
site: position

clothes: garments
cloths: fabrics

coarse: common, harsh
course: route

complement: addition, to add
compliment: to praise

congenial: kindred in taste
genial: cheerful

conscience: moral faculty
conscious: cognizant

consul: commercial
    representative
council: assembly
counsel: advice, attorney

contemptible: despicable
contemptuous: insolent

continual: in close succession
continuous: uninterrupted

corps: unit of organized
    establishment
corpse: dead body

credible: trustworthy
creditable: deserving of praise
credulous: inclined to believe

currant: raisin
current: motion

dairy: place for milk and its
    products
diary: daily record

desert: arid region; v.t., to
    leave, to abandon
dessert: course at end of meal

discreet: prudently silent
discrete: separate or distinct

disinterested: uninfluenced by
    personal advantage
uninterested: apathetic

dual: twofold
duel: combat

elegy: lament
eulogy: commendatory oration

emigrant: one who leaves
immigrant: one who enters

eminent: conspicuous or
    prominent
imminent: ready to take place

euphemism: softened statement
euphony: pleasant sound
euphuism: artificial statement

exceptional: uncommon
exceptionable: objectionable

factious: dissentient
factitious: artificial
fictitious: false
fractious: unruly

faint: swoon
feint: pretense

farther: applied to distance,
    space
further: applied to extent,
    degree

forceful: possessing power
forcible: violent

feat: deed
feet: terminals of legs

formally: conventionally
formerly: heretofore

forth: onward
fourth: ordinal of *four*

hanged: executed
hung: suspended

healthful: wholesome
healthy: well, vigorous

ingenious: clever
ingenuous: candid

indict: to charge
indite: to write

Complete Guide to Speech, Style and Grammar

inhumane: lacking in human kindness
inhuman (also *unhuman*): savage

later: afterward
latter: the second of two

lay (also past of *lie*): to place
lie: to recline

liable: responsible
libel: defame

liable: obliged
likely: probably

lightening: relieving
lightning: flashing of light

loose: unattached
lose: to miss

luxuriant: profuse
luxurious: costly, ornate

mantel: shelf
mantle: cloak

misogamist: marriage hater
misogynist: woman hater

noted: renowned
notorious: disgraceful

O: used in invocation
oh: exclamation

observance: act of custom
observation: attentive consideration

passed: crossed
past: bygone

persecute: to afflict
prosecute: to carry on

personal: private
personnel: group collectively employed

plain: level land
plane: level surface

practical: useful, skillful
practicable: feasible

precedence: priority
precedents: antecedents

principal: chief
principle: doctrine or belief

prodigy: wonder
progeny: offspring

propose: to offer
purpose: to resolve

prophecy: prediction
prophesy: to predict

quiet: undisturbed
quite: wholly

raise: to erect (in good use, not a noun)
rise: to ascend

recipe: formula
receipt: written acknowledgment

respectful: deferential
respective: individual

sciolist: pretender
scholiast: commentator

sensual: fleshly
sensuous: pertaining to the senses

sentiment: feeling
sentimentality: excessive feeling

stationary: fixed
stationery: paper

statue: image
stature: height
statute: law

specie: coin
species: variety

suit: apparel
suite: set

their: possessive of *they*
there: in that place

therefor: for that
therefore: hence

to: toward
too: also
two: the number

troop: a collection
troupe: company of actors

venal: mercenary
venial: excusable

waive: to relinquish
wave: to swing

weather: condition of atmosphere
whether: if

who's: contraction of *who is* or *who has*
whose: possessive of *who*

wont: accustomed, habitual
won't: will not

your: possessive of you
you're: contraction of *you are*

ACADEMIC ASSIGNMENTS

The Research Paper

A research, library, or term paper is a documented prose work resulting from an organized analysis of a subject. Such a paper presents the results of careful investigation of some chosen topic in an interesting, orderly, and clear manner. To produce an original paper a student searches with intelligence through varied sources, selecting facts that are essential to the stated subject. The student takes a relevant idea from one author, a telling quotation from another and, having gathered together a body of such information, will then, by using imagination and knowledge, create something new. It is written in the student's own words unless a direct quotation is attributed to its original author.

Steps to Follow

1. CHOOSE, THEN LIMIT YOUR SUBJECT. You will do best with a subject that interests you, that you can understand, that has sufficient information available about it, and that is limited in its scope so that it can be covered adequately in a paper of the assigned length.

2. SURVEY YOUR RESOURCES. Check the library's card catalog or computerized listing for books dealing with your proposed topic. Determining the key word to look under is a basic problem in library research. No matter what library tool you use—card catalog, *Reader's Guide*, indexes to books—you must ask yourself this question: "What key word will lead me to the information I seek?" The same key word does not always apply to every reference tool. For instance, the *Reader's Guide* may use "Impeachment," while the card catalog may use "Presidents—U.S.—Impeachment." Remember the topic may encompass many subject headings. For instance, the broad subject of "Crime and Criminals" would include these subject headings and many more: Crime prevention; Criminal law; Administration of justice; Juvenile delinquency; Murder; Organized crime; Police; Prisons; Punishment; Racketeering; Social ethics, etc.

Write down the call numbers for books you think you could use, then go to the shelves to find them. Look at books with similar call numbers. Scan tables of contents to see what the books are about. Check the indexes to see how many pages are devoted to the topic you are investigating. If only a few pages are cited, look at them and consider making any relevant notes so you do not have to cover this ground again. Books devoted to your subject or with longer passages devoted to it may be checked out and taken with you.

In the card catalog also note references to pamphlets and clippings in the library's Vertical File and to nonbook materials such as filmstrips and multimedia kits. Consider knowledgeable people in the field to interview. Systematically look at the various issues of the *Reader's Guide*, checking off each volume as you finish it. Many libraries now have computerized access to the *Reader's Guide*, their card catalog, and other indexes. Using the computer search equipment can save you hours of research time.

3. MAKE A PRELIMINARY STATEMENT OF OBJECTIVE (THESIS STATEMENT). At some point during your survey of resources, you may find there is not enough information on your topic. Change topics immediately. Expanding the topic to include a broader scope may suffice. Whether you broaden the topic or switch to another subject, repeat the previous steps.

If you have found too much information, you will need to narrow the topic. Surveying your resources helps you see the different facets of the topic. You might put together the following list of possible topics:

> The Supreme Court—No! Impossibly broad!
>
> Recent Supreme Court Decisions—No! Still impossible!
>
> Supreme Court Decisions Pertaining to School Desegregation—Still too big!
>
> The Effect of Supreme Court Decisions on Nashville Schools—OK
>
> Thesis Statement: Dramatic changes in the structure of Nashville's school system occurred in the 1950s, in 1971, and in 1983 as a result of Supreme Court decisions.

Making a preliminary thesis statement helps keep you on track. And honing your chosen objective to find all you need to know about it may prevent wasting your time on nonessential information.

4. MAKE A WORKING BIBLIOGRAPHY. Once you have settled on what you are looking for, it is time to begin gathering material in earnest. Set up a Working Bibliography on a sheet of notebook paper listing everything that might possibly be of use to you. Here you copy all magazine articles exactly as the information is given you in the *Reader's Guide*. Make notations of those unavailable in your school library so you can check the public library. Scratch off those that prove useless. Enter all books, periodicals, pamphlets, and non-print sources. The working bibliography is a good place to list all the varied subject headings you need to check to find available material. This is a valuable tool, so preserve it carefully until you have finished your paper.

5. SCAN YOUR MATERIAL. As you find information, glance through it quickly to see if it contains information you want. You must understand the material and then translate it into an intelligible presentation of your own. Ask yourself, "What is the author trying to say?" "What are the main points he is trying to make?" If the answers to these questions have a bearing on your thesis, prepare to go over the material more thoroughly.

6. MAKE A BIBLIOGRAPHY CARD—separate, complete, and accurate—for each source of information you consult. Do this before you take any notes from that source and keep your master bibliography cards separate from your note cards.

For a book, get your information from the title page and, if no date is listed there, the copyright date from the back of the title page. Book information includes author (full name, last name first), title, place of publication, publisher, and date.

For a magazine you must have the author of the article (if any); title of the article; name of magazine; its volume number and issue number, both in arabic numerals; its date; and the pages the article is found on, such as pp. 37–41.

7. TAKE GOOD NOTES. If they are prepared properly, writing the paper is relatively easy, and you should not have to consult your sources again. Follow this procedure:

(a) Write on 3 x 5 or 4 x 6 cards.
(b) Write on one side of the card only.
(c) Put only one idea from one source to a card.
(d) Include on each card four things—

(1) a slug, identification of the specific subject treated on the card;

(2) the source, shortened title or author's name so you know where you obtained the information;

(3) your notes;

(4) the exact page where the material appears.

Do not write down obvious, easily remembered, well known, or general information. As you read, stop to think what the main idea is. Close your eyes and say it in your own words. Write the notation on the note card. Check back to see that you have understood the idea correctly. Be careful to avoid misrepresentation by lifting material out of context or by twisting the interpretation to suit your own conclusion. Put the information in your own words, never using words in the book. However, if you think you would like to quote the material from your source, copy it exactly and enclose it in quotation marks.

On page 202 are samples of a bibliography card and a note card made from it.

8. During this reading process, MAKE A PRELIMINARY OUT-LINE, so you can see exactly what information you need on various points and how much you will need. (See "The Outline" on page 205.) Outline topics make good slugs for notecards.

9. CONTINUE READING AND NOTE TAKING. Remember the outline is like a skeleton which your paper will flesh out. The preliminary outline may show that your skeleton lacks an arm, or one arm is much smaller than the other. Your reading and note taking now can fill in what the outline revealed was needed.

10. WRITE YOUR THESIS STATEMENT IN ITS FINAL FORM. Remember the thesis tells exactly what your paper is about, what it is to cover; and the outline shows how you accomplish the objective of the thesis. In the preliminary stages you may need to adjust both the original thesis and the original outline. Now is the time to get your thesis in precise final form. Play with words, work to express your thesis so it will convey exactly the ideas you want it to in an interesting manner.

11. REVISE OUTLINE into its final form.

12. WRITE AN INTERESTING INTRODUCTION that (1) attracts the reader's attention; (2) states what the paper is about; and

Bibliography Card

Muir, Frank
<u>Christmas</u> <u>Customs</u> <u>& Traditions</u>
New York, Taplinger Publishing Company
1975

Note Card

Preparations - Cookery   Muir, p. 22
Stir Up Sunday - Sun. before Advent
last time to make Christmas
pudding to be ready in time.
Gets name from church. Collect
for that day which begins "Stir
up we beseech thee, O Lord, the
wills of thy faithful people ...."

(3) previews the main topics. Incorporate your thesis in the introduction.

13. SORT YOUR NOTE CARDS to conform to your outline.

14. WRITE THE PAPER in your words using formal, objective style.

Avoid the use of "you" and "I." The research paper is not an informal essay, although you need to make it interesting and may use imagination in making deductions and drawing conclusions.

Even though you are writing in your own words, you have used information supplied by others. You will also want to use direct quotations (but only sparingly, to emphasize an important point or as proof of your conclusions). These must be acknowledged. Use a footnote or an endnote to give credit for a direct quotation, to give credit for an original or unusually interesting opinion or interpretation which you have put in your own words, and to give credit for all statistics, figures, definitions, illustrations.

Have your endnote page beside you and make your endnotes as you write. Be specific but do not worry about exact form at this time, as you can go back and set your endnotes in precise form later. Just be sure your numbers coincide. Endnote [3] in your paper must refer to [3] on your endnote page.

The question always arises, "Since I knew nothing about this subject before researching it, do I have to footnote every piece of information used?" Obviously that would be impractical. If the ideas seem to be general knowledge of authorities in the field, do not footnote unless you are quoting exactly. (See "Footnotes and Endnotes" for exact details.)

Direct quotations are handled in two different ways. For a short quotation (one that would be three typed lines or less) enclose it in quotation marks and work it in smoothly as part of your own sentence.

A long quotation (one that is four lines or more of type) should be handled as this one from *Mansfield Park* by Jane Austen:

> She was an altered creature, quieted, stupefied, indifferent to everything that passed. The being left with her sister and nephew, and all the house under her care, had been an advantage entirely thrown away; she had been unable to direct or dictate, or even fancy herself useful.[2]

Complete Guide to Speech, Style and Grammar

15. WRITE A GOOD CONCLUSION that rounds out your paper, sums it up, and gives a feeling of completeness.

16. REVISE YOUR PAPER.

17. PROOFREAD your final draft. Double-check footnotes or endnotes for accuracy and for form.

18. MAKE YOUR BIBLIOGRAPHY. Arrange your bibliography cards according to the author's last name. If there is no author, alphabetize by the first word of the title (skipping *A, An,* and *The*. If the reference is published by an organization with no author, use the organization as author. Make your bibliography according to the prescribed forms. Often teachers want you to include in your bibliography only the sources you actually used in writing the paper, not a complete listing of sources you may have consulted. (See "Bibliography.")

19. MAKE THE TITLE PAGE. (See form, page 219.)

20. ASSEMBLE THE PAPER. The usual order is: (1) title page; (2) the paper itself; (3) endnotes; (4) bibliography.

Abbreviations

Abbreviations commonly found in doing research are the following:

ca., c.	about (circa)
ch., chs.	chapter, chapters
cf.	compare, confer
et al.	and others (*et alii* or *alibi*)
ed.	edited, edition, editor
e.g.	for example (*exempli gratia*)
f., ff.	and the following page, pages
illus.	illustrated
ibid.	in the same place (*ibidem*) (obsolete)
id.	the same (*idem*)
l., ll.	line, lines
i.e.	that is (*id est*)
loc. cit.	in the place cited (*loco citato*) (obsolete)
lit.	literally
MS, MSS	manuscript, manuscripts
N.B.	note well (*nota bene*)

n.d.	no date given
no., nos.	number, numbers
op. cit.	in the work cited *(opere citato)* (obsolete)
p., pp.	page, pages
trans.	translator, translation
viz.	namely *(videlicet)*
vol., vols.	volume, volumes

The Outline

An outline is to a paper what a road map is to a journey. The thesis statement states your destination, and the outline shows you how to get there. Thesis: I am going to Yazoo City, Mississippi, from Nashville, Tennessee. Outline: Take I-40 to Memphis; then I-55 toward Jackson; at Exit 181 go west on Highway 16. . . . The purpose of outlining is to prevent wandering off the subject; to give a quick overview of the essay; to insure proportionate space to each part; to aid in organizing and giving order to the essay; and to enable you to spot missing or irrelevant matter. Some ways to organize are by time, by space, by likenesses and differences, in order of importance, and by cause and effect.

An outline includes only main ideas and important points. Fill in the details when you write the paper.

Under any topic there must always be more than one subtopic. Subtopics are divisions of the topic above them, and you cannot divide anything into fewer than two parts. If you find yourself wanting to use a single subtopic, rewrite the topic above it so that this "sub idea" is included in the main topic.

    Wrong C. Hostesses
                    1. Those who nag

    Right   C. Nagging Hostesses

A subtopic must belong under the main topic beneath which it is placed. It must be closely related to the topic above it.

    Wrong A. Dull games
                    1. Bingo
                    2. Not enough refreshments

Complete Guide to Speech, Style and Grammar

Terms such as *Introduction, Body,* and *Conclusion* should not be included in the outline. Of course, you should have them as definite parts of your paper (though never so designated), but these are not topics that you intend to discuss.

There are two kinds of outlines: the topic and the sentence. The topic is composed of words or phrases throughout all divisions. It is used for conciseness and brevity, and no end punctuation is needed. A sentence outline uses sentences throughout its divisions, so end punctuation is needed. It is fuller, clearer, and more exact than a topic outline.

How to Prepare an Outline

To outline a chapter in a book is easy because the information was outlined before it was written. The difficult part of outlining is taking a large body of information and organizing it into a logical, coherent form. Here are some tips to help you do this for your research paper. Notice it is in sentence outline form.

I. Select the subject of your paper.
   A. Decide on a general topic.
      1. Survey available resources.
      2. Note the various aspects of the subject.
   B. Limit your topic to a narrow aspect that can be adequately covered in a paper of your designated length.
   C. Continue research and note taking.
   D. Write a thesis statement that exactly pinpoints your objective.

II. Make a rough draft of your outline.
   A. Jot down at random all the points about your paper that come to mind.
   B. Group similar ones together.
   C. Decide what pattern would be best to follow.
      1. It could be chronological.
      2. It could be spatial (geographical).
      3. It could be a study of contrasts or comparisons.
      4. It could be cause-and-effect.
      5. It could be a study of influences.
   D. Write a simple topic outline.

    1. Choose two to four most important points for the major divisions.
    2. Place remaining ideas as subtopics under them.
  E. Assess the result.
    1. Consider if you are fulfilling your thesis statement.
    2. Consider if you have covered the subject adequately.
    3. Check to see that each subtopic falls logically under its larger topic.
    4. Eliminate any material that does not fit.
      (a) This means irrelevant matter.
      (b) This means unnecessary matter (too detailed) for an outline.
    5. Determine if you need to look for additional information.
      (a) Should this information be for an added topic?
      (b) Should it be to expand on an existing topic?

III. Write the outline in final sentence form.
  A. Word the main topics to make them concise, clear, and parallel.*
  B. Fill in the subtopics by the same criteria.
  C. See that the outline is in correct outline form.

    Wrong How to Do the Laundry
              I. Sorting by colors
             II. To start the machine
           III. Proper water temperature
           IV. How to handle delicate fabrics

    Right How to Do the Laundry
              I. Sorting by colors
             II. Starting the machine
           III. Choosing proper water temperature
           IV. Handling delicate fabrics

---

*Parallelism means using similar wording for various divisions of equal rank.

Complete Guide to Speech, Style and Grammar

Picture of an Outline

Title of Paper

Thesis Statement: ....

I. Major division
   A. Subdivision
      1. Sub-subdivision
         a.
            (1)
                  (a)
                  (b)
            (2)
         b.
      2.
   B.
II.

Footnotes and Endnotes

The distinction has been made that footnotes are properly used in dissertations and endnotes are used in research papers. The difference is that footnotes appear at the bottom of the page containing the cited material, while endnotes are arranged on one or two pages at the end of the paper. It is much easier to do endnotes because in footnotes the writing has to be spaced very carefully to allow sufficient room at the bottom of the page. Teachers vary in which they require. People generally speak of footnotes to mean both those at the foot of the page and those at the end of the paper.

These instructions are for endnotes.

- Number them consecutively throughout the paper.
- In the body of your paper put a number slightly above the line *at the end* of the material to be acknowledged. No period follows an endnote number.
- On your endnote page put the same number as its corresponding number in the paper (again above the line and without a period). Indent the first line of each endnote and start the second line even with the left margin.
- The author's *given name* should be written *first*.

When the same source is repeated, it is not necessary to give the full information about that source a second time. Use a shortened form to identify the reference. Formerly Latin terms such as *ibid.*, *op. cit.*, and *loc. cit.* were used. These are now considered obsolete. When the same source is used a second or subsequent time, simply write the endnote number, then the author's last name, and then the page number on which the material can be found.

If you have made your bibliography cards properly, you will have all the information you will need for your endnotes, except for the exact page on which that bit of material was found, which will be on your note card. Never endnote for several pages in a source; the only time you would indicate two pages is when the sentence on the source page runs over onto a second page.

Examples of Endnotes

BOOKS

*One author
   ¹Robert W. Kirk, *First Aid for Pets* (New York: E. P. Dutton, 1978), p. 40.

*Two authors
   ²Mary Bray Wheeler and Genon Hickerson Neblett, *Hidden Glory: The Life and Times of Hampton Plantation, Legend of the South Santee* (Nashville: Rutledge Hill Press, 1983), pp. 21–22.

*Three authors
   ³Clarence L. Barnhart, Sol Steinmetz, and Robert K. Barnhart, *The Barnhart Dictionary of New English Since 1963* (New York: Harper & Row, 1973), p. 53.

*Four or more authors
With four or more authors, use the name of the first author followed by the expression *and others* or *et al*. The phrase *et al.* is italicized because it is in a foreign language.
   ⁴Geffredo Silvestri and others, *Quest for Space,* trans. Arnoldo Mondadori (New York: Cresent Books, 1987), p. 62.

*No author
   ⁵*Webster's Geographical Dictionary* (Springfield, Mass.: G. & C. Merriam Co., 1981), p. 535.

Complete Guide to Speech, Style and Grammar

*Organization as author
[6]U.S. Department of Commerce, Bureau of the Census, *Statistical Abstract of the United States 1982–83* (Washington, D.C., Government Printing Office, 1982), p. 1065.

*Editor as author
[7]Lois Decker O'Neill, ed., *The Women's Book of World Records and Achievements* (New York: Doubleday, 1979), p. 84.

*Two editors as authors
[8]Eugene Rabinowitch and Richard S. Lewis, eds., *Man on the Moon* (New York: Basic Books, Inc., Publishers, 1969), p. 103.

*Second and subsequent uses of a book
[9]Kirk, p. 41.

*Author and translator
[10]Homer, *The Iliad,* trans. Richmond Lattimore (Chicago: University of Chicago Press, 1951), pp. 326–7.

*Subsequent edition
[11]William Strunk, Jr., and E. B. White, *The Elements of Style,* 3rd ed. (New York: Macmillan Publishing Co., Inc., 1979), p. 17.

*Part of a multivolume series
[12]Phil Hardy, ed., *Science Fiction,* Vol. 2 of *The Film Encyclopedia* (New York: William Morrow and Company, Inc., 1984), p. 181.

PARTS WITHIN BOOKS

*An encyclopedia article
[13]"Jet Propulsion," *World Book Encyclopedia* (1979 ed.), vol. 11, p. 386.

*Short work from a collection
Poems, short stories, essays, and chapters are considered short works. The title is enclosed in quotation marks.

*A short work from a collection by one author
[14]Walt Whitman, "O Captain! My Captain!" *Complete Poetry and Selected Prose,* ed. James E. Miller, Jr. (Boston: Houghton Mifflin Company, 1959), p. 239.

*A short work from a collection by many authors
[15]Emily Dickinson, "465," in *The Norton Anthology of Poetry*, 3rd ed.—shorter, eds. Alexander W. Allison and others (New York: W. W. Norton & Company, 1983), p. 476.

*Long work from a collection
Novels, plays, and epic poems are considered long works. The title is underlined or italicized.

*A long work from a collection by several authors
[16]Tennessee Williams, *The Glass Menagerie*, in *Concise Anthology of American Literature*, 2nd ed., eds. George McMichael and others (New York: Macmillan Publishing Company, 1985), p. 1854.

*Named author of preface, etc.
[17]Richard E. Leakey, Introduction, *The Illustrated Origin of Species*, by Charles Darwin (New York: Hill and Wang, 1979), p. 21.

*Quoted material
[18]James Boswell, *The Life of Samuel Johnson*, quoted by Robert Byrne in *Cat Scan* (New York: Atheneum, 1983), p. 7.

PERIODICALS

*Magazine or journal article with an author
Note the volume number before the date.
[19]Michael M. Lombardo, "The Intolerable Boss," *Psychology Today*, 18 (January 1984), p. 45.

*Second and subsequent uses of the same article
[20]Lombardo, p. 46.

*Magazine article with no author
[21]"The Muffin-Mix Scare," *Time*, 123 (Feb. 13, 1984), p. 20.

*Second and subsequent uses of the same article
[22]*Time*, p. 22.

If you are quoting from several *different* issues of *Time*, include the date in parentheses: *Time* (Feb. 13, 1984), p. 22. This will indicate which issue you refer to.

*Newspaper article with a byline
[23]Patricia McCormack, "Special Diet Urged to Thwart Cancer," *Nashville Tennessean* (Feb. 11, 1984), Sec. D, p. 2.

*Newspaper article with no byline
[24]"Moslems Take West Beirut," *Nashville Banner* (Feb. 8, 1984), Sec. A, p. 1.

OTHER SOURCES

*Interview
[14]Richard Fulton, Mayor of Nashville, interviewed by Mary Smith (Metropolitan Courthouse, Nashville, Tenn.), 10 A.M., Jan. 15, 1984.

*Personal letter
[15]Personal letter from Lamar Alexander, Governor of Tennessee, to Jason Jones, Feb. 16, 1984.

*Thesis or dissertation
[21]James R. Purdue, "Adaptations of the Snowy Plover, *Charadrius Alexandrinus,* to an Inland Salt Plain" (unpublished Ph.D. dissertation, Graduate College, University of Oklahoma, 1974), p. 12.

TWO OR MORE WORKS BY SAME AUTHOR

If there are two or more works by the same author, or two or more authors with the same name, a shortened title of the cited work is used after the author's last name. Let us assume you are quoting from two books by Louise Davis, *Nashville Tales* and *Frontier Tales.*

*First citation
[17]Louise Littleton Davis, *Nashville Tales* (Gretna, La.: Pelican Publishing Co., 1981), p. 35.

*Second citation
[18]Davis, *Nashville,* p. 4.

Bibliography

References not cited in the endnotes are generally not included in the bibliography.

The forms and content of bibliographic entries are similar to those of endnotes; however, there are some important differences. In endnotes the arrangement is strictly numerical in the order the material is cited from the work; the author's first name comes first; the first line is indented and the second line is flush with the left-hand margin. In a bibliography, the arrangement is alphabetical by the author's last name, and the first line is flush with the left-hand margin but subsequent lines are indented. Current style does not transpose the first and last names of subsequent authors.

You will find slight variations, especially in punctuation, among the many handbooks available showing forms for footnotes and bibliographies. The important thing for you to do is to choose one source as your model and then be scrupulous in following it exactly so your paper is consistent throughout.

Examples of Bibliographic Entries

BOOKS

*One author
Kirk, Robert W. *First Aid for Pets*. New York: E. P. Dutton, 1978.

*Two authors
Wheeler, Mary Bray, and Genon Hickerson Neblett. *Hidden Glory: The Life and Times of Hampton Plantation, Legend of the South Santee*. Nashville: Rutledge Hill Press, 1983.

*Three authors
Barnhart, Clarence L., Sol Steinmetz, and Robert K. Barnhart. *The Barnhart Dictionary of New English Since 1963*. New York: Harper & Row, 1973.

*Four or more authors
With four or more authors, use the name of the first author followed by the expression *and others* or *et al*. The phrase *et al*. is italicized because it is in a foreign language.

Silvestri, Geffredo, and others. *Quest for Space*. Trans. Arnoldo Mondadori. New York: Cresent Books, 1987.

*No author
Webster's Geographical Dictionary. Springfield, Mass.: G. & C. Merriam Co., 1981.

Complete Guide to Speech, Style and Grammar

*Organization as author
U.S. Department of Commerce, Bureau of the Census. *Statistical Abstract of the United States 1982–83*. Washington, D.C.: Government Printing Office, 1982.

*Editor as author
O'Neill, Lois Decker, ed. *The Women's Book of World Records and Achievements*. New York: Doubleday, 1979.

*Two editors as authors
Rabinowitch, Euguene, and Richard S. Lewis, eds. *Man on the Moon*. New York: Basic Books, Inc., Publishers, 1969.

*Author and translator
Homer. *The Iliad*. Trans. Richmond Lattimore. Chicago: University of Chicago Press, 1951.

*Subsequent edition
Strunk, William, Jr., and E. B. White. *The Elements of Style*. 3rd ed. New York: Macmillan Publishing Co., Inc., 1979.

*Part of a multivolume series
Hardy, Phil, ed. *Science Fiction*. Vol. 2 of *The Film Encyclopedia*. New York: William Morrow and Company, Inc., 1984.

PARTS WITHIN BOOKS

*An encyclopedia article
"Jet Propulsion." *World Book Encyclopedia*, 1979 ed., vol. 11, p. 386.

*Short work from a collection
Poems, short stories, essays, and chapters are considered short works. The title is enclosed in quotation marks.

*A short work from a collection by one author
Whitman, Walt. "O Captain! My Captain!" *Complete Poetry and Selected Prose*. Ed. James E. Miller, Jr. Boston: Houghton Mifflin Company, 1959.

*A short work from a collection by many authors
Dickinson, Emily. "465." In *The Norton Anthology of Poetry*. 3rd ed.—shorter. Eds. Alexander W. Allison and others. New York: W. W. Norton & Company, 1983.

*Long work from a collection
Novels, plays, and epic poems are considered long works. The title
is underlined or italicized.

*A long work in a collection by several authors
Williams, Tennessee. *The Glass Menagerie*. In *Concise Anthology
of American Literature*. 2nd ed. Eds. George McMichael and
others. New York: Macmillan Publishing Company, 1985.

*Named author of preface, etc.
Leakey, Richard E. Introduction. *The Illustrated Origin of Species*.
By Charles Darwin. New York: Hill and Wang, 1979.

*Quoted material
Byrne, Robert. *Cat Scan*. New York: Atheneum, 1983.

PERIODICALS

*Magazine or journal article with an author
Note volume number before the date.
Lombardo, Michael M. "The Intolerable Boss." *Psychology Today*,
18 (January 1984), pp. 45–48.

*Magazine article with no author
"Muffin-Mix Scare." *Time*, 123 (Feb. 13, 1984), pp. 20–21.

*Newspaper article with a byline
McCormack, Patricia. "Special Diet Urged to Thwart Cancer."
Nashville Tennessean (Feb. 8, 1984), Sec. D, p. 2.

*Newspaper article with no byline
"Moslems Take West Beirut." *Nashville Banner* (Feb. 8, 1984),
Sec. A, p. 1.

OTHER SOURCES

*Interview
Fulton, Richard, Mayor of Nashville, interviewed by Mary Smith,
Metropolitan Courthouse, Nashville, Tenn., 10 A.M., Jan. 15,
1984.

*Personal letter
Alexander, Lamar, Governor of Tennessee, to Jason Jones, Feb. 16,
1984.

Complete Guide to Speech, Style and Grammar

*Thesis or dissertation

Purdue, James R. "Adaptations of the Snowy Plover, *Charadrius Alexandrinus,* to an Inland Salt Plain." Unpublished Ph.D. dissertation, Graduate College, University of Oklahoma, 1974.

TWO OR MORE WORKS BY SAME AUTHOR

If there are two or more works by the same author, then the name is replaced in the subsequent entries by an underline five spaces long:

Davis, Louise Littleton. *Frontier Tales*. Gretna, La.: Pelican Publishing Co., 1980.

_____. *Nashville Tales*. Gretna, La.: Pelican Publishing Co., 1981.

Alternate Forms of Documentation

A radically different form of documentation is commonly used in scientific papers. In this style, the references are inserted into the text in parentheses, instead of being at the bottom of the page or at the end. Generally, these only include the author's last name, the year of publication, and the page number where the information was found.

The following excerpt demonstrates the form, placement, and usage of this type of reference. In the first paragraph, the quotation is being documented; in the second, the information.

> The imaginative expectations of lunar voyages became increasingly realistic as scientists made new discoveries and developed new technologies to make the dream a reality. The earliest stories, starting in ancient Greece, tended to use demons or animals to carry people to the moon, but "as man's astronomical knowledge increased, . . . the fictional space voyages devised by his restless imagination became correspondingly more sophisticated" (von Braun, Ordway, and Dooling, 1985, pp. 8–9). In other words, writers incorporated new scientific discoveries into their stories, thereby creating more realistic adventures, which would seem plausible to their readers. These stories also raised expectations that, one day, people would actually travel to the moon.
>
> Humankind has long been fascinated by the moon. In ancient times, most peoples worshiped or revered the moon, associating it with gods. Then people started to dream of going there (Hurt, 1988, p. 22). . . .

Academic Assignments

Often in this type of paper, the author of another work will be given credit directly in the text. For example, the paper may be presenting several different ideas put forward by various individuals on one topic. In this case, it is usually clearer to give the name of the individual than to call the ideas "Idea A," "Idea B," and so on. When this happens, the citation is shortened so that the author's name is not repeated:

Willy Ley (1951, p. 13) said that atomic energy was needed for a manned lunar mission because chemical rockets were not powerful enough.

Sometimes in this type of paper, you will be using a source that has one or two main ideas developed throughout the work. If you put those ideas into your paper, you are in essence summarizing that author's work. In this case, you would use an inclusive reference because the idea is coming from the whole work, not just from one page. Therefore, there is no page number included in the reference:

The landing on the moon is generally considered the most historic part of the Apollo 11 mission. It was very tense for all involved because of several near-aborts. First, there were two computer overflow alarms, which were problems that had been thrown at the crew during a "disastrous simulation exercise" a month earlier. Next, the chosen landing site was covered with boulders, so Neil Armstrong took manual control to search for another site. They landed with less than ten seconds of fuel left (Hurt, 1988).

The form of the bibliography is also different in this method of citation, but the listing is alphabetical by each author's last name.

References

Hurt, H. (1988). *For all mankind*. New York: The Atlantic Monthly Press.

Ley, W. (1951, December). First spaceship by 1970! *Science Digest,* pp. 10–14.

von Braun, W.; Ordway, F. I.; & Dooling, D. (1985). *Space travel: A history*. New York: Harper & Row, Publishers.

Once again, the forms can vary somewhat from place to place and from time to time. The one illustrated above is the one used by the American Psychological Association and other social and behavioral sciences. The previous style illustrated is a more literary style, commonly used in English and literature classes. When a particular style is preferred, instructors or periodical editors provide a sheet of guidelines.

The Book Report/Review

Three conventional ways of writing about books are: (1) book reports, (2) book reviews, and (3) literary criticism. The book report is the traditional method whereby a teacher checks to see that an assignment has been completed and understood. It is the most elementary form. The third type, literary criticism, is an analysis, evaluation, and judgment, presupposing critical knowledge on the part of the critic and the reader.

The second type, the book review, is about halfway between the two, combining elements of both of the other types. Its purpose is (a) to inform the readership that a certain book is available; (b) to tell enough about the book to whet the appetite for someone to want to read it or allow the reader to decide that he does not want to read it; (c) to make some judgment about its merit, although many reviewers are not acknowledged literary critics.

Students in elementary and middle schools need a lot of practice in doing book reports so when they reach high school they can move up into reviewing and make a good start toward real critiquing.

The way to approach writing a standard book report varies depending on the kind of book and the teacher's objective in making the assignment, so the teacher will often give specific guidelines to follow. However, there are many helpful hints the wise student will utilize which can make the difference between an "A" and a "C" report.

Keep in mind always that a book report is a hybrid, part fact and part fancy. It gives hard information about the book, yet it is your own creation, giving your opinion and judgment of it. Any report should tell at the beginning the title and the author's full name. The publisher and the date of publication are also included in most written reports, but students often are instructed to omit this information if the report is to be read aloud in class. The book report should

Sample of Title Page

RAIN OF DEATH: THE IMPACT OF

ACID RAIN ON NATURAL RESOURCES

IN THE UNITED STATES

by

Nathan Elliott

American History

February 21, 1992

make clear exactly what kind of book is being reviewed (fiction, biography, factual book about science, current events, history, etc.). Each type is judged by different standards which will be discussed later.

But no matter what kind of book is read, good book reporters and good book reviewers always read with the review constantly in the back of their minds. They mark in the book (if it belongs to them) or they make notes as they read to help them remember important things they want to say about the book and to help them find pertinent passages to quote in the review.

These book report and review makers read imaginatively, which is a skill that is necessary to complete the act of writing. The greatest work ever written is only a piece of paper with words on it until a reader reacts to it. The reader actually helps create literature by responding to what the writer has to say. A thoughtful and imaginative reader considers both what the writer tries to say and how he says it. This gives him or her greater enjoyment in reading, and the critical skills develop with use, just as muscles do.

Usually when you finish a book you have a feeling. It may be of sorrow that the book has ended. It may be of satisfaction or even of exhilaration. It may be a let-down feeling or plain indifference. Before you lose these emotions, before they fade away, jot down random notes capturing these reactions to the book. Then let your thoughts simmer on the back burner before actually writing the review.

Reviewing Fiction

Most likely the majority of your class assignments for review will be in fiction, so you need to keep in mind these elements of literature as you read. First there is *characterization*. A writer may want to describe actions or ideas, but he must also describe the people who do the acting or have the ideas.

Then there is *motivation,* which means the reasons for the characters' actions. The writer should try to make his characters act like real people.

The *setting* is the place in which a character's story occurs. Literary characters, like the persons who read about them, do not exist in a vacuum. They act and react with one another, responding to the world in which they live.

The *plot* tells what happens to the characters in the story. It is built around a series of events that take place within a definite period of time. The leading character has a problem, faces the problem, and overcomes it or is overcome by it.

Theme is what the author is trying to say, the basic idea behind writing the novel, the statement the author wants to make to the world. Seldom is it expressed in direct words; more often it is implied by the entire work. Students often experience difficulty in understanding from the book what the author is trying to say above and beyond the simple story line of who did what to whom. The author may be saying that he thinks life is meaningless, that animals are superior to people, that love is the greatest power on earth, that all people need other people and cannot live alone, or whatever, *ad infinitum*. If you are in doubt about the theme, ask yourself if the main character learned (or failed to learn) an important lesson about life. Having identified such a lesson, ask yourself if this is the theme. If the book is assigned reading for the whole class, your teacher or general textbook may have already given you clues.

Style is the way a writer uses words to create literature, to evoke emotions, to describe beauty or ugliness, to make characters come to life, to make events seem real.

As a mature reader you will understand these elements of literature and will assess them as you read, for they will color your evaluation.

You are now ready to plan your review. You have your notes made during the reading and your notes taken when you finished, and you have allowed your thoughts to take form. Ask yourself these questions:

- What was the author's real goal in writing the book? What was his or her theme? What was I being led to see, feel, or think? Did my response match the theme? Did the author accomplish his or her objective?
- Was the plot convincing? Did the incidents follow one another logically so I felt the story really could have happened?
- Did the characters seem human? Did I really care what happened to them? Did they act like real people or like puppets on a string? Did I learn anything about human nature after meeting these characters?
- Was the dialogue believable? Was it in keeping with the person-

alities of the characters? Did the dialogue move the story along or hinder it?

- Did the setting come to life? Could I actually see in my mind's eye the places described? Did the author fill in with vivid details?
- Was the style suitable to the plot and theme? Did it blend with the book or was I conscious of inept wording so it detracted from the story?

Make notes of your answers to these questions, giving specific details to justify your reasons. Criticize where criticism is justified, but do not feel you must be critical to sound smart.

Summarize the plot briefly, never going into lengthy detail nor revealing an unexpected ending, which would spoil the suspense if someone else were to read it. Never, never give a blow-by-blow account of the action; you are not rewriting the book but are judging the elements of the book and evaluating it as a whole. You may describe one particular scene in detail to try to capture the flavor of the book for your audience.

Think about circumstances at the time the work was written. Harriet Beecher Stowe's *Uncle Tom's Cabin* was written to stir emotions against slavery. More recently Nadine Gordimer (*July's People, Something Out There*, etc.) has examined attitudes and assumptions between black people and white people in South Africa.

Take into consideration the exact nature of the book. If it is a historical novel, it is set in some specific place and period, so be sure to note the time, place, events, and historical persons involved. For instance, if you read the book *Tituba of Salem Village*, look up Tituba in an encyclopedia and point out that she was a real person and tell how the book followed (or did not follow) the actual events in her life. Read a little about the witchcraft trials in Salem, Massachusetts, so you can fix the book knowledgeably in its historical background.

Sometimes the title of the book needs explanation. If you read *The Magnificent Mutineers*, you should certainly include a paragraph about how mutineers, who are usually thought of as criminals, could be considered "magnificent."

Now ask yourself, What information do I want to get across to my readers about this book, what will *my* theme be? Take all your notes and form them into a logical outline that covers all that you want to say. Begin with the most factual parts and end with your own personal impressions.

Necessary for any good writing is a good introduction which entices the reader to read on and gives an overview of what is to come. Then the body of the work presents all the points the writer wishes to make. Equally critical is the conclusion that wraps up the writing, giving a feeling of completeness to the work.

The reviewer's own style of writing is important, with one word following another logically and interestingly, and with good paragraphs leading from one to the other smoothly. Use of transitional words or phrases between paragraphs helps the reader to follow the writer's meaning. All writing must be grammatically correct, devoid of misspelled words, and properly proofread.

Revise and polish your rough draft. Read the review over objectively. How do you think a reader of *your* work would evaluate it? Does it make a point? Does it give sufficient information for an outsider to form a valid opinion of the book? Is it dull? Is it a trustworthy evaluation? Be as thorough and critical of your own work as you were of the author's work!

Reviewing a Biography

In reviewing a biography you must do much more than just tell the facts of the person's life which anyone can look up in an encyclopedia. Do summarize the person's life, telling when and where he or she lived and why this person was a worthy subject for a book.

A main factor to consider is what the author was trying to say about the person and what area of his or her life the author stressed. For instance, a biography about Thomas Jefferson might focus on Jefferson the president and what he did during his administration, such as enlarging the country through the Louisiana Purchase. Or the author might aim at showing how multitalented he was in the sciences and the arts. Or the concentration could be on his role in the Revolution as the author of the Declaration of Independence. Perhaps the main thrust would be on the personality of Jefferson and his relationship with the people he loved.

Ask yourself these questions:

• Is the biographee presented as a real human being, with good traits and faults, or is this person made into a stereotype, someone who is not quite real?

- Do the times and places come alive? Is the setting made real?
- Does the author explain what factors influenced the person? What conditions, or events, or people helped make the person what he became?
- Are the conversations as recorded believable?
- How does the author's style help or hinder the reading of the book?
- Would I have liked to have known the main character?

Reviewing a Science Book

Here are some questions to ask yourself:

- Was the material easily understood? Did the author explain things clearly? Did I need more background to understand it or did the author write in too simple a manner?
- Were the facts accurate as far as I can tell?
- Were there enough illustrations, pictures, diagrams, and charts to help explain things?
- What are the author's qualifications? Is he or she a recognized authority in the field? How did the author obtain the information—by actual experience or by research?
- What new sort of knowledge did I learn from reading the book? Is it just new to me or is it brand new scientific information? If it is new, does everyone agree with the author in his assessment of it? For example, a book detailing how some scientists believe that birds are the direct descendants of dinosaurs would require relating this theory to older theories. Or a book about the discovery of "Lucy," a seven-million-year-old skeleton, would require fitting this information into opinions held by other scientists about how long humans have been on this earth. But a book describing the life cycle of a butterfly might present nothing new or controversial although the information in it was new to you and helped enlarge your knowledge of the world about you.

Reviewing History and Current Events

This type of book often deals with subjects from one point of view alone. What was the author's point of view? What was his or her purpose in writing it? Is only one side of a controversial question presented, or was it discussed from many angles? For instance, a book about nuclear weapons can be slanted to the author's feeling or it can show different perspectives.

- Did my attitude change as I read the book?
- Was the book written in a clear manner so I could understand the various implications discussed?
- Did I feel the author distinguished fact from interpretation? Could I tell when hard facts were being given, those that can be checked elsewhere, and when the author was giving an assessment of the facts? Were all the facts told, or were some omitted or distorted? (This is a difficult thing to pinpoint, but reading a book with this possibility in mind helps open your eyes to the insidious nature of propaganda.)
- What are the author's qualifications for writing the book?

A Précis

A précis is a concise summary in your own words of the essential points of a longer piece of writing, usually one-fourth to one-third as long as the original. Learning how to do this provides excellent training in reading for comprehension and in mastering the technique of clear, concise, and accurate writing. It is a useful skill, if mastered, and will be a valuable tool both for schoolwork and in the business world.

Fully recognize first of all that a précis is not a paraphrase, which is a restatement in different words of what the original said, often of the same length as or longer than the original. A précis, unlike a paraphrase, cuts wordage to the minimum, simplifying and getting to the essential meaning in very few words. It contains no details, examples, or illustrations, and it does not allow any comment or interpretation on your part. The French meaning of the word, "exact, terse," describes it accurately.

Follow these steps:

1. Read the selection quickly for a general overview.
2. Reread it paragraph by paragraph several times very thoughtfully.
3. In each paragraph look for the topic sentence and restate it, first to yourself, then write it down in your own words.

4. Combine these ideas into a statement of the whole. Eliminate any that do not directly bear on the main idea of the paper.

5. Revise your version, checking to see that it is absolutely accurate in accordance with the author's version and that it follows the original in the same sequence of thoughts and facts.

6. Go through your précis and cut it to one-fourth or one-third of the original length by tightening each sentence, cutting any extra words. Substitute a phrase for a clause or one word for a phrase.

Examples:

> **Wordy** If you do your studying right after school, you will be able to watch television at night.

> **Terse** Afternoon studying leaves night time free for TV watching.

> **Wordy** Miss Brown spoke to me in a pleasant manner.

> **Terse** Miss Brown spoke to me pleasantly.

Science Project Report

Writing a science project report involves a special format, although not all of the items listed below must be included for every project, as the nature of the investigation sometimes imposes limitations. However, knowing what can be required helps the student in planning and executing a successful project conducted according to approved scientific methods.

The writing must be clear and concise, using formal style, which allows no colloquial expressions, no contractions, and no first or second person (all forms of the words *you* and *I*). Define all terms that might need clarification.

1. *Title*. This should convey exactly what the report is about, being very specific and factual in wording. Cute or catchy titles are out of place. For example, "Sit, Lie Down, Play Dead" would not be a suitable title for a research report about how to train a dog. Instead, "Train a Dog to Follow Simple Commands" would be better.

2. *Abstract*. A one-paragraph summary of the report should

introduce the paper telling the purpose of the project, general methods or procedures used, and the main results produced or conclusions reached. The reason for writing the abstract is to allow another busy scientist to decide if he or she wishes to study the entire report.

3. *Introduction.* This includes the importance of the area under investigation, why you chose it, something of the historical background, and an overview of what other people have done in the field. This literary support requires using the *Reader's Guide* or other indexes to find references to what has already been done on the subject. You will need to document (give credit to) the sources you consulted. Although you may be required to use conventional footnotes, the more usual method in scientific publications is putting in parentheses within the text a shortened version of the source (Jones, *Science Reports,* 1984). The parenthetical citation refers to a more complete listing of the work in a bibliography which you will include following the paper itself.

4. *The Problem.* Clearly state what it is you planned to do. Tell if you were testing several hypotheses, were looking for a hypothesis, were suggesting a theory, or were reporting some observations made under certain specific, controlled conditions. If possible, include how your problem relates to other theories. A hypothesis is a tentative assumption made in order to draw out and test its logical consequences.

5. *Hypothesis.* State the hypothesis that you were testing and, if possible, what the results of your experiments will mean as to the acceptance or rejection of this hypothesis.

6. *Procedures.* Describe in detail exactly how you did your experiments so other people can do the same thing with the same results. List all equipment you used, a step-by-step account of procedures followed, an exact description of the conditions influencing the results. Include all failures as well as successes so others will not waste time doing things that will not work. Diagrams and drawings can be used.

7. *Observations and Interpretations.* Record chronologically, perhaps in diary form, the facts you observed as you were conducting your experiments. Compile tables or graphs to present statistics, measurements, and other numerical data.

Explain what your observations mean in connection with the hypothesis that was being tested.

8. *Conclusions.* Your hypothesis should be examined in light of your observations and interpretations so that the hypothesis may be rejected outright or accepted with reservations for more testing. Rarely does student work result in a fully accepted hypothesis.

9. *Generalizations.* Here you tell the implication or meaning of your research in relation to its larger field of science. Perhaps your study can suggest some new problems or further areas of study.

10. *Summary.* Write a brief summary of your investigation, listing the principal findings of the project.

Mechanical Details

Manuscript Guidelines

1. Use good quality bond paper, white, 8½ x 11 inches in size.
2. Use black ribbon and type on one side of the paper only.
3. Always make a carbon copy or photocopy your manuscript.
4. Double space the body of the manuscript, following the single spacing rules for long quotations, footnotes, endnotes, and bibliography entries.
5. The left margin should be 1½ inches wide; the right margin, as nearly as possible 1 inch wide; and the bottom margin, 1½ inches. This results in a page of 25 lines averaging about 10 words each, or a total of 250 words to a page.
6. On the first page, 12 spaces below the top of the paper, type the title, centered, in all capital letters.
7. Begin the paper proper three spaces below the title.
8. Indent each paragraph five spaces.
9. Do not number the first page, but do place a page number on each page of the paper beginning with page 2. Do not number outline, endnote, bibliography, or any appendix pages. The page number should be placed 1 inch from the top of the paper and 1 inch from the right margin. Do not use any punctuation with the number.

10. On all pages after the first, continue the body of the text two spaces below the page number.

11. One reason for dividing words at the ends of lines is to keep the right margin as even as possible. However, correct syllabication must be observed. Consult the dictionary.

12. Leave one space after a comma or a semicolon. Leave two spaces after any punctuation mark that ends a sentence. Leave two spaces after a colon when the next word or sentence begins with a capital letter.

13. Center any columns. Figures are usually aligned so the right margin will be in block form.

14. Do not "x" out mistakes. Correct neatly with a whitening agent.

15. Always proofread for typographical errors.

16. Enclose your paper in a folder or stiff paper cover.

Word Processor Use

The format described above also applies to papers written on word processors or in word processing programs. Many programs can automatically number pages, but some do not give a choice for the location of the numbers. Most instructors will accept any of the standard placements. If your program includes justification, turn it off. The irregular spacing made necessary by justification often makes the manuscript more difficult to read.

If you have access to a word processor, do not put off learning to use it. The ease with which corrections are made will save you hours in the preparation of any paper of four or more pages. If you are away at school or in a new job where such facilities are shared, make time to master the word processing immediately and dive into writing assignments so as not to be caught in the crunch that inevitably occurs just before deadline. As you write on the word processor, save your writing frequently; and, if you are using a personal computer, keep an eye on the capacity available in the file. Failure to heed this last warning may result in the loss of all or a substantial part of what you have written.

Handwritten Manuscripts

One of the most valuable skills a student can possess is to be able

Complete Guide to Speech, Style and Grammar

to type. If you have not had typing and must handwrite your paper, follow these rules.

1. Use standard notebook paper with wide-spaced lines, not paper torn from a spiral notebook.
2. Follow the typing rules as closely as possible.
3. Use the red line for the left margin space.
4. Write very legibly in blue-black or black ink.

LETTERS THAT MUST BE WRITTEN

Letter writing is essential to one's progress in life. Those people who attempt to bypass the necessary letters by using the telephone exclusively or by ignoring those situations when a letter is needed do themselves a great disservice. Granted, some letters are more difficult to write than others, but letter writing is a skill that can be learned.

Correspondence can be grouped in three major categories which reflect the purpose for each. These are the business of life, the personal life, and the working life:

- Letters required by the business of living frequently are impersonal in that you are writing to a stranger about a query, purchase, correction, or complaint.
- Personal letters include formal and informal correspondence to friends and acquaintances.
- Working or job-related letters apply to obtaining, holding, and terminating employment.

Letters for the Business of Life

These letters, although simple and impersonal, are essentially business letters. They should follow the usual format for business letters.

Parts of the Letter

There are seven basic parts of a letter. Business and other official letters usually require all seven. They are the following:

1. *Heading or return address.* The writer's address—engraved, printed, or typewritten at the top of the sheet—constitutes the heading of the letter. If the address does not appear on the stationery being used, it must be written or typed at the top of the sheet. Most business firms and other organizations have their names and addresses imprinted at the top of their letter sheets.
2. *Date line.* All letters must be dated. The usual place for a letter date is below the heading. Exact placement depends on

the style being used for the rest of the letter (see examples in the following pages). Spell out the month in the date line (for example, *January 25, 1991*). Never use such forms as January 25th, 1991 or 1/25/91.

3. *Inside address.* Business letters always carry the name and address of the recipient of the letter. This *inside address* is generally placed four to six lines below the date line, beginning flush with the left margin.

4. *Salutation.* The greeting *Dear* ____ is called the salutation. In business letters the salutation is almost always followed by a colon and is generally formal. Typical business salutations include the anonymous *Dear Sir or Madam* and the specific *Dear Mr. Jones.*

5. *Body.* The part of the letter which carries the message is called the body.

6. *Complimentary close.* Signaling the conclusion of the letter is the function of the complimentary close. The most common complimentary close for a business letter is *Sincerely* or *Sincerely yours.* The complimentary close is always followed by a comma. Note that although the first word begins with a capital letter the others do not.

7. *Signature.* All letters whether typed or handwritten must be signed by the writer. In business letters, the written signature is followed by a typed or printed signature so that the recipient is left in no doubt about the spelling of the writer's name. If the letter is written on behalf of an organization or employer, the writer's title is typed or written below the writer's name.

Other parts may be needed to carry additional information. Some offices use a *reference line* carrying a file, order, or policy number placed one to four lines below the date. If mail is to be sent by other than first-class postal service, a notation of delivery service is typed in capital letters flush with the left margin about two lines above the inside address. The designation *personal* or *confidential,* if required, is placed in the same area (and must be marked on the envelope). An *attention line* naming an individual is used only on a letter addressed to an organization. The attention line is typed two spaces below the inside address and two spaces above the salutation if there is one. A *subject line,* if used, is typed in all capitals three lines below the inside address. It may be flush left, centered, or aligned with paragraph indentations.

Options after the signature block include *executive and secretary/typist initials, enclosure notation,* and *carbon copy notation.* All are typed in the order listed, flush left with the margin, two lines apart beginning two lines after the signature block.

A list of special forms of address can be found on pages 253–256. These include appropriate salutations and complimentary closes.

Formats for Letters

In recent years, the block format and modified block have become the standard formats to use in preparing business letters on the typewriter or word processor. In the block style all parts of the letter are flush left with appropriate spacing between each part of the letter, and the paragraphs are not indented. The modified block format may center the heading or return address but more commonly places it in the upper right-hand corner of the type area. In this format, paragraphs are indented, and the complimentary close and signature touch the right margin. (See examples which follow, pages 238–241.)

If your letter is being written in longhand, use the traditional form with the heading or return address and date line in the upper right-hand area. The inside address and greeting are flush left with the margin, and the paragraphs of the body are indented without extra space between them. The closing and signature are usually centered. Or, you may use the new simplified format. Either way it helps the recipient if you print your name below your signature.

The simplified format was developed recently by the American Management Association. In this format, the salutation and complimentary close are omitted, but a subject line is essential. Usually typed in all capitals, it is a brief phrase of two to four words that identifies the topic of the letter. This line may also be used with a salutation. A similar but slightly different purpose is served by the reference line. The reference line is usually a number (an account number, for example, when writing to correct a charge account bill). The reference line is placed two lines below the salutation if one is used, or in that approximate position if no salutation is used. (An alternative placement is two lines below, and aligned with, the date.)

Complete Guide to Speech, Style and Grammar

Solving the Sex Question in Letter Writing

With more and more women holding prominent career positions, the traditional *Dear Sir* or the time-honored *Gentlemen* has fallen into disfavor for use when the identity of the recipient is unknown. Current practice suggests using *Dear Sir or Madam* or *Ladies and Gentlemen*.

However, a simpler solution is to use the title of the person addressed: *Dear Personnel Director; Dear Registrar; Dear Principal; Dear Public Service Commissioners.* The same idea can be used in writing to a company: *Dear Jones Bookstore; Dear Executive Tax Service.*

If it is known that the addressee is a woman, and her preference of titles is known, then address her as *Miss Mary Alston* or *Mrs. Joan Krantz* or *Ms. Sara Ledbetter.* However, in many cases the correct choice is unknown. If in doubt, incorporate her title in the salutation as *Dear Professor Caffey* or *Dear Director Smith.*

An alternative to these solutions is the use of the simplified letter format which omits both salutation and complimentary close.

Communicating Ideas in a Letter

A successful letter is one that wins a favorable response. When you write a thank-you letter, you seek a specific response—*I want Ann to realize how much I appreciate the silver tray she sent.* When you write a business letter, you also seek a specific response—*I want the bookkeeper at Greynolds, Inc., to understand that the 2% discount he took is not justified and that a check for $5.64 must be sent to me.* When you write a personal letter to a friend, you seek a much less tangible and much less specific response of friendship shared—*I want Tom to get pleasure and knowledge from the news I send and a deepened appreciation of our friendship.* In all of these types of letters, the success of the letter is judged by the response.

The Response Desired

So important is this response that the first principle of effective letter writing is: *Let the response you desire be your guide throughout the letter.*

A good practice is to pause a moment before beginning to write and answer the following questions:

Just why am I writing this letter?

Just how do I want my reader to feel when he finishes this letter?

In a particularly important letter, you may want to write out for yourself in a sentence or two the response you desire. But in most letters it will be enough if you get the response desired clearly in your own mind before you start writing.

The You-Attitude

When you have determined the desired response, you must next consider that goal from your reader's point of view. Imagine yourself the reader. Then select a plan for your letter, a set of ideas, a tone of approach, and a phrasing that would move *you* to the response desired.

This tactic of viewing a letter problem through the reader's eyes may be called the *you-attitude*. So important is the you-attitude that the second principle of effective letter writing is: *Let your reader's interests be your guide in the selection and phrasing of ideas.*

A letter which concentrates on the selfish interests of the writer is apt to be dull and generally ineffective. Readers respond best when their own interests are being considered. In writing personal letters, you should stick to subjects that will give pleasure to your reader. Respond to the main points of his or her last letter to you. Involve the reader as much as possible in what you say. Instead of saying: "I found the view from the bridge over the rushing waters very impressive," say: "If only you could have shared that view from the bridge with me. I know you would have thought, as I did, 'It's just like the Ausable River.'"

When you write business letters, you are always concerned with the advancement of some interest—getting a job, making a sale, collecting an account. Yet, these letters as well must be written with the you-attitude if they are to gain the response desired and win goodwill for the writer and his firm. A job applicant should tell how his training and experience will benefit the reader. The writer of a collection letter should stress the advantage his reader will gain through prompt payment—satisfaction in knowing his debts are paid or the protection of his credit standing.

Expression Skill

With the exception of formal correspondence, letters are best written in a natural conversational tone. After all, the letter substitutes for a person-to-person meeting and should employ language appropriate to such meetings. Stilted language, artificiality, or phrases designed to impress have no place in a letter.

Writing skill, however, is very important to the letter writer. Actually, a letter is *not* a person-to-person meeting, and it requires skill to convey an idea and a set of feelings precisely and naturally through the written word.

The need to write well leads to a further principle of effective letter writing: *Let your ideas and feelings find expression in language that is clear, persuasive, natural, thoughtful, and interesting.*

The basic method of improving your ability to express yourself in writing is to read good writing and to practice as much writing as possible. As you read good writing, notice how logical and constructive is the thought behind it. Notice how the writer phrases his or her ideas precisely. Notice how easily and naturally the writer expresses ideas. Such attention to the techniques of skillful writing will enhance your own writing skill.

When you practice writing, concentrate on the ideas and feelings you want your writing to convey, rather than on techniques and style. Think hard until you have an idea worthy of expression. Make yourself feel the mood you want to convey—cheeriness, sympathy, friendliness, or whatever that mood may be. Concentrate on that idea and feeling until the right phrasing comes to you. With an increase of experience, you will discover that you are acquiring skill, that the right words and phrasing come more and more readily.

When you concentrate on the ideas and feelings you want to convey, language will begin to flow; the trick is to keep it flowing. Your first attempt to express a business-letter idea may be, "Please do something about this." Obviously, this idea needs more definite thought and expression. If you concentrate on it, you will gain not only a clearer thought but also more precise expression of that thought, and you will be writing, "Please pick up the damaged table on Saturday morning."

You can speed up this skill-building process further if you bear in mind the writing principles discussed in other chapters of this book.

Watch These Expressions

accept, except Do not confuse. *I shall accept* (receive) *the letter. I shall except* (exclude) *this sum from the list.*

affect, effect   Do not confuse. *The news will affect* (influence) *his mood. The manager will effect* (bring about) *a new schedule. The effect* (the noun form meaning result) *of television is obvious*.

busy   In personal letters never write *I would have answered sooner but I was too busy* or any similarly rude expression.

beside, besides   Do not confuse. *The wastebasket is beside* (alongside of) *the desk. Who is going besides* (in addition to) *you?*

due to   Do not use *due to* in place of *because of* or *owing to*.

favor   Do not refer to a letter as a *favor* in such trite expressions as *Your favor of June 1 received*.

good, well   Do not use *good* as an adverb. *This program works well* (not good).

hoping   Avoid such letter endings as *hoping to hear from you*.

I am, I remain   Avoid these old-fashioned phrases in your letter closings.

its, it's   Do not confuse. *Every machine has its* (possessive) *own cover. It's* (it is) *going to be warm today*.

said   Avoid such expressions as *the said program* or *the said matter*.

thanking you   Avoid such expressions as *thanking you for your interest* followed by a complimentary close.

Avoid These Expressions

anticipating	trusting that this is satisfactory
as per, as regards	valued
at your earliest convenience	we are, we remain
awaiting, we await	we trust
beg	we wish to
duly noted	with due regard
enclosed please find	with reference to the matter
esteemed	yours
recent date	

Complete Guide to Speech, Style and Grammar

Query Letter in Block Format

555 Euclid Avenue
Tulsa, Oklahoma 00000
January 20, 1992

TasteBest Company
10 Dewhurst Drive
New York, NY 00000

Dear Sir or Madam:

Could you please provide standard nutritional
information for the original Smoothie Chocolate Chip
Cookie recipe that appears on the reverse side of the
package. Specifically I would like to know the following:

1. The number of servings per 12 ounce package
2. The number of pieces per serving
3. The calories, fat in grams, and sodium in milligrams
   per serving

Has your company ever developed a reduced calorie
version of this recipe?

You answer will be gratefully received.

Sincerely,

Sally Smith

Purchase Letter in Simplified Format

January 20, 1992

XYZ Press
1010 University Avenue
Hoboken, NJ 00000

BOOK ORDER

Please send me one copy of <u>Plan Now for College</u> by
Jane Grad and June Smith. My check for $9.95 is
enclosed.

Sally Smith
555 Euclid Avenue
Tulsa, Oklahoma 10101

Enclosure: $9.95 check

When ordering an item, it is best to put your return address next to
your name.

Complete Guide to Speech, Style and Grammar

Correction Request in Modified Block Format

555 Euclid Avenue
Tulsa, Oklahoma 00101
June 10,1992

Registrar
XYZ College
Woodland Avenue
College Town, MA 00000

Dear Registrar:

In the grade report I received yesterday, my final grade for General Chemistry 101 was a C, but this is not correct.

Going into the final exam, I was carrying a B+ in this class. The scores from the final exam were posted before I left campus last week. My grade was listed as a B; therefore, my overall average had to be a B, not a C.

The instructor for this course, Phyllis Newhouse, indicated in class that she would be out of town until classes resume next fall so I am writing to you in the hope that you can correct this error promptly.

I appreciate your action on this matter.

Sincerely,

Sally Smith

Letter of Complaint

2525 Austin Avenue
San Antonio, TX 00000

October 20, 1988

Attn: Customer Service
XYZ Company
65 Monroe Street
Newberry, TN 00000

XYZ toaster model R-10
-123456-789-987Z

Although I have only used this toaster occasionally on
weekends since I received it as a wedding gift in April, I
find that even on the lightest setting ordinary raisin
bread is burnt before it will pop up and turn off.

Please tell me where I can take this toaster for repair or
replacement. Such information probably accompanied
the appliance when I received it, but my husband is in
the armed services and I have moved three times since
the wedding.

I appreciate your help in returning this toaster to the
level of service I know you demand of all your products.

Sally Smith
(Mrs. John R. Smith)

Letters in Your Personal Life

When you write a letter—whether personal or business—those lines of writing become *you* in the mind of your reader. Your letters will, of course, vary in purpose and formality, as the occasion requires, yet each letter you write is, for your reader, like a face-to-face meeting with you.

Those letters which help us share with friends and relatives the joys of living are called *personal letters*. There is a single test for evaluating the personal letter: Does it provide the writer and the reader with shared satisfaction of friendship?

Note how Thackeray's daughter achieves the vividness of face-to-face contact in a letter:

> I have been imagining you in my favorite corner of my favorite city. Have you opened your windows and looked out, does it smell-rumble-taste Paris? I'm sure it does. Even the little tin water cans are unlike anything anywhere else.

The few principles of personal letter writing that do exist are designed to help writer and reader enjoy to the full the pleasures of correspondence:

1. Make your letters as cheerful and constructive as you can; nobody likes a complaining, gloomy, nagging letter.
2. Avoid any statement or hint that writing is a chore. It is impolite to tell a correspondent that you just could not get around to writing, that there is nothing to say, or that you are hastily dashing off a few lines.
3. Avoid putting into a letter any statement that could prove unbecoming if the letter were to fall into the hands of another. Remember, letters are permanent records.

Receive a Letter, Write a Letter

Personal letters are written because you think warmly of the person you are addressing and you want the other person to think warmly of you. When you receive a letter, you are obligated to answer. Failure to do so sends a message to the writer that you do not wish to continue the friendship.

Receive a Gift, Write a Letter

When you receive a gift, whether from a close friend, an associate at work, or a distant relative, it is not sufficient to thank the person orally. A thank-you note should be written as soon as possible after you receive the gift. Such notes do not need to be elaborate but should be written thoughtfully. The gift should be mentioned specifically whether it is a silver tray, a book, or a gift of money. Sometimes people wonder how to handle a cash gift without violating good taste. The following example would be an appropriate thank-you letter for a graduation gift.

The Thank-You Note

June 10, 1991

Dear Uncle Henry,

Your generous check arrived today. Thank you. Thank you. As you have probably heard—I think Dad's been bragging—I have a scholarship to Duke that will cover most of my expenses this fall, so I am going to use your gift for those extras that make life fun (hot fudge sundaes, admission to the swimming pool, phone calls home, etc.) while I am traveling with a church service project this summer.

Thanks again. I just wish you were here so I could hug you. Everyone should have an uncle like you.

Your niece,
Kim

Complete Guide to Speech, Style and Grammar

Enthusiasm takes this thank-you note beyond an obligation and makes the giver feel appreciated, and that is the purpose of the letter.

Sincerity is even more important. If you are having trouble wording a thank-you letter, try to envision the other person selecting and sending you the gift. Keep the you-attitude:

August 23, 1991

Dear Martha,

How thoughtful of you! The bookends you sent Bob and me were put to use immediately. Since both of us are continuing our degree work at State, I don't think you could have found a gift that we would use more than these. Every time I see them, I am reminded of you and the glorious summer we spent studying at the Art Institute.

We are expecting you to come for a visit when you return from Asia.

Fondly,

Susan

Be a Guest, Write a Letter

Despite assurances to the contrary, a great deal of work goes into having a guest or guests in the home. If you have been a guest, you need to acknowledge this hospitality in a bread-and-butter note. This is a thank-you letter specifically written to a person after you have been a guest in his or her home.

These letters are usually brief and contain reference to at least one thing or event that was particularly appreciated. The formality of the salutation and signature in the following example imply that the writer and the hostess either do not know each other well or are of two different generations.

The Bread-and-Butter Note

Dear Mrs. Parsons,

That Saturday morning sunrise over the valley, those gay voices of the twins, and that stimulating table talk are still with me. Every moment of the weekend was perfect, but one—departure. How I hated to have it end!

I loved every moment at Oakridge Manor and I want to thank you very much for a wonderful time.

Sincerely,
Harvey Henderson

Complete Guide to Speech, Style and Grammar

Responding to Formal Invitations

Very formal affairs—weddings, receptions, and formal dinners—still require a formal correspondence ritual. Guests are invited in a nonpersonal, formal manner, as is to be seen in the example below. The invitations are usually engraved or printed; they may be written in longhand. Guests responding to such invitations employ the same formal, nonpersonal language that they find in the invitation, but the responses are always handwritten.

INVITATION

Mr. and Mrs. Eugene Parsons
request the honor of your presence
at the marriage of their daughter
Sue Ellen
to
Mr. Harvey Henderson
on Saturday, the first of June
at ten o'clock
Saint Mark's Church
New York

ACCEPTANCE

Thomas Olderbach accepts with pleasure
the kind invitation of Mr. and Mrs. Eugene Parsons
to the marriage of their daughter
Sue Ellen to Mr. Harvey Henderson
on Saturday, the first of June at ten o'clock
Saint Mark's Church
New York

Likewise, any invitation which has the notation R.S.V.P. or which includes a meal requires a response. If a return card or telephone number has been included, you may use them to satisfy your social obligation. It is never correct, however, to ignore an invitation or to accept an invitation and subsequently not attend. In the case of illness, one should contact the host or hostess as soon as possible.

The Letter of Condolence or Sympathy

The death of someone close to a friend, co-worker, or acquaintance of long standing requires a short sympathetic letter. There are a few guidelines to follow:

1. Express your sympathy briefly.
2. Mention the person who died.
3. If the deceased was known to you personally, say something complimentary about them.
4. If appropriate and sincere, offer to help the person to whom you are writing.

It is a matter of personal choice whether you use the word *death*. Two examples follow. In the first, all the persons mentioned were friends. In the second, a co-worker's father has died.

The Letter of Condolence

Dear Mary,

Bill and I were shocked and saddened to learn of Jim's death when we arrived here after several weeks visiting the children. Jim was such a kind person. Our son still talks about the Scout trips he took the boys on.

We'd like you to consider spending the winter with us here in Florida. Since Bill still works in tax preparation, you and I would be free to spend our days however we wish. Do call me at 555-3457 to let us know when to meet your plane or if there is anything at all that we can do to help.

                                        Sincerely,
                                        Maggie

Dear Jim,
  I was sorry to learn of your father's death. You have
my deepest sympathy. May you find comfort in knowing
that all of us at the office care.

                          Sincerely,
                          Elizabeth

Letters Related to Work

Letters are used frequently in the process of obtaining employment. A resumé should never be sent to a prospective employer without a focused but brief cover letter. Follow-up letters after an interview can make a difference. People who help you obtain employment, especially those who write letters of reference, should be thanked. And when it is time to move on, your resignation should be put in writing.

Writing Intriguing Cover Letters

You will need a cover letter whenever you send a resumé or application form to a potential employer. The letter should capture the employer's attention, show why you are writing, indicate why your employment will benefit the company, and ask for an interview. The kind of specific information that must be included in a letter means that each must be written individually. Each letter must also be typed perfectly, which may present a problem. Word processing equipment helps.

Frequently only the address, first paragraph, and specifics concerning an interview will vary. These items are easily changed on word processing equipment and memory typewriters. If you do not have access to such equipment, you might be able to rent it. Or you might be able to have your letters typed by a resumé or employment services company listed in the yellow pages. Be sure you know the full cost of such a service before agreeing to use one.

The Cover Letter

15 Hilton House
College de l'Art Libre
Smallville, CO 77717

March 18, 1987

Ms. Collette Recruiter
Rest Easy Hotels
1500 Suite Street
Megapolis, SD 99999

Dear Ms. Recruiter:

The Rest Easy Hotels always served as landmarks for
me when I traveled through this country and Europe. I
would like to contribute to their growth, especially their
new chain, the Suite Rest Hotels that feature reception
rooms for every guest. I have had many jobs working
with people and have always enjoyed this aspect of my
experience. Knowing its importance to your company, I
believe I would be an asset to the Rest Easy Hotels.

During the week of March 31, I will be visiting
Megapolis and would like to speak with you concerning
your training program for hotel managers. I will call
your secretary to confirm an appointment.

The enclosed resumé outlines my education and
experience.

Sincerely yours,

Allison Springs
(888) 736-3550

Complete Guide to Speech, Style and Grammar

Salutation

Each letter should be addressed by name to the person you want to talk with. That person is the one who can hire you. This is almost certainly not someone in the personnel department, and it is probably not a department head either. It is most likely to be the person who will actually supervise you once you start work. Call the company to make sure you have the right name. And spell it correctly.

Opening

The opening should appeal to the reader. Cover letters are sales letters. Sales are made after you capture a person's attention. You capture the reader's attention most easily by talking about the company rather than yourself. Mention projects under development, recent awards, or favorable comments recently published about the company. You can find such information in the business press, including the business section of local newspapers and the many magazines that are devoted to particular industries. If you are answering an ad, you may mention it. If someone suggested that you write, use their name (with permission, of course).

Body

The body of the letter gives a brief description of your qualifications and refers to the resumé, where your sales campaign can continue.

Closing

You cannot have what you do not ask for. At the end of the letter, request an interview. Suggest a time and state that you will confirm the appointment. Use a standard complimentary close, such as "Sincerely yours," leave three or four lines for your signature, and type your name. Either type your phone number under your name or place the phone number in the body of the letter, but finding it there will be more difficult should the reader wish to call you.

The Follow-Up Letter

The most effective way to follow up an interview is with a well-written letter that restates your potential usefulness to the employer.

Letters That Must Be Written

This is not a thank-you note; you are simply continuing your campaign to present yourself as the best applicant for the opening.

Be professional in your preparation of this letter. The following guide may be helpful:

1. Use the full name of the company, the interviewer and his or her title. Do not abbreviate anything.
2. Use a subject line such as "Interview for (job title) opening on (date of interview)."
3. Use a formal greeting even if the interviewer asked you to use a first name during the interview.
4. To open the body of the letter, express appreciation for the interview with such words as "Thanks again for taking the time to discuss the opening in (name of department or area such as *sales* or *finance*)." Another possibility is "It was a pleasure meeting you Thursday to discuss the opening in the circulation department of University Publishing Company." Then say something about the discussion or add to it in such a way as to remind the reader of your qualifications.
5. In the body, talk about the company. Use what you learned in the interview to praise the company and build a connection between yourself and the company.
6. Make your last paragraph a dignified but specific request for the position. This might be "This position is exactly what I have been hoping to find, and I look forward to hearing from you soon." Or "This is an exciting opportunity, and I hope to hear from you next week."

Thank Your References

As soon as you accept an offer, inform those people who let you use them as references. Thank them for their help; without it you probably would not have received the offer. The best way to do this is with a letter.

If there are others who told you about an opening or answered your questions about their employer and the opening you sought, write them a letter of appreciation also.

Tell the people who were not references for this position but were for others that you have found work and thank them for all they did.

Complete Guide to Speech, Style and Grammar

The Letter of Resignation

Resignations should be written. The letter may be prepared after you have told your supervisor or you may carry it with you when you tell this person. Do not risk the supervisor finding out from someone else. (Prepare the letter yourself—away from the office if necessary to preserve confidentiality.)

A resignation letter should contain the following:

1. The effective date of the resignation.
2. A reason for leaving. This does not need to be your primary reason, but it should be acceptable. Acceptable reasons for leaving include career advancement, change in career direction, going back to school, poor health, family needs, etc.
3. Praise something about the company or the working situation. You want to leave on a pleasant note as you do not know when you will need a recommendation. This is not the time to praise yourself.

The resignation letter will go into your permanent personnel file. It will most probably be there long after you leave your next job and

---

Forms of Address

PERSON	INSIDE ADDRESS
President	The President The White House Washington, DC 20500
Senator	The Honorable John Doe United States Senate Washington, DC 20510
Representative	The Honorable Jane Doe The House of Representatives Washington, DC 20515
Governor	The Honorable John Doe Governor of New York Albany, NY 00000

---

the one after that. An angry or spiteful letter will do you no good, and it very likely will do you harm. Like the other employment-related letters, this one should be formal. Use your supervisor's last name preceded by Mr., Ms., or other title of preference in the salutation. Punctuate it with a colon. Sign your full name.

Other Letters in Business

The letter is an important tool in business, government, the professions, and other administrative work. For all practical purposes, the great variety of business letters may be classified under four basic headings:

1. *Letters that handle routine business.* Most business letters have a simple, routine mission; they carry needed details and short statements of information from business to business. Letters that order goods, acknowledge orders, and handle remittances make up the bulk of mail interchanged by business organizations. The main qualities these routine letters must possess are brevity and clearness. They must be complete in supplying all details as to style, color, price, conditions, procedures, and the like.

SALUTATION	COMPLEMENTARY CLOSE
Mr. President:	Respectfully yours,
or Dear Mr. President:	*or* Respectfully,
Sir: Madam:	Very truly yours,
or Dear Senator Doe:	Sincerely yours,
	or Sincerely,
Sir: Madam:	Very truly yours,
or Ms. Doe:	Sincerely yours,
	or Sincerely,
Sir: Madam:	Respectfully yours,
or Dear Governor Doe:	Very truly yours,
	Sincerely yours,
	or Sincerely,

Complete Guide to Speech, Style and Grammar

PERSON	INSIDE ADDRESS
Mayor	The Honorable Jane Doe Mayor of the City of Troy City Hall Troy, CO 00000
College Registrar	The Registrar Finn University Tobin City, NJ 00000
Rabbi	Rabbi John Doe . . . .
Protestant clergy	The Reverend Jane Doe . . . .
Priest	The Reverend John Doe . . . .
Nun	Sister Lioba, O.S.B.* . . . . (*Indicate order)
Woman Formally in a Business Letter	Ms. Mary Doe . . . .
Man Formally in a Business Letter	Mr. John Doe . . . .
Business Firm	Perfect Corporation . . . .
Man or Woman in a Social or Personal Letter	(No inside address needed, but be certain to use Mr., Mrs., Miss, Dr., or other title of courtesy before name on the envelope.)

SALUTATION	COMPLEMENTARY CLOSE
Sir: Madam: *or* Dear Mayor Doe:	Very truly yours, Sincerely yours, *or* Sincerely,
Dear Sir or Madam: *or* Dear Registrar:	Very truly yours, *or* Sincerely yours,
Dear Rabbi Doe:	Respectfully yours, *or* Sincerely yours,
Reverend Sir: *or* Dear Ms. Doe:	Respectfully yours, *or* Sincerely yours,
Reverend Sir: *or* Dear Father Doe:	Respectfully yours, *or* Sincerely yours,
Dear Sister Lioba:	Respectfully yours, Faithfully yours, *or* Sincerely yours,
Dear Ms. Doe:	Yours truly, Sincerely yours, *or* Sincerely,
Dear Mr. Doe:	Yours truly, Sincerely yours, *or* Sincerely,
Ladies and Gentlemen:	Sincerely,
Dear Mr. Jones, Dear Mrs. Doe, Dear Tom, Dear Jane, *or in friendly letters any familiar salutation in good taste.*	Sincerely, *or any more intimate closing in good taste, such as* Affectionately yours, Lovingly,

Complete Guide to Speech, Style and Grammar

2. *Letters that grant requests.* Many business letters are written to grant requests; they supply information sought by other businessmen and the public; they send out samples and booklets; they open charge accounts; they make adjustments. When a request is granted, it should be done graciously and with goodwill, usually in the opening sentence of the letter. The middle of the letter can then supply the necessary detail. The ending is usually a further statement of goodwill.

3. *Letters that deny requests.* Many business letters have to deny requests. The best tactics for making a denial are (a) open with a statement that the reader will find agreeable—*We appreciate very much your detailed description of your recent experience with our Toast-Browner;* (b) give reasons for the denial; (c) make the denial; (d) seek the goodwill of the reader.

4. *Letters that persuade and sell.* Many business letters have a persuasive mission; they must move the minds and wills of their readers. Some of them must assist in selling goods and services; some of them must collect money; some of them must debate issues. All of them must employ techniques of persuasion.

   The sales letter is usually constructed on a patterning of steps which lead to the sale—attention, desire, conviction, and action.

A useful resource for personal and business use is *Lifetime Encyclopedia of Letters* by Harold E. Meyer (Prentice Hall: Englewood Cliffs, N.J. 07632).

WRITING AN EFFECTIVE RESUMÉ

A resumé is a way for you to show an employer what you know and what you have done; but most importantly it is a way to show what you can do. After all, you are going to get a job. It is just a question of which one.

Employers want to hire people who can do the job. To learn who these people are, they may use resumés, application forms, written tests, performance tests, medical examinations, and interviews. Reference checks are customary for applicants who reach the "finalist" stage and sometimes are done as a matter of course for all applicants. You can use each of these different evaluation procedures to your advantage, but quite often the resumé (and the related application form) is the key that allows you to move on to the next stage of the application process.

Creating Effective Resumés and Application Forms

Resumés and application forms are two ways to achieve the same goal: To give the employer written evidence of your qualifications. When creating a resumé or completing an application form, you need two different kinds of information: Facts about yourself and facts about the job you want. With this information in hand, you can present the facts about yourself in terms of the job. You have more freedom with a resumé—you can put your best points first and avoid blanks. But, even on application forms, you can describe your qualifications in terms of the job's duties.

Know Thyself

Begin by assembling information about yourself. Some items appear on virtually every resumé or application form, including the following:

- Current address and phone number—if you are rarely at home during business hours, try to obtain an answering machine. Leave a message that would reflect well on you. This is not the time for jokes! Alternatively, you may want to give the phone number of a friend or relative who will take messages for you.

- Job sought or career goal.
- Experience (paid and volunteer)—date of employment, name and full address of the employer, job title, starting and finishing salary, and reason for leaving (moving, returning to school, and seeking a better position are among the readily accepted reasons).
- Education—the school's name, the city in which it is located, the years you attended it, the diploma or certificate you earned, and the course of studies you pursued.
- Other qualifications—hobbies, organizations you belong to, honors you have received, and leadership positions you have held.
- Office machines, tools, and equipment you have used and skills that you possess.
- Skills and achievements—more than duties and responsibilities. What have you accomplished? What are your marketable strengths? These are most likely related to your work experience but could be related to your education or outside interests.

Other information, such as your Social Security number, is often asked for on application forms but is rarely presented on resumés. Application forms might also ask for a record of past addresses and for information that you would rather not reveal, such as a record of convictions. If asked for such information, you must be honest. Honesty does not, however, require that you reveal disabilities that do not affect your overall qualifications for a job.

Know Thy Job

Next, gather specific information about the jobs you are applying for. You need to know the pay range (so you can make their top your bottom), education and experience usually required, hours and shifts usually worked. Most importantly, you need to know the job duties (so that you can describe your experience in terms of those duties). Study the job description. Some job announcements, especially those issued by a government, even have a checklist that assigns a numerical weight to different qualifications so that you can be certain as to which is the most important; looking at such announcements will give you an idea of what employers look for even if you do not wish to apply for a government job. If the announcement or advertisement is vague, call the employer to learn what is sought.

Once you have the information you need, you can prepare a resumé. You may need to prepare more than one master resumé if you are going to look for different kinds of jobs. Otherwise, your resumé will not fit the job you seek.

Two Kinds of Resumés

The way you arrange your resumé depends on how well your experience seems to prepare you for the position you want. Basically, you can either describe your most recent job first and work backwards (reverse chronology) or group similar skills together. No matter which format you use, the following advice applies generally.

- Use specifics. A vague description of your duties will make only a vague impression.
- Identify accomplishments. If you headed a project, improved productivity, reduced costs, increased membership, or achieved some other goal, say so.
- Use action verbs. Combine the specifics and the accomplishments with action verbs. For example, supervised staff of 7; increased sales by 35 percent in two years; set new standard in assembling 2,000 widgets on schedule without a flaw.

Appearance Counts

After you have drafted a resumé, choose an attractive format and follow these guidelines.

- Type your resumé, using a standard typeface. (Printed resumés are becoming more common, but employers do not indicate a preference for them.)
- Keep the length down to two pages at the most.
- Remember your mother's advice not to say anything if you cannot say something nice. Leave all embarrassing or negative information off the resumé—but be ready to deal with it in a positive fashion at the interview.
- Proofread the master copy carefully.
- Have someone else proofread the master copy carefully.
- Have a third person proofread the master copy carefully.

- Use the best quality photocopying machine and good white or off-white paper.

The following information appears on almost every resumé.

- Name.
- Phone number(s) at which you can be reached or receive messages.
- Address.
- Job or career sought.
- References—often just a statement that references are available suffices. If your references are likely to be known by the person who reads the resumé, however, their names are worth listing.
- Experience.
- Education.
- Special talents.
- Personal information—height, weight, marital status, physical condition. Although this information often appears, it is not important to recruiters. In fact, employers are prohibited by law from asking for some of it. If some of this information is directly job related—the height and weight of a bouncer is important to an employer, for example—list it. Otherwise, save space and put in more information about your skills.

Reverse chronology is the easiest method to use. It is also the least effective because it makes when you did something more important than what you can do. It is an especially poor format if you have gaps in your work history, if the job you seek is very different from the job you currently hold, or if you are just entering the job market. Use such a resumé when you have progressed up a clearly defined career ladder and want to move up a rung.

Resumés that are not in reverse chronological order may be called functional, analytical, skill oriented, creative, or some other name. The differences are less important than the similarity, which is that all stress what you can do. The employer can see immediately how you will fit the job. This format also has advantages for many job hunters because it camouflages gaps in paid employment and avoids giving prominence to irrelevant jobs.

You begin writing a functional resumé by determining the skills the employer is looking for. Again, study the job description for this information. Next, review your experience and education to see when you demonstrated the ability sought. Then prepare the resumé itself, putting first the information that relates most obviously to the job. The result will be a resumé with headings such as "Engineering," "Computer Languages," "Communications Skills," or "Design Experience." These headings will have much more impact than the dates that you would use on a chronological resumé.

If you have decided to change fields or you are not certain what skills you have, plan to spend some time thoughtfully answering some questions. Simply list as many brief answers as you can to the following: What tasks do I enjoy most? What tasks do I dislike most? What do I do best? What do I do poorly? What characteristics do I possess (for example, cheerful, competitive, friendly)? How do others perceive me? (You may want to look at past performance reviews or teacher evaluations.) What do I want from the workplace (for example, protection from extremes of weather, outdoor work, independent activity [the opposite of close supervision], collegial structure, non-smoking or smoking building, etc.)? Generate a page of answers for each question if possible; don't settle for less than eight items on any list but try to be comprehensive.

Taking each list separately rank the three to five answers that are the most important to you. Put the number one next to the task you enjoy most of the tasks you have listed, two next to your next favorite, and so on for each list of answers.

Allison Springs
15 Hilton House
College de l' Art Libre
Smallville, CO 77717

(888) 736-3550

Job sought: Hotel Management Trainee

Skills, education, and experience

<u>Working with people:</u>   All the jobs I have had involve
working closely with a large variety of people on many
different levels. As Vice President of the Junior Class, I
balanced the concerns of different groups in order to
reach a common goal. As a claims interviewer with a
state public assistance agency, I dealt with people under
very trying circumstances. As a research assistant with
a law firm, I worked with both lawyers and clerical
workers. And as a lifeguard (5 summers), I learned how
to manage groups of people.

<u>Effective communication:</u>   My campaign for class
office, committee projects, and fund raising efforts
(which netted $15,000 for the junior class project),
relied on effective communication in both oral and
written presentations.

<u>Organization and management:</u>   My participation in
student government has developed my organizational
and management skills. In addition, my work with the
state government and a law office has made me familiar
with organizational procedures.

Chronology

September 1983 to present	Attended College de l'Art Libre in Smallville, Colorado. Will earn a Bachelor of Arts degree in political science. Elected Vice President of the Junior Class, managed successful fund drive, directed Harvest Celebration Committee, served on many other committees, and earned 33 percent of my college expenses.
January 1987 to present	Work as research assistant for the law office of McCall, McCrow, and McCow, 980 Main Street, Westrow, Colorado 77718. Supervisor: Jan Eagelli (666) 654-3211
September 1986 to December 1986	Worked as claims interviewer intern for the Department of Public Assistance of the State of Colorado, 226 Park Street, Smallville, Colorado 77717. Supervisor: James Fish (666) 777-7717.
1980-1985	Worked as lifeguard during the summers at the Shilo Pool, 46 Waterway, Shilo, Nebraska 77777.

Recommendations available on request

Fit Yourself to a Form

Some large employers, such as fast-food restaurants and government agencies, make more use of application forms than of resumés. The forms suit the style of large organizations because people find information more quickly if it always appears in the same place. However, creating a resumé before filling out an application form will still benefit you. You can use the resumé when you send a letter inquiring about a position. You can submit a resumé even if an application is required; it will spotlight your qualifications. And the information on the resumé will serve as a handy reference if you must fill out an application form quickly. Application forms are really just resumés in disguise anyway. No matter how rigid the form appears to be, you can still use it to show why you are the person for the job being filled.

At first glance, application forms seem to give a job hunter no leeway. The forms certainly do not have the flexibility that a resumé does, but you can still use them to your best advantage. Remember that the attitude of the person reading the form is not, "Let's find out why this person is unqualified," but, "Maybe this is the person we want." Use all the parts of the form—experience blocks, education blocks, and others—to show that that person is you.

Here's some general advice on completing application forms.

- Request two copies of the form. If only one is provided, photocopy it before you make a mark on it. You will need more than one copy to prepare rough drafts.
- Read the whole form before you start completing it.
- Prepare a master copy if the same form is used by several divisions within the same company or organization. Do not put the specific job applied for, date, and signature on the master copy. Fill in that information on the photocopies as you submit them.
- Type the form if possible. If it has lots of little lines that are hard to type within, type the information on a piece of blank paper that will fit in the space, paste the paper over the form, and photocopy the finished product. Such a procedure results in a much neater, easier to read page.
- Leave no blanks; enter n/a (for "not applicable") when the information requested does not apply to you; this tells people checking the form that you did not simply skip the question.

- Carry a resumé and a copy of other frequently asked information (such as previous addresses) with you when visiting potential employers in case you must fill out an application on the spot. Whenever possible, however, fill the form out at home and return it with a resumé and a cover letter that point up your strengths.

When all your choices are complete, you will have the information about yourself that you need to evaluate your potential job satisfaction in a new field or in an old one. You should also have a good start on sorting out the skills you wish to emphasize in your resumé. Look at the resumés reproduced in this section, not only for format, but for possible headings and action verbs. Note that the skill resumés include a chronology too.

If you want additional help on analyzing your skills and different jobs, your local library has a wealth of information. You may want to consult *What Color Is Your Parachute?* by Richard N. Bolles. It is revised frequently and published in both paperback and hardback editions by Ten Speed Press. The same author has written *The New Quick Job Hunting Map* (revised 1990; Ten Speed Press).

There are a number of books on writing winning resumés including the very helpful *Jeff Allen's Best: The Resumé* by Jeffrey G. Allen (New York: John Wiley & Sons, 1990). This is part of a down-to-earth paperback series that also includes *Jeff Allen's Best: Get the Interview* and *Jeff Allen's Best: Win the Job*.

FOREIGN WORDS AND PHRASES

In a language like English, whose vocabulary is at least 80 percent borrowed from other language sources, it is not always easy to judge whether a word or expression should be considered as "foreign" or "naturalized." The choice is easier when it comes to full sentences and sayings. The chief sources of our foreign words and phrases are French and Latin. Other heavy contributors are Italian (particularly for musical terms), German, Greek, and Spanish. But English is a ready borrower and adapter, and we find in our list contributions from other European languages (Russian, Dutch, Scandinavian, Portuguese, etc.); from Semitic tongues, such as Hebrew and Arabic; from languages of Asia, such as Japanese, Chinese, Persian, and Turkish; from the tongues of the American Indians; and even from languages of the far Pacific, notably Hawaiian.

In each case, we have given the pronunciation of the word or expression with an approximation to the language of origin, even where usage has established a current English pronunciation; for instance, while there is a current English pronunciation of a Latin term like *bona fide*, our transcription approximates the sound of the original Latin because the current pronunciation is already commonly known.

The system of transcription is for the most part self-explanatory. Place the stress on the syllable that appears in capitals. Pronounce: *ah* like the *a* in *father*; *eh* like the *e* in *met*; *eye* as in *eye*; *oh* like the *o* in *or*; *oo* as in *fool*; *ee* as in *seen*; *ow* as in *fowl*; *zh* like the *s* in *pleasure*; *aw* as in *awe*; *ay* as in *lay*.

In French words, *āh, ēh, āw, ūh* represent the four French nasal sounds of *an, vin, on, un,* respectively; shut off completely the passage between nose and mouth, so that your breath-stream is forced into the nose, and pronounce at the same time *ah, eh, aw, uh*. The transcription *ö* represents a sound halfway between the *e* of *met* and the *o* of *or* (for which the French spelling is *eu* or *oeu*); the transcription *ü* represents a sound intermediate between the *oo* of *fool* and the *ee* of *seen* (purse lips for *oo*, and try to say *ee*). In German words, *kh* represents the sound of *ch* in *ach,* ç, the sound of *ch* in *ich* (the nearest English approximately is the *h* of *huge*).

Abbreviations for the names of the source language are as follows:

F	French	J	Japanese
L	Latin	Ch	Chinese
It	Italian	Du	Dutch
Sp	Spanish	Pers	Persian
G	German	Swed	Swedish
Pt	Portuguese	Yid	Yiddish
R	Russian	Arab	Arabic
Gk	Greek	Turk	Turkish
Sk	Sanskrit	Hind	Hindi
Heb	Hebrew	Norw	Norwegian

Other languages of rare occurrence (Hungarian, Irish, Welsh, Icelandic, Basque, Egyptian, Hawaiian, etc.) are left unabbreviated.

The translations given are sometimes literal, but more often aim at rendering the meaning of the foreign word or expression.

The italicized words and expressions are still considered "foreign." These words should be underlined in the original manuscript and italicized when printed. Not all authorities will agree with this list. When you "naturalize" a word or phrase, be prepared to defend your act. A quick rule to follow is: If the word or phrase does not appear in one of the major dictionaries, then it is still "foreign."

A

à bon marché (a bāw mar-SHAY), cheap, a bargain (F)

a cappella (ah kahp-PEHL-lah), church style, without accompaniment (It)

accelerando (ah-chay-lay-RAHN-doh), with increasing speed (It)

achtung (AKH-toong), attention (G)

adagio (ah-DAH-joh), slowly (It)

ad astra per aspera (ahd AH-strah pehr AH-speh-rah), to the stars through difficult places (L)

addendum (ahd-DEHN-doom) (pl. **addenda,** ahd-DEHN-dah), to be added (L)

adeste fideles (ah-DEHS-teh fee-DEH-lehs), Come, ye faithful (L)

ad hoc (ahd HOHK), for this, for this purpose (L)

Complete Guide to Speech, Style and Grammar

adieu (a-DYÖ), farewell, good-bye (F)

ad infinitum (ahd een-fee-NEE-toom), to infinity, on and on (L)

adiós (ah-DYOHS), farewell, good-bye (Sp)

ad lib(itum) (ahd LEE-bee-toom), at pleasure (usually abbr. ad lib) (L)

ad nauseam (ahd NOW-seh-ahm), to the point of disgust (L)

ad rem (ahd REHM), to the thing, pertinent (L)

ad valorem (ahd wah-LOH-rehm), in proportion to value or valuation (L)

affaire de coeur (a-FEHR duh KÖR), love affair (F)

affaire d'honneur (a-FEHR daw-NÖR), matter involving honor (F)

aficionado (ah-fee-thyoh-NAH-doh), fan, enthusiast (Sp)

a fortiori (ah fohr-tee-OH-ree), with greater reason, all the more (L)

agenda (ah-GHEHN-dah), things to be done (L)

agent provocateur (a-ZHÄH praw-vaw-ka-TÖR), one who provokes others into unlawful actions (F)

agio (AH-joh), ease; currency differential (It)

Agnus Dei (AHG-noos DEH-ee), Lamb of God (L)

agora (AH-goh-rah), marketplace (Gk)

aguardiente (ah-gwahr-DYEHN-teh), firewater, brandy (Sp)

aide-de-camp (EHD duh KÄH), field aide, assistant (F)

à la (a la), in the fashion (à la française, French style) (F)

à la carte (a la KART), according to the menu, picking out individual items (F)

alameda (ah-lah-MEH-dah), poplar grove (Sp)

à la mode (a la MAWD), in the fashion (F)

alcázar (ahl-KAH-thahr), fortress, fortified palace (Arab-Sp)

al fresco (ahl FRAYS-koh), in the open air (It)

alias (AH-lee-ahs), otherwise, at another time (L)

alibi (AH-lee-bee), elsewhere (L)

allegro (ahl-LAY-groh), quick, lively, merry (It)

alma mater (AHL-mah MAH-tehr), fostering mother, school or college (L)

aloha oe (ah-LOH-hah OH-eh), farewell to you (Hawaiian)

alpenstock (AHL-pen-shtok), iron-tipped staff used in mountain climbing (G)

alpha-omega (AHL-fah OH-may-gah), beginning and end (Gk)

alter ego (AHL-tehr EH-goh), another self, close and inseparable friend (L)

alto (AHL-toh), low female voice (used for *contralto,* "counter high") (It)

alumnus, alumna; pl. -ni, -nae (ah-LOOM-noos, ah-LOOM-nah; -neye; -nee), male, female graduate of an institution (L)

amabile (ah-MAH-bee-lay), amiable, pleasing (It)

amicus curiae (ah-MEE-koos KOO-ree-eye), friend of the court (L)

amour propre (a-MOOR PRAW-pruh), self-love, pride (F)

ancien régime (āh-SYĒH ray-ZHEEM), old, prerevolutionary regime (F)

angst (AHNXT), anxiety (G)

animato (ah-nee-MAH-toh), animated, with spirit (It)

anno Domini (AHN-no DOH-mee-nee), in the year of our Lord (abbr. A.D.) (L)

anschluss (AHN-shloos), annexation, union (G)

ante bellum (AHN-teh BEHL-loom), before the war (L)

ante meridiem (AHN-teh meh-REE-dee-ehm), abbr. A.M.; before noon, morning (L)

antipasto (ahn-tee-PAH-stoh), appetizer, hors d'oeuvre (It)

apartheid (a-PART-hayt), South African policy of racial segregation (Du)

apéritif (a-pay-ree-TEEF), appetizer, before-meal drink (F)

aplomb (a-PLAW̄), self-possession, poise (F)

a posteriori (ah pohs-teh-ree-OH-ree), with hindsight, reasoning backwards from observed facts (L)

appassionato (ahp-pahs-syoh-NAH-toh), passionately (It)

Après moi le déluge! (a-PREH MWAH luh day-LÜZH), after me the deluge, I don't care what happens after I'm gone (F)

a priori (ah pree-OH-ree), reaching conclusions before gathering facts (L)

apropos (a praw-POH), opportunely, by the way, with regard to (F)

aquavit (ah-kwah-VEET), brandy (Swedish, from Latin *aqua vitae,* water of life)

arbiter elegantiarum (AHR-bee-tehr eh-leh-gahn-tee-AH-room), arbiter of style or taste (L)

argot (ar-GOH), slang, thieves' cant (F)

argumentum ad hominem (ahr-goo-MEHN-toom ahd HOH-mee-nehm), diversion of a discussion to the personality of the opponent (L)

aria (AH-ryah), vocal solo passage in an opera (It)

---

arista (AH-rees-tah), the best, honors group in a high school (Gk)

arpeggio (ahr-PAY-joh), notes of chord played in harplike succession (It)

arroz con pollo (ahr-ROHTH kohn POH-lyoh), chicken with rice and condiments (Sp)

ars gratia artis (AHRS GRAH-tee-ah AHR-tees), art for art's sake (L)

ars longa, vita brevis (AHRS LOHN-gah, WEE-tah BREH-wees), art is long, but life is fleeting (L)

attaché (a-ta-SHAY), diplomatic official attached to an embassy (F)

au courant (oh koo-RĀH), posted, informed (F)

auf wiedersehen (owf VEE-duhr-zayn), good-bye, till we meet again (G)

au gratin (oh gra-TĒH), baked with crumbs or cheese on top (F)

au jus (oh ZHÜ), in its natural juice or gravy (F)

aurea mediocritas (OW-ray-ah meh-dee-OH-kree-tahs), the golden mean (L)

au revoir (oh ruh-VWAHR), good-bye, till we meet again (F)

aurora borealis (ow-ROH-rah boh-ray-AH-lees), the northern lights (L)

aut Caesar aut nullus (owt KEYE-sahr owt NOOL-loos), either everything or nothing (L)

autobahn (OW-toh-bahn), automobile highway (G)

auto da fé (OW-toh dah FEH), burning at the stake on a charge of heresy (Pt)

avant-garde (a-VĀH-GAHRD), in the van or forefront (F)

Ave atque vale! (AH-weh AHT-kweh WAH-leh), hail and farewell (L)

Ave Caesar, morituri te salutamus (AH-weh KEYE-sahr, moh-ree-TOO-ree teh sah-loo-TAH-moos), Hail, Caesar, we who are about to die salute you (L)

Ave Maria (AH-weh mah-REE-ah), Hail, Mary (L)

à votre santé! (a VAW-truh SĀH-tay), to your health! (F)

ayatollah (eye-uh-TOH-luh), religious leaders in the Shiite Muslim hierarchy second only to the *imans* (Pers)

B

babushka (BAH-boosh-kuh), scarf over the head, tied under the chin "little grandmother" fashion (R) *baklava* (or *paklava*) (bah-KLAH-vah), Turkish pastry made with nuts and honey (Turkish)

bakshish (BAHK-sheesh), tip, money, bribe (Pers)

balalaika (buh-luh-LEYE-kuh), three-stringed triangular guitar (R)

bambino (bahm-BEE-noh), baby, child (It)

banderilla (bahn-deh-REE-lyah), dart with streamer used in bull-fight (Sp)

banzai (BAHN-zeye), cheer or battle cry, "ten thousand years" (J)

bar mitzva (BAHR-MEETS-vah), confirmation ceremony (Heb)

baroque (ba-RAWK), irregular in shape, over-ornamental (F)

barrio (BAH-ree-oh), district (now an Hispanic neighborhood in a city where Hispanics are a minority) (Sp)

bas-relief (bah-ruh-LYEHF), sculpture with figures projecting from background (F)

basso profundo (BAHS-soh proh-FOON-doh), deep bass voice (It-L)

bathos (BAH-thos), false pathos; an anticlimax (Gk)

beau geste (BOH ZHEHST), fine gesture or deed (F)

beau monde (BOH MAWD), high society (F)

beaux arts (BOH-ZAHR), fine arts (F)

béchamel (bay-sha-MEHL), rich white sauce (F)

bel canto (behl KAHN-toh), fine singing (It)

belladonna (behl-lah-DAWN-nah), lovely lady, poisonous plant, eye-drug (It)

belles-lettres (behl-LEH-truh), literature, the humanities (F)

berceuse (behr-SÜZ), cradle-song, lullaby (F)

béret (bay-REH), flat, round cap (F)

bête noire (BEHT NWAHR), black beast, pet abomination (F)

bêtise (beh-TEEZ), foolish act or word (F)

beurre noir (BÖR NWAHR), black butter sauce (F)

billet-doux (bee-YEH DOO), love note or letter (F)

bisque (BEESK), rich soup (F)

bistro (bee-STROH), cabaret, wine shop (F)

blanc mange (BLAH MAHZH), white pudding (F)

blasé (bla-ZAY), jaded, satiated, bored (F)

blintzi (BLEEN-tsy), cheese or meat wrapped in pancake (Yid)

blitzkreig (BLITZ-kreek), lightning war; swift, sudden attack (G)

B'nai B'rith (BNEYE BREETH), sons of the covenant, Jewish service organization (Heb)

Complete Guide to Speech, Style and Grammar

bocce (BAW-chay), an Italian bowling game (It)

boeuf á la mode (BÖF a la MAWD), larded and pot-roasted beef (F)

Boer (BOOR), peasant or settler in South Africa (Du)

bohême (boh-EHM), gypsy-like, unconventional living (F)

bolero (boh-LEH-roh), a Spanish dance (Sp)

Bolsheviki (buhl'-shuh-vee-KEE), Maximalists, Lenin-led Communists (R)

bombe glacée (BAWB gla-SAY), frozen dessert (F)

bona fide (BOH-nah FEE-day), in good faith (L)

bon ami (BAW-na-MEE), good friend (F)

bonanza (boh-NAHN-thah), windfall, run of luck (Sp)

bonbon (Baw-BAW), candy (F)

bon gré mal gré (baw-GRAY mal-GRAY), willy-nilly (F)

bon jour, bon soir (baw zhur, baw swahr), good morning, good evening (F)

bon marché (baw mar-SHAY) (*see* à bon marché)

bon mot (baw MOH), witticism (F)

bon vivant (baw-vee-VAH), one who likes to live well (F)

bon voyage (baw-vwa-YAHZH), a happy trip (F)

borsch (BAWRSHCH), Russian beet soup, usually with sour cream (R)

boudoir (boo-DWAHR), lady's private sitting room (F)

bouffant (boo-FAH), puffed out, full (F)

bouillabaisse (boo-ya-BEHS), seafood soup (F)

bourgeoisie (boor-zhwah-ZEE), middle class (F)

bravo, brava (BRAH-voh, BRAH-vah), cry of approval; hired killer (It)

brie (BREE), a creamy French cheese (F)

brioche (bree-AWSH), bun, light roll (F)

brut (BRÜ), raw, unadulterated (F)

bund (BOONT), league; union, organization (G)

bushido (BOO-shee-doh), code of honor of *samurai* class (J)

C

ca. See *circa*

cabala, kabala (kahb-ah-LAH), Hebrew occult religious philosophy (Heb)

---

cacciatora (kah-chah-TOH-rah), hunter style (It); more properly *alla cacciatora*

caciocavallo (kah-choh-kah-VAHL-loh), piquant Italian cheese (It)

cacique (kah-THEE-kay), American Indian chief, political leader (Carib-Sp)

caesura (keye-SOO-rah), break in line of poetry (L)

café (ka-FAY), coffee shop, saloon (F); —**au lait** (oh LEH), coffee with milk; —**noir** (NWAHR), black coffee

caffè espresso (kah-FEH ays-PREHS-soh), strong black coffee, machine-made (It)

calvados (kal-va-DOHS), apple brandy from the French region of the same name (F)

camaraderie (ka-ma-rad-REE), loyalty, comradeship, good fellowship (F)

camarilla (ka-mah-REE-lyah), clique, group of special advisors (Sp)

camembert (ka-māh-BEHR), a soft French cheese (F)

camino real (kah-MEE-noh reh-AHL), royal or main highway (Sp)

camorra (kah-MAWR-rah), Neapolitan secret society (It)

campanile (kahm-pah-NEE-lay) bell tower (It)

campesino (kahm-peh-SEE-noh), rustic, peasant (Sp)

campo santo (KAHM poh SAIIN-toh), graveyard, cemetery (It)

canaille (ka-NA-yuh), rabble (F)

canapé (ka-na-PAY), open sandwich served as appetizer (F)

canard (ka-NAHR), duck, hoax (F)

canasta (kah-NAHS-tah), basket, card game (Sp)

cannelloni (kahn-nayl-LOH-nee), large hollow macaroni stuffed with meat (It)

cantabile (kahn-TAH-bee-lay), singable, in singing style (It)

cantata (kahn-TAH-tah), musical composition for solos or choruses (It)

canton (kāh-TĀW), political subdivision of Switzerland (F)

cap-à-pied (ka-pa-PYEH), head-to-foot armor (F)

capriccio (kah-PREE-choh), free musical composition, caprice (It)

carabiniere (kah-rah-bee-NYEH-ray), Italian military policeman (It)

carioca (kah-RYOH-kah), native of Rio; Brazilian dance (Pt)

carpe diem (KAHR-peh DEE-ehm), "seize the day"; make hay while the sun shines (L)

Complete Guide to Speech, Style and Grammar

carte blanche (KART BLĀHSH), free hand; authorization to act as one will (F)

cartel (kar-TEHL), monopoly trust; organized group of business interests (F)

cartouche (kar-TOOSH), cartridge; oval space for inscription of name of Egyptian Pharaoh (F)

casus belli (KAH-soos BEHL-lee), occurrence giving rise to war (L)

caudillo (kow-DEE-lyoh), chief, leader (Sp)

cause célèbre (KOHZ say-LEH-bruh), famous or sensational trial (F)

causerie (kohz-REE), chat, informal talk (F)

cavatina (kah-vah-TEE-nah), short song (It)

caveat (KAH-weh-aht), let (him) beware (L); —**emptor** (EHMP-tohr), let the buyer beware

cave canem (KAH-weh KAH-nehm), beware of the dog (L)

certiorari (kehr-tee-oh-RAH-ree), "to be ascertained"; writ to procure records (L)

c'est-à-dire (seh-ta-DEER), that is to say (F)

c'est la vie (seh-la-VEE), that's life (F)

ceteris paribus (KEH-teh-rees PAH-ree-boos), other things being equal (L)

chacun à son goût (sha-KŪH a-sāw-GOO), everyone to his taste (F)

chacun pour soi (sha-KŪH poor SWAH), every man for himself (F)

chaise longue (SHEHZ LĀWG), reclining chair or sofa (F)

champignon (shāh-pee-NYAW̄), mushroom (F)

chanteuse (shāh-TŌZ), female singer (F)

chargé d'affaires (shar-ZHAY da-FEHR), minor government official temporarily replacing a higher diplomat (F)

charivari (sha-ree-va-REE), mock serenade or raucous music (F)

chasseur (sha-SÖR), hunter; light-infantryman; footman (F)

château (sha-TOH), castle, palace (F)

chef (de cuisine) (SHEF duh kwee-ZEEN), head cook (F)

chef d'oeuvre (SHEH DÖ-vruh), masterpiece (F)

Cherchez la femme! (shehr-SHAY la FAM), look for the woman in the case (F)

chérie (shay-REE), dearie, sweetheart (F)

chevaux-de-frise (shuh-VÖH duh FREEZ), barrier of spikes in timber (F)

chez (SHAY), at the home of (F)

chianti (KYAHN-tee), Italian wine (It)

chiaroscuro (kyah-roh-SKOO-roh), light and dark effect (It)

chic (SHEEK), elegant, elegance (F)

cid (THEED), chieftain, leader (Sp, from Arab *sayyid*)

ci-git (see-ZHEE), here lies (F)

cinquecento (cheen-kway-CHEHN-toh), 16th century (It)

circa (KEER-kah), about, approximately; abbr. ca. (L)

civis Romanus sum (Kee-wees roh-MAH-noos SOOM), I am a Roman citizen (L)

Civitas Dei (KEE-wee-tahs DEH-ee), the City of God (L)

clair de lune (KLEHR duh LÜN), moonlight (F)

claret (kla-REH), light red wine (F)

clef (KLAY or KLEHF), key (F)

clique (KLEEK), set; group (F)

clôture (kloh-TÜR), closure of debate (F)

cocido (koh-THEE-doh), Spanish stew (Sp)

coda (KOH-dah), tail; concluding musical passage (It)

Code Napoléon (KAWD na-poh-lay-ÄW), code of civil law of France of 1804, applied with modifications in Louisiana (F)

codex (KOH-dehks), body of laws; manuscript on parchment (L)

cogito, ergo sum (KOH-ghee-toh, EHR-goh SOOM), I think, therefore I exist (L)

cognac (kaw-NYAK), French brandy (F)

cognoscenti (erroneous for *conoscenti*, koh-noh-SHEHN-tee), experts (It)

coiffeur (kwa-FÖR), hairdresser (F)

coiffure (kwa-FUR), hairstyle (F)

coloratura (koh-loh-rah-TOO-rah), embellishment in vocal music; soprano (It)

commando (koh-MAHN-doh), raiding troops (Du, from Pt)

comme ci, comme ca (kawm SEE, kawm SA), so-so (F)

comme il faut (kawm eel FOH), proper; properly; in the right fashion (F)

commedia dell'arte (kohm-MEH-dyah dayl-LAHR-tay), guild players' comedy, often improvised (It)

commissar (kuhm-mee-SAHR), government official (R, from F *commissaire*)

communiqué (kaw-mu-nee-KAY), official statement or dispatch (F)

compote (käw-PAWT), stewed fruit (F)

Complete Guide to Speech, Style and Grammar

con amore (kohn ah-MOH-ray), lovingly (It)

concerto (kohn-CHEHR-toh), musical composition for solo instrument(s) with orchestral accompaniment (It)

concierge (käw-SYEHRZH), janitor, superintendent (F)

concordat (käw-kawr-DAH), pact, agreement (F from Latin *concordatus*)

condottiere (kohn-doht-TYEH-ray), Italian Renaissance leader of mercenary troops (It)

confetti (kohn-FEHT-tee), candies; plaster or paper imitations used at feasts (It)

confrère (käw-FREHR), colleague; associate (F)

conga (KAWN-gah), Latin-American dance (Sp or Pt)

con moto (kohn MAW-toh), with movement; fast (It)

connoisseur (kaw-neh-SÖR), expert; one who knows (F)

conquistadores (kohn-kees-tah-DOH-rehs), conquerors (Sp)

console (käw-SAWL), ornamental bracket for supporting shelf; table with ledges (F)

consommé (käw-saw-MAY), concentrated meat broth (F)

consortium (kohn-SOHR-tee-oom), international finance control group (L)

contra (KOHN-trah), against (abbr. con; L)

contrabasso (kohn-trah-BAHS-soh), double-bass viol (It)

copula (KOH-poo-lah), connective; the verb "to be" or a similar verb (L)

coq au vin (KAWK oh VĒH), chicken braised in wine (F)

coquetterie (kaw-keht-REE), flirtatiousness (F)

coram populo (KOH-rahm POH-poo-loh), publicly (L)

cordillera (kohr-dee-LYEH-rah), mountain range (Sp)

cornu copiae (KOHR-noo KOH-pee-eye), horn of plenty (L)

corona (koh-ROH-nah), crown (L)

corps de ballet (KAWR duh ba-LEH), ballet troupe (F)

corpus (KOHR-poos), body; collection (L)

corpus delicti (KOHR-poss deh-LEEK-tee), the body or tangible evidence of a crime (L)

corpus juris (KOHR-poos YOO-rees), the body of the law; collection of laws (L)

corrida (kohr-REE-dah), bullfight (Sp)

corrigenda (kohr-ree-GHEHN-dah), things to be corrected (L)

cortège (kawr-TEHZH), procession (F)

corvée (kawr-VAY), forced labor (F)

cosi cosi (koh-SEE koh-SEE), so-so (It)

coterie (kawt-REE), small, intimate group or circle (F)

coup de grâce (KOO-duh GRAHS), death-blow (F)

coup de main (KOO duh MĒH), sudden blow (F)

coup d'état (KOO day-TAH), seizure of government by sudden stroke (F)

couturier (koo-tü-RYAY), dressmaker (F)

crèche (KREHSH), crib, manger, public nursery (F)

credenza (kray-DEHN-tsah), small table or cupboard (It)

credo (KREH-doh), belief, article of faith, creed (L)

crème de menthe (KREHM duh MĀHT), peppermint liqueur (F)

crêpe (KREHP), thin cloth of silk, rayon, wool, etc. (F)

crêpe suzette (KREHP sü-ZEHT), thin pancake (F)

crescendo (kray-SHEHN-doh), gradual increase in loudness or intensity (It)

critique (kree-TEEK), criticism (F)

croissant (krwa-SĀH), crescent-shaped roll (F)

Croix de Guerre (KRWAH duh GHEHR), war cross, French military decoration (F)

croquette (kraw-KEHT), fried meat or fish, covered with bread crumbs (F)

croupier (kroo-PYAY), man who rakes in stakes at gambling table (F)

crux (KROOKS), cross; main point at issue (L)

cucaracha (koo-kah-RAH-chah), cockroach (Sp)

cui bono? (KOO-ee BOH-noh), to whose advantage? (L)

cul-de-sac (KÜL-duh-SAHK), blind alley, dead end (F)

cum grano salis (koom GRAH-noh SAH-lees), with a grain of salt (L)

cum laude (koom LOW-deh), with praise, with honor (L)

curé (kü-RAY), parish priest (F)

curriculum (koor-REE-koo-loom), year's course of studies (L); —**vitae** (WEE-teye), outline of one's life

czar (more precisely *tsar*, TSAHR), Russian emperor, autocrat (R)

czardas (more precisely *csárdás*, CHAHR-dahsh), Hungarian dance (Hungarian)

D

da capo (dah KAH-poh), from the start (It)

dal segno (dahl SAY-nyoh), from the sign (It)

décolleté (day-kawl-TAY), low-necked (F)

de facto (deh FAHK-toh), in existence, in actuality (L)

de gustibus non est disputandum (deh GOOS-tee-boos nohn EHST dees-poo-TAHN-doom), there is no arguing about tastes (L)

Dei gratia (DEH-ee GRAH-tee-ah), by the grace of God (L)

déjeuner (day-zhö-NAY), lunch, breakfast (F)

déjà vu (day-zhah VUE), a sense of having seen before (F)

de jure (deh YOO-reh), legally, legitimately (L)

dele (DEH-leh), erase, strike out, delete; abbreviation (L)

démarche (day-MAHRSH), diplomatic approach, step (F)

dementia praecox (deh-MEHN-tee-ah PREYE-kohks), adolescent mental illness (L)

demi-tasse (duh-MEE-TAHS), small cup of coffee (F)

demi-monde (duh-MEE-MAWD), fringe of society (F)

de mortuis nihil nisi bonum (deh MOHR-too-ees NEE-heel NEE-see BOH-noom), say nothing but good about the dead (L)

denarius (deh-NAH-ree-oos), Roman silver coin (L)

denier (duh-NYAY), small coin, unit of weight for hosiery (F)

dénouement (day-noo-MÃH), unraveling, solution of plot (F)

de novo (deh NOH-voh), anew, again from the start (L)

Deo volente (DEH-oh woh-LEHN-teh), God willing (L)

de profundis (deh proh-FOON-dees), out of the depths (L)

de rigueur (duh ree-GÖR), indispensable, required (F)

dernier cri (dehr-NYAY KREE), latest style, last word (F)

(los) desaparecidos (los dehs-ah-PAH-reh-SEE-dohs), the disappeared, those kidnapped and presumably murdered by the Argentine junta which overthrew Isabel Perón (Sp)

descamisado (dehs-kah-mee-SAH-doh), shirtless; follower of Evita Perón (Sp)

déshabillé (day-za-bee-YAY), in state of informal undress (F)

desideratum (deh-see-deh-RAH-toom; pl. **desiderata,** deh-see-deh-RAH-tah), what is desired (L)

détente (day-TÃHT), release of strained relations (F)

de trop (duh TROH), in excess, superfluous, not wanted (F) *deus ex machina* (DEH-oos ehks MAH-kee-nah), outside intervention to solve a crisis (L)

Deus vobiscum (DEH-oos woh-BEES-koom), God be with you (L)

diaspora (dee-AHS-poh-rah), dispersion, scattering (particularly of Jews after destruction of Jerusalem) (Gk)

dictum (DEEK-toom), saying, pronouncement (L)

diminuendo (dee-mee-noo-EHN-doh), diminishing in volume (It)

dirndl (DEERNDL), peasant-girl dress (G)

diseur (fem. diseuse; dee-ZÖR, dee-ZÖZ), monologist (F)

diva (DEE-vah), female opera singer (It)

divertissement (dee-vehr-tees-MAH), lively piece between acts (F)

divide et impera (dee-WEE-deh eht EEM-peh-rah), divide and conquer (L)

doge (DAW-jay), medieval ruler of Venice (It)

dogma (DOHG-mah), belief, article of faith (Gk)

dolce far niente (DOHL-chay FAHR NYEHN-tay), sweet idleness (It)

dolce stil nuovo (DOHL-chay STEEL NWAW-voh), sweet new literary style of 14th century (It)

Dominus vobiscum (DOH-mee-noos woh-BEES-koom), the Lord be with you (L)

don (DOHN), tutor at English universities; Spanish and Italian title of respect, Mafia leader (It, Sp)

donna (DAWN-nah), lady, woman (It)

doppelgänger (DOH-pehl-gheng-uhr), ghostly double (G)

dossier (daw-SYAY), file (F)

double entendre (DOO-bläh-TĀH-druh), expression with double meaning (F)

dramatis personae (DRAH-mah-tees pehr-SOH-neye), cast of characters (L)

droshky (DRAWSH-kee), cab, carriage (R)

duce (DOO-chay), leader (It)

dueña (DWEH-nyah), chaperone (Sp)

duomo (DWAW-moh), cathedral (It)

dybbuk (DEE-book), bewitched person; evil spirit entering living body (Heb)

E

eau de vie (OH duh VEE), brandy (F)

ecce homo (EHK-keh HOH-moh), behold the man (L)

échelon (aysh-LĀW), steplike formation of troops, any hierarchical arrangement (F)

éclat (ay-KLAH), success, prestige (F)

Edda (EHD-dah), old Scandinavian poetry (Icelandic)

edelweiss (AY-duhl-veyes), white Alpine flower (G)

editio princeps (eh-DEE-tee-oh PREEN-kehps), original edition (L)

eisteddfod (ay-STETH-vohd), musical or poetic contest (Welsh)

élan (ay-LĀH), sparkle, liveliness (F)

el dorado (ehl doh-RAH-doh), fabulous South American land of gold (Sp)

Eli (EH-lee), my God (Heb)

Elohim (eh-loh-HEEM), God, Supreme Being (Heb)

embarras du choix (āh-ba-RAH dü SHWAH), trouble making up one's mind (F)

embonpoint (āh-baw-PWĒH), plumpness (F)

emeritus (eh-MEH-ree-toos), retired with honor (L)

émigré (ay-mee-GRAY), emigrated, exiled (F)

en bloc (āh BLAWK), together; as a unit (F)

en brochette (āh braw-SHEHT), on a skewer (F)

enceinte (āh-SĒHT), pregnant, with child (F)

en coquille (āh kaw-KEE-yuh), served in a shell (F)

enfant gâté (terrible) (āh-FAH gah-TAY, teh-REE-bluh), spoiled child, brat (F)

en masse (āh MAHS), all together, in a mass (F)

ennui (āh-NWEE), boredom (F)

en passant (āh pa-SĀH), incidentally; by the way (F)

entente (āh-TĀHT), understanding; international agreement, alliance (F)

entr'acte (āh-TRAKT), between the acts (F)

entrée (āh-TRAY), entrance; main dish (F)

entre nous (āh-truh-NOO), between us (F)

envoi (āh-VWAH), postscript (F)

épater le bourgeois (ay-pa-TAY luh boor-ZHAWAH), to bedazzle and befuddle people (F)

epaulette (ay-poh-LEHT), shoulder piece (F)

e pluribus unum (eh PLOO-ree-boos OO-noom), one out of many (L)

ergo (EHR-goh), therefore, consequently (L)

Erin go bragh (EH-reen goh BRAH), Ireland forever (Ir)

errare humanum est (ehr-RAH-reh hoo-MAH-noom EHST), to err
  is human (L)

erratum (pl. **errata**; ehr-RAH-toom, ehr-RAH-tah), error, mistake
  (L)

ersatz (EHR-zatz), substitute, synthetic (G)

escargots (ehs-kar-GOH), snails (F)

espada (ehs-PAH-dah), sword; the matador who kills the bull with a
  sword (Sp)

esprit de corps (ehs-PREE duh KAWR), spirit of loyalty to one's
  group (F)

et alii (eht AH-lee-ee); abbr. et. al., and others (L)

et cetera (eht KEYE-teh-rah); abbr. etc., and others, and other
  things (L)

ethos (EH-thos), custom, national character (Gk)

et passim (eht PAHS-seem), abbr. et pass., and everywhere, scattered throughout a work (L)

et tu Brute? (eht TOO, BROO-teh), you, too, Brutus? (L)

étude (ay-TÜD), study; short musical composition (F)

et uxor (eht OOK-sohr), abbr. et ux., and wife (L)

eureka! (EH-OO-reh-kah), I have found it! (Gk)

ewig weibliche (AY-vik VEYEB-li-çe), eternal feminine (G)

ex cathedra (ehks KAH-theh-droh), authoritatively, pontifically (L)

excelsior (ehks-KEHL-see-ohr), ever higher (L)

exempli gratia (ehk-SEHM-plee GRAH-tee-ah), abbr. e.g., for instance (L)

ex libris (ehks LEE-brees), from among the books of (L)

ex officio (ehks ohf-FEE-kee-oh), by virtue of his office (L)

ex nihilo (ehks NEE-hee-loh), out of nothing (L)

exposé (ehks-paw-ZAY), statement, explanation, revelation (F)

ex post facto (ehks pohst FAHK-toh), after the fact (L)

ex tempore (ehks TEHM-poh-reh), without previous preparation (L)

ex voto (ehks WOH-toh), as a vow; tablet or inscription recording an
  accomplished vow (L)

F

fait accompli (FEH-ta-kolaw-PLEE), thing already done (F)

falsetto (fahl-SAYT-toh), excessively high tone (It)

Complete Guide to Speech, Style and Grammar

fandango (fahn-DAHN-goh), Spanish dance (Sp)

farina (fah-REE-nah), flour or meal (L)

faute de mieux (FOHT duh MYÖ), for lack of anything better (F)

faux pas (FOH PAH), false step, blunder (F)

feis (FAYS), Irish song festival (Ir)

femme de chambre (FAM duh SHĀH-bruh), chambermaid (F)

femme fatale (FAM fa-TAL), enchantress, "vamp" (F)

festina lente (fehs-TEE-nah LEHN-teh), make haste slowly (L)

festschrift (FEHST-shrift), memorial or commemorative volume (G)

fiacre (FYA-kruh), cab (F)

fiancé, fiancée (fyāh-SAY), male, female who is engaged to be married (F)

fiasco (FYAHS-koh), failure (It)

fiat (FEE-aht), administrative order without legislative authorization (L)

fiesta (FYEHSH-tah), festival (Sp)

filet mignon (fee-LEH mee-NYĀW), tenderloin steak (F)

film noir (feelm NWARH), dark, mystery movies of the late 1950s (F)

financière (fee-nāh-SYEHR), spicy stew (F)

fin de siècle (FĒH duh SYEH-kluh), end of the century; decadence (F)

fine champagne (FEEN shāh-PAH-nyuh), brandy (F)

fines herbes (FEEN ZEHRB), minced chives, parsley, etc. (F)

finis (FEE-nees), end (L)

finocchio (fee-NAWK-kyoh), fennel (It)

flagrante delicto (flah-GRAHN-teh day-LIHK-toh), caught in the act (L)

fleur de lis (FLÖR duh LEE), lily emblem of France (F)

foie gras (FWAH GRAH), goose liver (F)

fondue (fāw-DÜ), melted cheese (F)

force majeure (FAWRS ma-ZHÖR), superior force (F)

fortissimo (fohr-TEES-see-moh), very loud (It)

foulard (foo-LAHR), neckerchief of silk fabric (F)

franc-tireur (frāh-tee-RÖR), sniper, guerrilla fighter (F)

frappé (fra-PAY), whipped, semifrozen (F)

frau (FROW), lady, madam, Mrs. (G)

fräulein (FROY-leyen), Miss, young lady (G)

fresco (FRAYS-koh), mural painting (It)

fricassé (free-ka-SAY), diced meat in thick sauce (F)

frijoles (free-HOH-lehs), kidney beans (Sp)

friseur (free-ZÖR), hairdresser (F)

fritos (FREE-tohs), fried potatoes, etc. (Sp)

fromage (fraw-MAZH), cheese (F)

führer (FÜ-ruhr), leader (G)

G

gabelle (ga-BEHL), salt tax (F)

gaffe (GAF), bad blunder (F)

gala (GAH-lah), festive (It)

garbanzos (gahr-BAHN-thohs), chick-peas (Sp)

garçon (gar-SĀW), boy, waiter (F)

garni (gar-NEE), garnished (F)

gâteau (gah-TOH), cake (F)

gaucherie (gohsh-REE), awkward or tactless action (F)

gaucho (GOW-choh), South American cowboy (Sp)

gaudeamus igitur (gow-deh-AH-moos EE-ghee-toor), let us there-fore rejoice (L)

gazpacho (gath-PAH-choh), Spanish cold soup (Sp)

gefilte fish (guh-FEEL-tuh FISH) stuffed fish (Yiddish)

geheime Staatspolizei (guh-HEYE-muh SHTATS-poh-lee-tseye), abbr. Gestapo; secret state police (G)

geisha (GAH-shah), Japanese professional female entertainer (J)

gemütlichkeit (guh-MÜT-liç-keyet), congeniality, coziness (G)

gendarme (zhäh-DARM), policeman, constable, state trooper (F)

generalissimo (jay-nay-rah-LEES-see-moh), general-in-chief (It)

genre (ZHĀHR), kind, sort, species (F)

gestalt (guh-SHTAHLT), shape, form, pattern (G)

gestapo (guh-STAH-poh), see geheime Staatspolizei

gesundheit (guh-ZOONT-heyet), (good) health (G)

gigolo (zhee-goh-LOH), man paid to be dancing partner or compan-ion (F)

glacé (gla-SAY), iced, sugared (F)

glasnost (GLAHZ-nohst), openness (R)

glissando (glees-SAHN-doh), gliding (F–It)

glockenspiel (GLOK-uhn-shpeel), carillon (G)

Complete Guide to Speech, Style and Grammar

gloria in excelsis Deo (GLOH-ree-ah een ehks-KEHL-sees DEH-oh), glory to God on high (L)

gnocchi (NYAWK-kee), flour or potato small dumplings (It)

golem (GOH-lehm), robot created for an evil purpose (Heb)

goniff (GOH-nif), thief (Yiddish)

gorgonzola (gohr-gohn-TSAW-lah), Italian green mold cheese (It)

Gott mit uns! (GAWT mit OONS), God is with us! (G)

Gott sei dank! (GAWT zeye DAHNK), thanks be to God (G)

goulash (more properly *gulyás,* GOO-LYAHSH), Hungarian meat stew (Hungarian)

goy (GOY) Gentile, non-Jewish (Heb)

graf (GRAHF), count (G)

grande dame (GRÄHD DAHM), great lady (F)

grand prix (GRÄH PREE), first prize (F)

granita (grah-NEE-tah), ice pudding (It)

gratin (gra-TĒH), dish prepared with cheese or bread crumbs (F)

gratis (GRAH-tees), free, without charge (L)

gringo (GREEN-goh), U.S. American (Sp)

gruyère (grü-YEHR), Swiss cheese (F)

guru (GOO-roo), teacher (Hindi)

gusto (GOOS-toh), taste, enjoyment (It)

H

habeas corpus (HAH-beh-ahs KOHR-poos), you may have the body; writ to bring someone into court (L)

hacienda (ah-THYEHN-dah), plantation (Sp)

Hadassah (hah-DAHS-sah), Jewish women's organization (Heb)

haiku (HEYE-koo), traditional Japanese verse of seventeen syllables (J)

hallelujah (hah-lay-LOO-yah), praise the Lord (Heb)

hanukkah (HAH-nook-kah), dedication, feast of lights (Heb)

hapax legomenon (HAH-pahks leh-GOH-meh-non), something said only once (Gk)

hara-kiri (HAH-rah-kee-ree), belly-cutting, ceremonial suicide (J)

haricots verts (ah-ree-KOH VEHR), green beans (F)

hasenpfeffer (HAH-zehn-pfef-fuhr), marinated hare (G)

Hasidim (khah-SEE-deem), Jewish religious sect (Heb)

haute couture (OHT koo-TÜR), group of high-fashion dress designers (F)

Foreign Words and Phrases

hegira (more properly *hijra,* HEEJ-rah), Mohammed's flight; escape; moving day (Arab)

heimweh (HEYEM-vay), homesickness (G)

hetaira, **hetaera** (HEH-teye-rah), courtesan (Gk)

hiatus (hee-AH-toos), split, break, gap (L)

hic jacet (HEEK YAH-keht), here lies (L)

hidalgo (ee-DAHL-goh), nobleman, man of gentle birth (Sp)

hierba maté (YEHR-bah mah-TEH), Paraguayan tea (Sp)

hodie mihi, cras tibi (HOH-dee-eh MEE-hee, KRAHS TEE-bee), today to me, tomorrow to you (L)

hoi polloi (hoy pohl-LOY), the many, rabble (Gk)

homard (aw-MAHR), lobster (F)

hombre (OHM-breh), man (Sp)

homo homini lupus (HOH-moh HOH-mee-nee LOO-poos), man is a wolf to his fellowman (L)

homo sapiens (HOH-moh SAH-pee-chns), man as a thinking animal; genus and species (written correctly: *Homo sapiens*) (L)

honni soit qui mal y pense (aw-NEE SWAH kee MAHL ee PĀHS), evil to him who evil thinks (F)

honoris causa (hoh-NOH-rees KOW-sah), bestowed in recognition of merit (L)

horribile dictu (hohr-REE-bee-leh DEEK-too), horrible to relate (L)

hors de combat (AWR duh kōh-BAH), disabled, out of the fight (F)

hors d'oeuvres (AWR DÖ-vruh), appetizers, relishes (F)

hôtel de ville (hoh-TEHL duh VEEL), town hall (F)

houri (HOO-ree), Mohammedan nymph of paradise (Pers)

hukilau (hoo-kee-LAH-OO), feast (Hawaiian)

hula-hula (HOO-lah-HOO-lah), Hawaiian dance (Hawaiian)

humanum est errare (hoo-MAH-noom EHST ehr-RAH-reh), to err is human (L)

hybris or **hubris** (HOO-brees), transgression of moral law; act of defiance (Gk)

hysteron proteron (HOOS-teh-rohn PROH-teh-rohn), putting the cart before the horse (Gk)

I

ibidem (ee-BEE-dehm), abbr. ibid.; in the same place (L)

idée fixe (ee-DAY FEEKS), preconceived notion (F)

Complete Guide to Speech, Style and Grammar

idem (EYED-ehm), same (L)

id est (EED EHST), abbr. i.e.; that is (L)

Iesus Nazarenus Rex Iudaeorum (YEH-soos nah-zah-REH-noos REHKS yoo-deye-OH-room), abbr. I.N.R.I.; Jesus of Nazareth King of the Jews (L)

ignis fatuus (EEG-nees FAH-too-oos), will-of-the-wisp (L)

illuminati (eel-loo-mee-NAH-tee), enlightened ones, deep thinkers (L)

imam (EYE-mahm), religious leader descended from Mohammed, prayer leader of a mosque (Arab)

imbroglio (eem-BRAW-lyoh), mix-up, mess (It)

impedimenta (eem-peh-dee-MEHN-tah), baggage, hindrances (L)

imprimatur (eem-pree-MAH-toor), license to print, sanction (L)

in absentia (een ahb-SEHN-tee-ah), in one's absence (L)

in articulo mortis (een ahr-TEE-koo-loh MOHR-tees), on the point of death (L)

in camera (een KAH-meh-rah), in chambers; in private (L)

incognito (een-KAW-nyee-toh), in disguise, not revealing one's identity (It)

incommunicado, (een-koh-moo-nee-KAH-doh), cut off from communication with the outside (Sp)

index expurgatorius (EEN-dehks ehks-poor-gah-TOH-ree-oos), list of forbidden books (L)

in esse (een EHS-seh), in being, existing (L)

in extenso (een ehks-TEHN-soh), in full (L)

in extremis (een ehks-TREH-mees), on the point of death (L)

influenza (een-floo-EHN-tsah), respiratory disease, flu (It)

in folio (een FOH-lee-oh), once-folded sheet of printing (L)

infra (EEN-frah), below (L)

ingénue (ēh-zhay-NÜ), innocent feminine character (F)

in hoc signo vinces (een hohk SEEG-noh WEEN-kehs), in this sign you will conquer (L)

in loco parentis (een-LOH-koh pah-REHN-tees), in the place of a parent (L)

in medias res (een MEH-dee-ahs REHS), into the thick of things, without introduction (L)

in memoriam (een meh-MOH-ree-ahm), in memory of (L)

innamorata, innamorato (een-nah-moh-RAH-toh), female, male lover (It) *in primis* (een PREE-mees), among the first (L)

in quarto (een KWAHR-toh), printing sheet folded twice (L)

in re (een REH), in the matter of (L)

in rem (een REHM), proceedings against a thing rather than a person (L)

in saecula saeculorum (een SEYE-koo-lah seye-koo-LOH-room), for ever and ever (L)

intaglio (een-TAH-lyoh), decoration cut into a stone (It)

integer vitae scelerisque purus (EEN-teh-ghehr WEE-teye skeh-leh-REES-kweh POO-roos), upright in life and free of guilt (L)

intelligentsia (een-tehl-lee-GHEHN-tsyah), informed intellectual people collectively (R)

inter alia (EEN-tehr AH-lee-ah), among other things (L)

inter alios (EEN-tehr AH-lee-ohs), among others (L)

intermezzo (een-tayr-MEH-dzoh), music played during intermission (It)

inter nos (EEN-tehr NOHS), between us (L)

in toto (een TOH-toh), completely, entirely (L)

intra muros (EEN-trah MOO-rohs), within the walls (L)

in vino veritas (een WEE-noh WEH-ree-tahs), in wine is the truth (L)

in vitro (een WEE-troh), in glass, in a test tube

ipse dixit (EEP-seh DEEK-seet), he himself said it; the master has spoken (L)

ipso facto (EEP-soh FAHK-toh), by the very fact (L)

ite, missa est (EE-teh, MEES-sah EHST), go, the service is finished (L)

izvestiya (eez-VYEHS-tee-yuh), news, information (R)

J

jai-alai (HAH-ee ah-LAH-ee), Basque ball game (Basque)

jardinière (zhar-dee-NYEHR), mixed vegetables; ornamental flower pot (F)

je ne sais quoi (zhuh nuh SEH KWAH), I don't know what (F)

jeu d'esprit (ZHÖ dehs-PREE), witticism (F)

jeunesse dorée (zhö-NEHS daw-RAY), gilded youth, elegant young people (F)

jihad (JEE-hahd), holy war (Arab)

Complete Guide to Speech, Style and Grammar

jinni (JEEN-nee), supernatural being that can take human shape (Arab)

jinrickisha (JEEN-REEK-shah), man-drawn two-wheeled cab (J)

jodhpur (JOHD-poor), a kind of riding breeches (Hind)

joie de vivre (ZHWAH duh VEE-vruh), joy of being alive (F)

jongleur (zhāw-GLÖR), ministrel, juggler (F)

judo (JOO-doh), Japanese system of self-defense (J)

jujutsu (JOO JOO-tsoo), see judo (J)

junta (HOON-tah), administrative council or committee (Sp)

Jupiter Pluvius (YOO-pee-tehr PLOO-wee-oos), Jupiter of the rain (L)

jus gentium (YOOS GHEHN-tee-oom), law of nations, international law (L)

K

ka (KAH), the soul (Egypt)

kabuki (KAH-boo-kee), Japanese form of drama (J)

kaddish (KAHD-deesh), prayer for the dead (Heb)

kaffeeklatsch (kahf-FAY-klahtch), gathering for coffee and chatting (G)

kamikaze (KAH-mee-kah-zeh), divine wind; suicide dive bomber (J)

kaput (kah-POOT), finished, done for (G)

karate (kah-RAH-teh), a style of fighting with bare hands and feet (J)

katzenjammer (KAHT-suhn-yahm-muhr), hangover; discordant noise (G)

kibbutz (keeb-BOOTS), Israeli collective farm settlement (Heb)

kibitzer (KIB-its-uhr), onlooker at game, offering unwanted advice; meddler (Yid)

kimono (KEE-moh-noh), Japanese outer garment with sash and loose sleeves (J)

kirsch, kirschwasser (KEERSH-VAHS-suhr), cherry brandy (G)

kismet (KEES-meht), fate, lot, will of Allah (Turk)

kitsch (KIHCH), trashy creation designed for popular taste (G)

Knesset (KNEHS-seht), unicameral Israeli parliament (Heb)

koine (koy-NAY), language common to a large area (Gk)

koinos topos (koy-NOHS toh-POHS), commonplace (Gk)

Foreign Words and Phrases

kolkhoz (kuhl-KHAWS), collective farm (R)

Kol Nidre (KOHL NEE-dray), all vows; prayer of atonement; melody to which prayer is sung (Heb)

kommandatura (kohm-mahn-dah-TOO-rah), command headquarters (G)

kopek (more properly *kopeika*, kuh-PYEY-kuh), small Russian coin (R)

kraal (KRAHL), South African village or enclosure (Du, from Pt *curral*).

Kremlin (more properly *kreml', KRYEHML'),* citadel of Moscow, seat of government (R)

kriegspiel (KREEK-shpeel), war game (G)

kulak (koo-LAHK), fist, tightwad, well-to-do peasant (R)

kultur (kool-TOOR), civilization, culture German style (G)

Kulturkampf (kool-TOOR-KAHMPF), Prussia's struggle to dominate Catholic Church (G)

Kuomintang (GWOH-meen-tahng), national people's party of China (Ch)

L

la belle dame sans merci (la BEHL DAM SÄH mehr-SEE), the beautiful lady without mercy (F)

labor omnia vincit (LAH-bohr OHM-nee-ah WEEN-keet), labor overcomes everything (L)

lagniappe (la-NYAP), small present to purchaser with purchase (F from Sp from Quechua)

laissez faire (leh-SAY FEHR), let things alone, noninterference (F)

lapsus calami (LAHP-soos KAH-lah-mee), slip of the pen (L)

lapsus linguae (LAHP-soos LEEN-gweye), slip of the tongue (L)

largo (LAHR-goh), broad, slow tempo (It)

laudator temporis acti (low-DAH-tohr TEHM-poh-rees AHK-tee), one who praises the good old days (L)

lebensraum (LAY-buhns-rowm), living space, the rationale used by Germany in the 1930s to annex other countries (G)

legato (lay-GAH-toh), bound, with no pause between notes (It)

Légion d'Honneur (lay-ZHÄW daw-NÖR), military and civil order (F)

lei (LAY), wreath of flowers worn around the neck (Hawaiian)

leitmotiv (LEYET-moh-teef), guiding theme (G)

lento (LEHN-toh), slow tempo (It)

lèse-majesté (LEHZ-ma-zhehs-TAY), treason, offense against ruler (F)

l'état, c'est moi! (lay-TAH seh MWAH), *I* am the state! (F)

Liederkranz (LEE-duhr-krahnts), singing society; type of cheese (G)

Limburger (LEEM-boor-guhr), type of cheese (G)

lingua franca (LEEN-gwah FRAHN-kah), international or common language in multilingual area (L or It)

lira (LEE-rah), Italian unit of currency (It)

literati (lee-teh-RAH-tee), educated or cultured people, literary men (L)

loggia (LAWJ-jah), portico projecting from a building (It)

logos (LOH-gohs), word (Gk)

Lorelei (LOH-ah-leye), siren whose singing is a lure to sailors (G)

luau (loo-AH-oo), Hawaiian banquet (Hawaiian)

lycée (lee-SAY), high school (F)

M

macabre (ma-KAH-bruh), gruesome (F)

macédoine (ma-say-DWAHN), mixture of fruits or vegetables (F)

macho; machismo (MAH-choh, mah-CHEEZ-moh), male; assertion of male superiority through sexual feats and violence (Sp)

mademoiselle (mad-mwah-ZEHL), young lady, Miss (F)

Madonna (mah-DAWN-nah), my Lady; the Virgin Mary (It)

maestoso (mah-ays-TOH-soh), majestic (It)

maestro (mah-AYS-troh), master, teacher (It)

Mafia (MAH-fyah), Sicilian secret organization (It)

Magna Charta (or Magna Carta; MAHG-nah KAHR-tah), Great Charter; English Bill of Rights (L)

magna cum laude (MAHG-nah koom LOW-deh), with great praise or distinction (L)

magnifico (mah-NYEE-fee-koh), magnificent; great man (It)

magnum bonum (MAHG-noom BOH-noom), great good; great benefit (L)

magnum opus (MAHG-noom OH-poos), great work, masterpiece (L)

Foreign Words and Phrases

maharajah (mah-hah-RAH-jah), great king (Hind)

maharani (mah-hah-RAH-nee), great queen (Hind)

mahatma (mah-HAHT-mah), great soul, teacher (Sk)

mais où sont les neiges d'antan? (MEH-ZOO sāw lay NEHZH dāh-TĀH), but where are the snows of yesteryear? (F)

maitre d'hôtel (MEH-truh doh-TEHL), head steward, head butler (F)

major domo (MAH-yohr DOH-moh), chief steward, head servant (L)

maladroit (ma-la-DRWAH), awkward, tactless (F)

mal de mer (MAL duh MEHR), seasickness (F)

malentendu (ma-lāh-tāh-DÜ), misunderstanding (F)

malgré lui (mal-GRAY LWEE), in spite of himself (F)

mañana (mah-NYAH-nah), tomorrow (Sp)

mandamus (mahn-DAH-moos), we order; legal writ (L)

manicotti (mah-nee-KAWT-tee), stuffed pasta rolls (It)

manifesto (mah-nee-FEHS-toh), declaration (It)

maraca (mah-RAH-kah), gourd used as musical instrument (Sp)

mardi gras (mar-DEE GRAH), Shrove Tuesday, carnival that day (F)

mare nostrum (MAH-reh NOHS-troom), our sea, the Mediterranean (L)

mariachi (mahr-ee-AH-chee), Mexican band (Mexican Sp)

mariage de convenance (ma-RYAZH duh kaw-vuh-NĀHS), marriage of convenience (F)

marimba (mah-REEM-bah), wooden xylophone (Sp)

marina (mah-REE-nah), settled seashore (It)

marrons glacés (ma-RŌH gla-SAY), candied chestnuts (F)

marsala (mahr-SAH-lah), Sicilian sweet wine (It)

masseur, masseuse (ma-SÖR, ma-SÖZ), male, female massage expert (F)

matador (mah-tah-DOHR), bullfighter who kills bull with sword (Sp)

maté (mah-TEH), see hierba maté

materia medica (mah-TEH-ree-ah MEH-dee-kah), drugs, pharmacology (L)

matzo, pl. **matsoth** (MAH-sah, MAH-tsoth), Passover unleavened bread (Heb)

maxixe (mah-SHEE-shuh), Brazilian dance (Pt)

mazuma (mah-ZOO-mah), money (Yid)

mazurka (mah-ZOOR-kah), Polish dance (Pol)

mazzeltov (MAH-zuhl-tohv), congratulations, good luck (Heb)

mea (maxima) culpa (MEH-ah MAHK-see-mah KOOL-pah), my (greatest) fault (L)

meerschaum (MEHR-showm), mineral substance for making smoking pipes (G)

mein kampf (meyen KAHMPF), my battle, my struggle (G)

mélange (may-LÄHZH), mixture (F)

mêlée (meh-LAY), mix-up, fight, brawl (F)

memorabilia (meh-moh-rah-BEE-lee-ah), things worth remembering (L)

ménage (may-NAHZH), household (F)

ménage à trois (may-NAHZH ah TRWAH), a threesome (F)

menorah (meh-NOH-rah), Jewish seven-candle candelabrum (Heb)

mens sana in corpore sano (MEHNS SAH-nah een KOHR-poh-reh SAH-noh), a sound mind in a sound body (L)

meringue (muh-RĒHG), beaten and baked egg whites (F)

mesa (MEH-sah), tableland, plateau (Sp)

mésalliance (may-za-lee-ÄHS), marriage with a person of inferior social position (F)

mestizo (mehs-TEE-thoh), a person of mixed blood, especially of European and Native American ancestry (Sp)

métier (may-TYAY), trade, craft (F)

mezzo (MEH-dzoh), half, moderate (It)

midi (mee-DEE), midday, south (F)

miles gloriosus (MEE-lehs gloh-ree-OH-soos), braggart, swaggerer (L)

minestrone (mee-nehs-TROH-nay), vegetable soup (It)

mirabile dictu (mee-RAH-bee-leh DEEK-too), wonderful to relate (L)

mirabile visu (mee-RAH-bee-leh WEE-soo), wonderful to see (L)

mirabilia (mee-rah-BEE-lee-ah), wonderful things (L)

mise en scène (MEE-zäh-SEHN), stage setting (F)

miserere (mee-seh-REH-reh), have mercy (L)

modicum (MOH-dee-koom), proper or small measure (L)

modus operandi (MOH-doos oh-peh-RAHN-dee), way of working (L) *modus vivendi* (MOH-doos wee-WEHN-dee), way of living (together) (L)

mores (MOH-rehs), customs, folkways, conventions (L)

mot juste (MOH ZHÜST), the right word for the occasion (F)

moue (MOO), pout, grimace (F)

mousse (MOOS), frozen whipped dessert (F)

muchacha; muchacho (moo-CHAH-chuh; moo-CHAH-cho), girl, boy (Sp)

mufti (MOOF-tee), civilian judge; civilian garb (Arab)

mullah (MUH-lah), powerful Muslim leaders (Arab)

mutatis mutandis (moo-TAH-tees moo-TAHN-dees), with the appropriate changes (L)

muzhik (moo-ZHEEK), Russian peasant (R)

N

naiveté (na-eev-TAY), innocence, guilelessness (F)

née (NAY), born; having as a maiden name (F)

négligée (nay-glee-ZHAY), loose indoor robe for women (F)

nemesis (NEH-meh-sahs), retribution, one who punishes (L from G)

n'est-ce pas? (nehs PAH) isn't it so? (F)

ne plus ultra (neh PLOOS OOL-trah), no further (L)

nihil obstat (NEE-hcel OHB-staht), there is no impediment (L)

nil admirari (NEEL ahd-mee-RAH-ree), be surprised at nothing (L)

nil desperandum (NEEL dehs-peh-RAHN-doom), never despair (L)

n'importe (nēh-PAWRT), it doesn't matter (F)

Nirvana (neer-VAH-nah), extinction; oblivion; Buddhist paradise (Sk)

Nisei (NEE-say), second-generation Japanese-Americans (J)

nisi (NEE-see), unless (L)

noblesse oblige (naw-BLEHS aw-BLEEZH), high rank involves responsibility (F)

Noël (naw-EHL), Christmas (F)

nolle prosequi (NOHL-leh PROH-seh-kwee), I will prosecute no further (L)

nolo contendere (NOH-loh kohn-TEHN-deh-reh), no contest (L)

nom de guerre (NŌH duh GHEHR), pseudonym (F)

nom de plume (NŌH duh PLÜM), pen name (F)

Complete Guide to Speech, Style and Grammar

non compos mentis (nohn KOHM-pohs MEHN-tees), insane, not sound in mind (L)

non sequitur (nohn SEH-kwee-toor), it does not follow; logical inconsistency (L)

nota bene (NOH-tah BEH-neh; abbr. n.b.), note well (L)

note verbale (NAWT vehr-BAHL), verbal communication on diplomatic matter (F)

novella (noh-VEHL-lah), short story (It)

nuncio (NOON-chyoh), Papal envoy (It)

O

obbligato (ohb-blee-GAH-toh), solo passage, not to be omitted (It)

obiit (OH-beet) he, she died (L)

obiter dictum (OH-bee-tehr DEEK-toom), spoken incidentally (L)

objet d'art (awb-ZHEH DHAR), object of art (F)

odium (OH-dee-oom), hatred; blame (L)

olla podrida (OH-lyah poh-DREE-dah), stew, hodge-podge (Sp)

omnia mutantur, nos et mutamur in illis (OHM-nee-ah moo-TAHN-toor NOHS eht moo-TAH-moor een EEL-lees), all things change, and we change with them (L)

omnia vanitas (OHM-nee-ah WAH-nee-tahs), all is vanity (L)

omnia vincit amor (OHM-nee-ah WEEN-keet AH-mohr), love overcomes everything (L)

omnium gatherum (OHM-nee-oom GA-ther-um), miscellaneous collection (L and mock L)

onus probandi (OH-noos proh-BAHN-dee), the burden of proof (L)

opéra bouffe (oh-pay-RAH BOOF), comic opera, musical comedy (F)

opera omnia (OH-peh-rah OHM-nee-ah), all the works (L)

operetta (oh-pay-RAYT-tah), light opera, musical comedy (It)

opus (OH-poos), work (L)

opus citatum (OH-poos kee-TAH-toom), abbr. op. cit.; the work previously cited (L)

ora et labora (OH-rah eht lah-BOH-rah), pray and work (L)

ora pro nobis (OH-rah proh NOH-bees), pray for us (L)

oratorio (Oh-rah-TAW-ryoh), musical drama on sacred topic (It)

osso buco (AWS-soh BOO-koh), marrow bone of veal (It)

---

o tempora! o mores! (OH TEHM-poh-rah OH MOH-rehs), O, times and customs! (L)

outré (oo-TRAY), extreme, excessive (F)

oyer and terminer (oh-YEHR tehr-mee-NEHR), higher criminal court (Old F)

oyez (oh-YEHTS), hear ye! (Old F)

P

paella (pah-EH-lyah), South Spanish dish of rice and meat or fish (Sp)

palette (pa-LEHT), artist's color-mixing board (F)

palio (PAH-lyoh), Siena horserace (It)

pampa (PAHM-pah), grassy plain in Argentina (Sp, from Quechua)

panache (pa-NASH), plume; a swagger, flourish (F)

panem et circenses (PAH-nehm eht keer-KEHN-sehs), bread and games (L)

papier-mâché (pa-PYAY-mah-SHAY), paper pulp, cardboard (F)

par excellence (pa-rehk-seh-LĀHS), to a superlative degree (F)

parfait (par-FEH), ice cream with syrup or fudge (F)

pariah (PAH-ree-ah), outcast, rejected (Tamil)

pari passu (PAH-ree PAHS-soo), side by side, evenly (L)

parmigiana (pahr-mee-JAH-nah), Parma style, with melted cheese and tomato (It)

parmigiano (pahr-mee-JAH-noh), Parma cheese, usually for grating (It)

parti pris (par-TEE PREE), preconceived idea (F)

paso doble (PAH-soh DOH-bleh), two-step, Spanish dance (Sp)

passacaglia (pahs-sah-KAH-lyah), slow Italian dance or music (It)

passim (PAHS-seem), abbr. pass.; scattered everywhere (L)

pâté (pah-TAY), paste (F); *—de foie gras* (duh FWAH GRAH), goose-liver paste

pater familias (pah-tehr-fah-MEE-lee-ahs), head of family (L)

Pater Noster (PAH-tehr NOHS-tehr), Our Father, Lord's Prayer (L)

pater patriae (PAH-tehr PAH-tree-eye), father of his country (L)

patio (PAH-tyoh), courtyard, inner courtyard (Sp)

pâtisserie (pah-tees-REE), pastry (F)

patois (pa-TWAH), local dialect (F)

Complete Guide to Speech, Style and Grammar

pax romana (PAHKS roh-MAH-nah), Roman peace, enforced peace (L)

pax vobiscum (PAHKS woh-BEES-koom), peace be with you (L)

peineta (pay-NEH-tah), tall comb (Sp)

per annum (pehr AHN-noom), by the year (L)

per capita (pehr KAH-pee-teh), by the head, apiece (L)

per diem (pehr DEE-ehm), by the day (L)

per se (pehr SEH), in itself, inherently (L)

persona non grata (pehr-SOH-nah nohn GRAH-tah), not acceptable diplomatic representative (L)

Pesach (PAY-sakh), Passover (Heb)

peseta (peh-SEH-tah), Spanish coin (Sp)

peso (PEH-soh), Latin American unit of currency (Sp)

petit bourgeois (puh-TEE boor-ZHWAH), lower middle class (F)

petitio principii (peh-TEE-tee-oh preen-KEE-pee-ee), begging the question (L)

petits fours (puh-TEE FOOR), little sponge or pound cakes (F)

petits pois (puh-TEE PWAH), green peas (F)

phobia (FOH-bee-ah), fear, hatred (Gk)

pianissimo (pyah-NEES-see-moh), very softly (It)

piano (PYAH-noh), softly (It)

pibroch (PEE-brokh), bagpipe (Gaelic)

picador (pee-kah-DOHR), mounted bullfighter with lance (Sp)

piccolo (PEEK-koh-loh), small flute (It)

pièce de résistance (PYEHS duh ray-zees-TĀHS), main course, out-standing item (F)

pied à terre (pee-ehd-ah-TEHR), a country homeowner's apartment in the city (F)

pilaf (pee-LOW), Oriental rice dish (Pers)

piroshki (pee-RAWSH-kee), stuffed puffcakes (R)

pirouette (pee-roo-EHT), spin on one foot or in air (F)

più (PYOO), more (It)

pizzicato (pee-tsee-KAH-toh), plucking the strings of a musical in-strument (It)

plaza de toros (PLAH-thah deh TOH-rohs), bullring (Sp)

plus ca change, plus c'est la même chose (PLÜ sa SHÄHZH PLÜ seh la mehm SHOHZ), the more it changes, the more it's the same thing (F)

poco a poco (POH-koh ah POH-koh), little by little, carefully (Sp)

Foreign Words and Phrases

pogrom (puh-GRAWM), devastation, massacre (R)

point d'appui (PWĒH da-PWEE), fulcrum, support point (F)

polenta (poh-LEHN-tah), thick gruel of corn, chestnuts, etc. (It)

pollice verso (POHL-lee-keh WEHR-soh), thumbs down (L)

poltergeist (POHL-tuhr-geyest), racketing or prank-playing ghost (G)

pommes frites (PAWM FREET), fried potatoes (F)

poncho (POHN-choh), blanket with opening for head (Sp)

pons asinorum (POHNS ah-see-NOH-room), bridge of donkeys; hard problem for beginners (L)

portico (PAWR-tee-koh), covered gallery open on one side (It)

portmanteau (PAWRT-mäh-TOH), traveling bag (F)

posada (poh-SAH-dah), inn (Sp)

posse (comitatus) (POHS-seh koh-mee-TAH-toos), force of a county, sheriff and assistants (L)

post bellum (pohst BEHL-loom), after-war (L)

post hoc, ergo propter hoc (pohst HOHK EHR-goh PROHP-tehr HOHK), after, therefore in consequences of something else (L)

post meridiem (pohst meh-REE-dee-ehm), abbr. p.m., P.M.; after noon (L)

post mortem (pohst MOHR-tehm), after death, autopsy (L)

post scriptum (pohst SKREEP-toom), abbr. P.S., written after main letter (L)

potage (paw-TAHZH), soup (F)

potpourri, pot-pourri or **pot pourri** (poh-poo-REE), mixture, medley (F)

pourparler (poor-par-LAY), talk, negotiations (F)

préciosité (pray-syoh-zee-TAY), excessive refinement (F)

première danseuse (pruh-MYEHR däh-SÖZ), first female dancer (F)

prestissimo (prays-TEES-see-moh), very fast (It)

prima donna (PREE-mah DAWN-nah), female opera star; anyone who wants to be first (It)

prima facie (PREE-mah FAH-kee-eh), at first glance, on the face of it (L)

primus inter pares (PREE-moos EEN-tehr PAH-rehs), first among equals (L)

prix fixe (PREE FEEKS), fixed price, included in one price (F)

Complete Guide to Speech, Style and Grammar

pro bono publico (proh BOH-noh POO-blee-koh), for the public good (L)

pro et con(tra) (PROH eht KOHN-trah), for and against (L)

profanum vulgus (proh-FAH-noom WOOL-goos), the fickle crowd (L)

pro forma (proh FOHR-mah), as a matter of form (L)

propaganda (proh-pah-GAHN-dah), that which is to be spread (L)

pro rata (proh RAH-tah), in proportion, in accordance with fixed rate (L)

prosciutto (proh-SHOOT-toh), salted Italian-style ham (It)

prosit (PROH-seet), to your health or success (L)

protégé (praw-tay-ZHAY), one taken under another's sheltering wing (F)

pro tempore (proh TEHM-poh-reh), abbr. pro tem; temporarily (L)

provolone (proh-voh-LOH-nay), a hard, smooth Italian cheese (It)

puchero (poo-CHEH-roh), South American stew (Sp)

pudenda (poo-DEHN-dah), genital organs (L)

pueblo (PWEH-bloh), village, town (Sp)

puissance (pwee-SĀHS), power (F)

pulque (POOL-kah), alcoholic beverage of Mexico (Sp from Nahuatl)

pundit (PUN-deet), man of learning (Hind)

purdah (PUR-dah), veil, feminine seclusion (Hind)

purée (pu-RAY), thick cream soup; mash till all solids are a thick liquid (F)

Purim (POO-reem), Jewish feast of deliverance (Heb)

putsch (POOCH), abortive revolutionary attempt (G)

Q

qua (KWAH), considered as, in the capacity of (L)

quasi (KWAH-see), as if, as though (L)

que será será (KEH seh-RAH seh-RAH), what will be will be (Sp)

quidnunc (KWEED-nunk), what now, gossip, newsmonger (L)

quid pro quo (KWEED proh KWOH), something in return for something else (L)

¿quién sabe? (KYEHN SAH-veh), who knows? (Sp)

qui s'excuse s'accuse (KEE sehks-KÜZ sa-KÜZ), he who excuses himself accuses himself (F)

qui vive (KEE VEEV), on the alert, watchful (F)

qui va là? (KEE va LA), who goes there? (F)

quod erat demonstrandum (KWOHD EH-raht deh-mohn-STRAHN-doom), which was to be proved (L)

quod vide (KWOHD WEE-deh), abbr. q.v.; which see (L)

quondam (KWOHN-dahm), former, formerly (L)

quorum (KWOH-room), majority of legislative body for voting purposes (L)

quot homines, tot sententiae (KWOHT HOH-mee-nehs TOHT sehn-TEHN-tee-eye), as many opinions as there are people (L)

quo vadis? (KWOH WAH-dees), where are you going? (L)

R

ragoût (ra-GOO), spicy stew (F)

raison d'état (reh-ZŌH day-TAH), reason of state (F)

raison d'être (reh-ZŌH DEH-truh), reason for existing (F)

rajah (RAH-jah), king, ruler (Sk)

rallentando (rahl-layn-TAHN-doh), slowing up (It)

rani (RAH-nee), queen (Sk)

rapprochement (ra-prawsh-MĀH), reestablishing of friendly relations (F)

rara avis (RAH-rah AH-wees), rare bird (L)

rathskeller (RAHTS-KEHL-luhr), basement restaurant and bar (G)

re (REH), in the matter of (L)

realia (reh-AH-lee-ah), materials for teaching foreign cultures (L)

Reconquista (reh-kohn-KEES-tah), reconquest of Spain from the Moors (Sp)

recto (REKH-toh), on the right-hand page (L)

regata (ray-GAH-tah), Venetian gondola race (It)

répondez s'il vous plaît (ray-pōh-DAY seel voo PLEH), abbr. R.S.V.P.; please reply (F)

requiem (REH-kwee-ehm), rest; prayer for dead (L)

requiescat in pace (reh-kwee-EHS-kaht een PAH-keh), abbr. r.i.p.; may he or she rest in peace (L)

residuum (reh-SEE-doo-oom), remnant, residue (L)

résumé (ray-zü-MAY), summary (F)

ricksha (REEK-shaw), see *jinrickisha*

ricotta (ree-KAWT-tah), soft white Italian cheese (It)

Complete Guide to Speech, Style and Grammar

rigor mortis (REE-gohr MOHR-tees), stiffness of death (L)

rinascimento (ree-nah-shee-MAYN-toh), rebirth (It)

ris de veau (REE duh VOH), sweetbreads (F)

risorgimento (ree-sohr-jee-MAYN-toh), Italian movement for unity (It)

risotto (ree-SAWT-toh), Italian rice dish (It)

rissolé (ree-saw-LAY), golden brown (F)

ritardando (ree-tahr-DAHN-doh), slowing up (It)

Roma caput mundi (ROH-mah KAH-poot MOON-dee), Rome, head of the world (L)

Rosh Hashanah (ROHSH hah-shah-NAH), head of year, New Year's Day (Heb)

rota (ROH-tah), wheel; Papal court (L)

rôti (roh-TEE), roast (F)

rôtisserie (roh-tees-REE), grill restaurant (F)

rotunda (roh-TOON-dah), circular building with dome (L)

roulette (roo-LEHT), gambling wheel (F)

rubaiyat (ROO-beye-yaht), quatrains, poems (Arab)

rucksack (RUK-zahk), knapsack (G)

rupee (ROO-pee), Indian currency (Hind)

S

sabotage (sa-baw-TAHZH), intentional damage to arrest production (F)

sabra (SAH-brah), native Israeli (Heb)

sachet (sa-SHEH), small bag of perfume (F)

safari (sah-FAH-ree), hunting trip in Africa (Arab)

sahib (SAH-heeb), sir, master, title of respect (Arab)

sake (SAHK-ee), usually heated alcoholic rice drink (J)

salaam (sah-LAHM), peace, form of greeting (Arab)

salame, pl. -mi (sah-LAH-meh, -mee), spiced sausage (It)

salon (sa-LA̅W̅), drawing room, exhibition room (F)

salus populi suprema lex (SAH-loos POH-poo-lee soo-PREH-mah LEHKS), the welfare of the people is the supreme law (L)

salve (SAHL-weh), volley, salute (F); hail (L)

samba (SAHM-bah), Brazilian dance (Pt. from Am. Indian)

samovar (suh-muh-VAHR), Russian tea urn (R)

samurai (SAH-moo-reye), Japanese feudal nobleman (J)

sanctum sanctorum (SAHNK-toom sahnk-TOH-room), holy of holies (L)

sangfroid (sāh-FRWAH), coolness in the face of danger (F)

sans façon (sāh fa-SAW), unceremoniously (F)

sans gêne (sāh ZHEHN), without embarrassment, nervy (F)

sans souci (sāh soo-SEE), carefree, free from worry (F)

sarape (sah-RAH-peh), Mexican poncho-like shawl worn mostly by men (Sp)

sari (SAH-ree), Hindu female costume (Hindi)

sartor resartus (SAHR-tohr reh-SAHR-toos), tailor retailored, tit for tat (L)

Saturnalia (sah-toor-NAH-lee-ah), Roman December festival (L)

sauerbraten (ZOW-uhr-BRAH-tuhn), marinated roast (G)

sauerkraut (ZOW-uhr-krowt), pickled cabbage (G)

sauté (soh-TAY), fried in small amount of fat (F)

sauve qui peut (SOHV kee PO), every man for himself (F)

savoir faire (sa-VWAHR FEHR), tact, ability to do the right thing (F)

savoir vivre (sa-VWAHR VEE-vruh), knowledge of how to behave and get along (F)

sayonara (SAH-yoh-nah-rah), good-bye (J)

scherzo (SKAYR-tsoh), lively, jesting musical composition (It)

schlemiel (shluh-MEEL), easy mark, dumbbell (Yid)

schmalz (SHMAHLTS), fat; silly sentimentality (G)

schnapps (SHNAHPS), brandy, whiskey (G)

schnitzel (SHNIT-suhl), cutlet (G)

schnorrer (SHNOHR-ruhr), beggar (Yid)

schrecklichkeit (SHREHK-liç-keyet), frightfulness, policy of deliberate atrocity (G)

scilicet (SKEE-lee-keht), that is to say, to wit (L)

séance (say-ÄHS), session, sitting (F)

sec (SEHK), dry (F)

sehnsucht (ZEHN-ZOOKHT), longing, nostalgic feeling (G)

semper fidelis (SEHM-pehr fee-DEH-lees), forever faithful (L)

semper paratus (SEHM-pehr pah-RAH-toos), ever ready (L)

senatus populusque romanus (seh-NAH-toos poh-poo-LOOS-kweh roh-MAH-noos), abbr. S.P.Q.R., the Roman Senate and people (L)

Complete Guide to Speech, Style and Grammar

se non è vero, è ben trovato (say nohn eh VAY-roh, eh behn troh-VAH-toh), if it isn't true, it's a good lie (It)

sforzando (sfohr-TSAHN-doh), with force or vigor (It)

shah (SHAH), king of Persia (Pers)

shalom (shah-LOHM), peace, form of Hebrew or Israeli greeting (Heb)

shashlik (SHAHSH-leek), meat on skewer (R)

skeikh (SHEYEKH), old man, religious leader (Arab)

shekel (SHEH-kehl), unit of weight or money (Heb)

shillalagh (shil-LAY-lee), cudgel (Irish)

Shinto (SHEEN-toh), way of the gods; Japanese religion (J)

shish kebab (SHEESH keh-BAHB), lamb on skewer (Turk)

shlock (SHLAHK), trashy merchandise, junk (Yid)

shtick (SHTIHK), characteristic show business bit, one's line of business (Yid)

sic (SEEK), thus, precisely as it appears (L)

sic semper tyrannis (SEEK SEHM-pehr tee-RAHN-nees), may it always go thus with tyrants (L)

sic transit gloria mundi (SEEK TRAHN-seet GLOH-ree-ah MOON-dee), thus passes away the world's glory (L)

Siglo de Oro (SEE-gloh deh OH-roh), golden century (Sp)

s'il vous plait (seel voo PLEH), please (F)

similia similibus curantur (see-MEE-lee-ah see-MEE-lee-boos koo-RAHN-toor), like is cured with like (L)

sine die (SEE-neh DEE-eh), without assigning a day (L)

sine qua non (SEE-neh KWAH NOHN), indispensable requisite or condition (L)

Sinn Fein (SHIN FAYN), we ourselves; Irish revolutionary movement (Irish)

si vis pacem, para bellum (see wees PAH-khem, PAH-rah BEHL-loom), if you want peace, prepare for war (L)

skoal (SKOHL), to your health (Norw)

slalom (SLAH-lum), downhill skiing race on a zigzag course (Norw)

smörgasbord (SMOR-gus-boord), table of appetizers and other foods (Swed)

soi-disant (swah-dee-ZĀH) self-styled (F)

soirée (swah-RAY), evening gathering (F)

solfeggio (sohl-FAY-joh), singing by notes (It)

sombrero (sohm-BREH-roh), hat (Sp)

sotto voce (SOHT-toh VOH-chay), in an undertone (It)

soubriquet (soo-bree-KEH), nickname (F)

soufflé (soo-FLAY), puffed up, baked custard (F)

soupçon (soop-SAW), suspicion, dash, trace (F)

soviet (suh-VYEHT), council of delegates (R)

spa (SPAH), watering place (Belgian place name)

spoor (SPOHR), track of animal (Du)

spumone, pl. **-ni** (spoo-MOH-nay, -nee), Italian ice cream (It)

sputnik (SPOOT-neek), co-traveler, space satellite (R)

staccato (stahk-KAH-toh), having short notes (It)

stanza (STAHN-tsah) room; subdivision of poem (It)

status quo (STAH-toos KWOH), existing or previously existing state of affairs (L)

stet (STEHT), let it stand, disregard correction (L)

strudel (SHTROO-duhl), type of cake (G)

stucco (STOOK-koh), mixture of lime and pulverized stone (It)

studio (STOO-dyoh), study; place for studying or working (It)

Sturm und Drang (SHTOORM oont DRAHNG), storm and stress (G)

sub judice (soob YOO-dee-keh), not yet decided (L)

subpoena (soob-POY-nah), under penalty; required appearance in court (L)

sub rosa (soob ROH-sah), under cover; in secret (L)

succès d'estime (sük-SEH dehs-TEEM), favored by critics and experts, but not by mass (F)

sui generis (SOO-ee GEH-neh-rees), in a class by itself; unique (L)

sukiyaki (SKEE-yah-kee), Japanese dish of meat and vegetables (J)

summa cum laude (SOOM-mah koom LOW-deh), with the highest praise (L)

summum bonum (SOOM-moom BOH-noom), the supreme good (L)

suo nomine (SOO-oh NOH-mee-neh), in his own name (L)

Sûreté (sur-TAY), security; French security police (F)

suum cuique (SOO-oom kwoo-EE-kweh), to each his own (L)

svaraj (SVAH-rahj), self-rule, independence (Sk)

T

table d'hôte (TA-bluh DOHT), regular menu, no choice (F)

tabula rasa (TAH-boo-lah RAH-sah), empty slate (L)

Complete Guide to Speech, Style and Grammar

tamale (tah-MAH-leh), Mexican dish of cornmeal, meat, and red pepper wrapped in corn husks (Sp)

tant mieux (pis) (TĀH MYÖ PEE), so much the better (worse) (F)

tarantella (tah-rahn-TEHL-lah), swift Italian dance (It)

Te Deum Laudamus (TEH DEH-oom low-DAH-moos), Thee, God, we praise; a hymn of thanksgiving (L)

tempo (TEHM-poh), time, rate, rhythm, beat (It)

tempus fugit (TEHM-poos FOO-gheet), time is fleeting (L)

terminus (a quo, ad quem) (TEHR-mee-noos ah KWOH, ahd KWEHM), limit or boundary from which or to which (L)

terra cotta (TEHR-rah KAWT-tah), baked clay, earthenware (It)

terra firma (TEHR-rah FEER-mah), solid ground, mainland (L)

terra incognita (TEHR-rah een-KOHG-nee-tah), unknown land (L)

tertium quid (TEHR-tee-oom KWEED), a third factor (L)

tête-à-tête (TEH-ta-TEHT), face to face; intimate conversation (F)

thé dansant (TAY dāh-SĀH), afternoon tea and dance (F)

thesaurus (teh-SOW-roos), treasure collection; idea dictionary (L)

timbale, timballo (teh-BAL, teem-BAHL-loh), baked in a mold (F, It)

timeo Danaos et dona ferentes (TEE-meh-oh dah-NAH-ohs eht DOH-nah feh-REHN-tehs), I fear the Greeks even when they bear gifts (L)

toga (TOH-gah), loose, flowing robe of Romans (L)

toreador, torero (toh-reh-ah-DOHR, toh-REH-roh), bullfighter (Sp)

torso (TOHR-soh), upper part of body without head (It)

Totentanz (TOH-tuhn-tahnts), dance of death (G)

touché (too-SHAY), touched; remark that strikes home (F)

toujours (too-ZHOOR), always, forever (F)

toupet (too-PEH), wig, false hair (F)

tour de force (TOOR duh FAWRS), special feat of dexterity, skill, strength, or ingenuity (F)

tournure (toor-NUR), roundness, gracefulness of line (F)

tout de suite (TOO duh SWEET), at once (F)

tovarishch (tuh-VAH-reeshch), comrade (R)

traduttore, traditore (trah-doot-TOH-ray, trah-dee-TOH-ray), a translator is a traitor (It)

trauma (TROW-mah), blow, wound, injury (Gk)

tricolore (tree-kaw-LAWR), French flag, red, white, and blue (F)

Trimurti (tree-MOOR-tee), Hindu trinity: Brahma, Vishnu, and Shiva (Sk)

troika (TROY-kuh), vehicle drawn by three horses (R)

troppo (TRAWP-poh), too much (It)

trouvère (troo-VEHR), minstrel (F)

tsar (see czar)

tu quoque (TOO KWOH-kweh), you, too (L)

tutti-frutti (TOOT-tee FROOT-tee), all fruits, mixed fruits (It)

U

ubique (oo-BEE-kweh), everywhere (L)

ukaze (oo-KAHS), imperial edict (R)

ukulele (oo-koo-LEH-leh), Hawaiian guitar (Hawaiian)

ultima Thule (OOL-tee-mah TOO-leh), faraway, mythical locality (L)

ultimo (mense) (OOL-tee-moh), abbr. ult; last (month) (L)

ultra (OOL-trah), beyond, outside of (L)

ultra vires (OOL-trah WEE-rehs), beyond one's strength or capacity (L)

(d)'un certain age (däh sehr-TÃH nahzh), of a certain age, middle-aged (F)

und so weiter (oont ZOH VEYE-tuhr), and so forth; etc. (G)

uno animo (OO-noh AH-nee-moh), with one mind (L)

urbi et orbi (OOR-bee eht OHR-bee), to the city and to the world (L)

ut supra (OOT SOO-prah), as above (L)

V

vade mecum (WAH-deh MEH-koom), a book carried as a constant companion, a handbook (L)

vae victis (WEYE WEEK-tees), woe to the vanquished (L)

vale (WAH-leh), good-bye, farewell (L)

valuta (vah-LOO-tah), currency, foreign exchange (It)

vaquero (bah-KEH-roh), cowboy (Sp)

Veda (VEH-dah), knowledge, book of knowledge (Sk)

veld (FEHLT), open grassy country (Du)

veni, vidi, vici (WEH-nee WEE-dee WEE-kee), I came, I saw, I conquered (L)

verbatim (wehr-BAH-teem), word for word (L)

verbum sat sapienti (WEHR-boom SAHT sah-pee-EHN-tee), a word to the wise is sufficient (L)

verein (fehr-EYEN), union, club (G)

vermicelli (vayr-mee-CHEHL-lee), thin spaghetti (It)

versus (WEHR-soos), abbr. vs.; against (L)

Via Crucis (WEE-ah KROO-kees), the Way of the Cross (L)

vibrato (vee-BRAH-toh), with vibration (It)

vice versa (WEE-keh WEHR-sah), the other way around (L)

vide (WEE-deh), see (L)

videlicet (wee-DEH-lee-keht), abbr. viz.; to wit, namely (L)

vignette (vee-NYEHT), illustration, short essay (F)

vinaigrette (vee-neh-GREHT), seasoned with vinegar (F)

vin ordinaire (VĒH nawr-dee-NEHR), common table wine (F)

viola da gamba (VYAW-lah dah GAHM-bah), large viol (It)

virtuoso (veer-too-AW-soh), master performer or singer (It)

vis-à-vis (vee-za-VEE), face to face (F)

vista (VEES-tah), view, panorama (It)

viva voce (WEE-wah WOH-keh), orally, by word of mouth (L)

vive (VEEV) long live (F)

vodka (VAWT-kuh), grain spirits (R)

volaille (vaw-LA-yuh), fowl (F)

vol-au-vent (VAW-loh-VĀH), large, light patty; baked pastry shell (F)

volte-face (VAWLT-FAS), about face; reversal (F)

vomitorium (woh-mee-TOH-ree-oom), exit of large public building (L)

von (FUN), of, from, prefix to noble family name (G)

voortrekker (FOHR-TREHK-kuhr), early settler, pioneer (Du)

vox clamantis in deserto (WOHKS klah-MAHN-tees een deh-SEHR-toh), the voice of one shouting in the wilderness (L)

vox populi, vox Dei (WOHKS POH-poo-lee, WOHKS DEH-ee), the voice of the people is the voice of God (L)

vraisemblance (vreh-sāh-BLĀHS), likelihood, verisimilitude (F)

vulgo (WOOL-goh), commonly, popularly (L)

V

wagon-lit (va-GŌH-LEE), railroad sleeping car (F)

wahini (wah-HEE-nee), woman (Hawaiian)

Foreign Words and Phrases

wanderlust (VAHN-duhr-loost), desire for travel (G)
weltanschauung, weltansicht (VEHLT-ahn-show-ung, VEHLT-ahn-ziçt), general outlook, conception of things (G)
weltschmerz (VEHLT-shmehrts), sorrow for the world, pessimism (G)
wunderbar (VOON-duhr-bahr), wonderful (G)
wurst (VOORST), sausage (G)

X

xenophobia (KSEH-noh-FOH-bohs), fear or hatred of the foreign (Gk roots)

Y

Yahweh (YAH-vch), Jchovah, God (Heb)
yoga (YOH-gah), yoking; restraint; Hindu philosophy (Sk)
yogi (YOH-ghee), follower of Yoga (Sk)
Yom Kippur (YOHM keep-POOR), day of atonement, Hebrew holiday (Heb)

Z

zabaione (dzah-bah-YOH-nay), custard mixed with Marsala wine (It)
zeitgeist (TSEYET-gheyest), spirit of the times (G)
zwieback (TSVEE-bahk), toasted biscuit (G)

PROOFREADER'S MARKS

The following marks are standard for printers but are also often used in correcting early drafts.

⊙	Insert period	*s. c.*	Small caps—used in margin
↑	Insert comma	═	Small caps—used in text
:	Insert colon	*rom.*	Roman type
;	Insert semicolon	*caps.*	Caps—used in margin
?	Insert question mark	≡	Caps—used in text
!	Insert exclamation mark	*c+sc*	Caps & small caps—used in margin
=/	Insert hyphen	≣	Caps & small caps—used in text
✓	Insert apostrophe	*l.c.*	Lowercase—used in margin
✓/✓	Insert quotation marks	/	Used in text to show deletion or substitution
⊬	Insert 1-en dash	*ᵉ↑*	Delete
⊼	Insert 1-em dash	*ᵈ↑*	Delete and close up
#	Insert space	*w.f.*	Wrong font
ld>	Insert ( ) points of space	⊂	Close up
∨	Superior	⊐	Move right
∧	Inferior	⊏	Move left
(/)	Parentheses	⊓	Move up
⊏/⊐	Brackets	⊔	Move down
□	Indent 1 em	‖	Align vertically
□□	Indent 2 ems	═	Align horizontally
¶	Paragraph	⊐⊏	Center horizontally
no ¶	No paragraph	⊓⊔	Center vertically
tr	Transpose—used in margin	*eq.#*	Equalize space—used in margin
∿	Transpose—used in text	✓✓✓	Equalize space—used in text
sp	Spell out	,.....	Let it stand—used in text
ital	Italic—used in margin	*stet.*	Let it stand—used in margin
___	Italic—used in text	Ⓧ	Letter(s) not clear
b. f.	Boldface—used in margin	∧	Caret—General indicator used to mark position or error.
ᨓ	Boldface—used in text		

Sample Marked Proof

TYPOGRAPHICAL ERRORS

It does not appear that the earliest printers had any method of correcting errors before the form was on the press, The learned correctors of the first two centuries of printing were not proofreaders in our sense they were rather what we should term office editors, Their labors were chiefly to see that the proof corresponded to the copy, but that the printed page was correct in its latinity, that the words were there, and that the sense was right. They cared but little about orthography, bad letters, or purely printers' errors, and when the text seemed to them wrong they consulted fresh authorities or altered it on their own responsibility. Good proofs, in the modern sense, were, impossible until professional readers were employed, men who had first a printer's education, and then spent many years in the correction of proof. The orthography of English, which for the past century has undergone little change, was very fluctuating until after the publication of Johnson's Dictionary, and capitals, which have been used with considerable regularity for the past 80 years, were previously used on the miss or hit plan The approach to regularity, so far as we have, may be attributed to the growth of a class of professional proofreaders, and it is to them that we owe the correctness of modern printing. More errors have been found in the Bible than in any other one work. For many generations it was frequently the case that Bibles were brought out stealthily, from fear of governmental interference. They were frequently printed from imperfect texts, and were often modified to meet the views of those who published them. The story is related that a certain woman in Germany, who was the wife of a printer, and had become disgusted with the continual assertions of the superiority of man over woman which she had heard, hurried into the composing room while her husband was at supper and altered a sentence in the Bible, which he was printing, so that it read Narr instead of Herr, thus making the verse read "And he shall be thy fool" instead of "And he shall be thy lord." The word not was omitted by Barker, the king's printer in England in 1632, in printing the seventh commandment, He was fined £3,000 on this account.

INDEX

Index

Index